THE CANADIANS

THE OLD WEST

THE CANADIANS

By the Editors of

TIME-LIFE BOOKS

with text by

Ogden Tanner

TIME-LIFE BOOKS / ALEXANDRIA, VIRGINIA

Time-Life Books Inc.
is a wholly owned subsidiary of

TIME INCORPORATED

Founder: Henry R. Luce 1898-1967

Editor-in-Chief: Henry Anatole Grunwald
President: J. Richard Munro
Chairman of the Board: Ralph P. Davidson
Executive Vice President: Clifford J. Grum
Chairman, Executive Committee: James R. Shepley
Editorial Director: Ralph Graves
Group Vice President, Books: Joan D. Manley
Vice Chairman: Arthur Temple

TIME-LIFE BOOKS INC.

Managing Editor: Jerry Korn
Executive Editor: David Maness
Assistant Managing Editors: Dale M. Brown
(planning), George Constable, Martin Mann,
John Paul Porter, Gerry Schremp (acting)
Art Director: Tom Suzuki
Chief of Research: David L. Harrison
Director of Photography: Robert G. Mason
Assistant Art Director: Arnold C. Holeywell
Assistant Chief of Research: Carolyn L. Sackett
Assistant Director of Photography: Dolores A. Littles

Chairman: John D. McSweeney
President: Carl G. Jaeger
Executive Vice Presidents: John Steven Maxwell,
David J. Walsh
Vice Presidents: George Artandi (comptroller);
Stephen L. Bair (legal counsel); Peter G. Barnes;
Nicholas Benton (public relations); John L. Canova;
Beatrice T. Dobie (personnel); Carol Flaumenhaft
(consumer affairs); James L. Mercer (Europe/South
Pacific); Herbert Sorkin (production);
Paul R. Stewart (marketing)

THE OLD WEST

EDITORIAL STAFF FOR "THE CANADIANS"
Editor: George G. Daniels
Picture Editor: Patricia Hunt
Text Editors: Virginia Adams, Anne Horan,
Gerald Simons
Designers: Bruce Blair, Edward Frank
Staff Writers: Don Earnest, Sally French,
Stuart Gannes, Gregory Jaynes, David Johnson,
Frank Kappler, John Manners
Chief Researchers: June O. Goldberg,
Martha T. Goolrick
Researchers: Peggy Bushong, Muriel Clarke,
Jane Coughran, Tonna Gibert, Harriet Heck,
Beatrice Hsia, Thomas Lashnits, Donna Lucey,
Robert Stokes, Scot Terrell, Reiko Uyeshima,
Gretchen Wessels
Design Assistants: Deanna Lorenz, Michelle Clay

EDITORIAL PRODUCTION
Production Editor: Douglas B. Graham
Operations Manager: Gennaro C. Esposito,
Gordon E. Buck (assistant)
Assistant Production Editor: Feliciano Madrid
Quality Control: Robert L. Young (director),
James J. Cox (assistant), Daniel J. McSweeney,
Michael G. Wight (associates)
Art Coordinator: Anne B. Landry
Copy Staff: Susan B. Galloway (chief),
Michele Lanning, Barbara F. Quarmby, Celia Beattie
Picture Department: Alex George
Traffic: Kimberly K. Lewis

THE AUTHOR: Ogden Tanner has been a feature writer for the *San Francisco Chronicle*, associate editor of *House and Home*, assistant managing editor of *Architectural Forum* and an editor with TIME-LIFE BOOKS. For this volume he traveled extensively throughout Western Canada researching the region's rich history.

THE COVER: French-Canadian *voyageurs* guide their fragile, 36-foot birchbark canoe down a series of fearsome rapids in the 1860s. Among the passengers amidships is the artist, Frances Ann Hopkins *(on right in a straw boater)*, the talented wife of a Hudson's Bay Company official, who accompanied her husband on many wilderness expeditions. The frontispiece: Members of an 1871 railroad survey party are photographed dragging a dugout log canoe out of British Columbia's North Thompson River at the start of a long, back-breaking portage around a stretch of impassable white water.

CORRESPONDENTS: Elisabeth Kraemer (Bonn); Margot Hapgood, Dorothy Bacon, Lesley Coleman (London); Susan Jonas, Lucy T. Voulgaris (New York); Maria Vincenza Aloisi, Josephine du Brusle (Paris); Ann Natanson (Rome). Valuable assistance was also provided by: Judy Aspinall (London); Carolyn T. Chubet, Miriam Hsia, Christina Lieberman (New York); Mimi Murphy (Rome).

Other Publications:

LIBRARY OF HEALTH
CLASSICS OF THE OLD WEST
THE EPIC OF FLIGHT
THE GOOD COOK
THE SEAFARERS
THE ENCYCLOPEDIA OF COLLECTIBLES
THE GREAT CITIES
WORLD WAR II
HOME REPAIR AND IMPROVEMENT
THE WORLD'S WILD PLACES
THE TIME-LIFE LIBRARY OF BOATING
HUMAN BEHAVIOR
THE ART OF SEWING
THE EMERGENCE OF MAN
THE AMERICAN WILDERNESS
THE TIME-LIFE ENCYCLOPEDIA OF GARDENING
LIFE LIBRARY OF PHOTOGRAPHY
THIS FABULOUS CENTURY
FOODS OF THE WORLD
TIME-LIFE LIBRARY OF AMERICA
TIME-LIFE LIBRARY OF ART
GREAT AGES OF MAN
LIFE SCIENCE LIBRARY
THE LIFE HISTORY OF THE UNITED STATES
TIME READING PROGRAM
LIFE NATURE LIBRARY
LIFE WORLD LIBRARY
FAMILY LIBRARY:
   HOW THINGS WORK IN YOUR HOME
   THE TIME-LIFE BOOK OF THE FAMILY CAR
   THE TIME-LIFE FAMILY LEGAL GUIDE
   THE TIME-LIFE BOOK OF FAMILY FINANCE

For information about any Time-Life book, please write:
Reader Information
Time-Life Books
541 North Fairbanks Court
Chicago, Illinois 60611

Time-Life Books.
   The Canadians/by the editors of Time-Life Books; with text by
Ogden Tanner. —Alexandria, Va.: Time-Life Books, c 1977.
   240 p.: ill.; 29 cm. — (The Old West)
   Bibliography: p. 236-237.
   Includes index.
   1. Canada — History — To 1763 (New France)
   2. Canada — History — 19th century.
I. Tanner, Ogden.   II. Title.   III. Series: The Old West
(New York)
F1030.T6   1977   971   76-26845
ISBN 0-8094-1543-7
ISBN 0-8094-1542-9 lib. bdg.
ISBN 0-8094-1541-0 retail ed.

CONTENTS

Members of a government survey party crossing the plains bivouac along the North Saskatchewan River.

1|A primeval northland as big as Europe

The vast Canadian wilderness, which stretched from the Great Lakes to the Pacific Ocean, yielded with great reluctance to the French and British adventurers who went west in search of furs, then gold and finally farmland. The immense territory, greater in area than all Western Europe, embraced every extreme of terrain and climate, from prairies where summer temperatures could reach 110° F., to a bleak north country locked in ice. Some of the tallest, most forbidding peaks of the Rocky Mountains and coastal range barred the route to the Pacific Ocean, and immense tracts of what appeared to be flatland were merely floating layers of quaking muskeg.

The westbound pioneers traveled in a fascinating variety of ways. During winter, men slogged along on snowshoes, carrying their goods on their backs or on dog sleds. In summer, many frontiersmen used pack horses or high-wheeled, single-axle Red River carts *(below)*, which were light enough to traverse the muddy plains and tundra.

But the most common means of travel was the canoe. Paddling through Canada's far-flung network of rivers and lakes, with intermittent portages, *voyageurs* made epic journeys covering thousands of miles, taking in supplies, bringing out furs — and planting the first crude settlements. Canada's two coasts were not linked by transcontinental railroad until 1885, and it may be several centuries before the great wild land can be truly declared tamed.

Beneath a newly completed telegraph line, a freight wagon negotiates the cut through Great Bluff on British Columbia's Cariboo Road in 1865. The 18-foot-wide wagon road running 400 miles from Fort Yale on the Fraser River into the Cariboo gold fields took three years to complete.

A Tyrolean-hatted frontiersman lounges on the bluff outside Fort Edmonton in the summer of 1871. The trading post, perched on a height above the North Saskatchewan River, was a major supply point on the plains for fur brigades and, later, settlers heading to and from the Rockies.

Eight hands tense as their supply scow noses over a white-water chute in the north-flowing Slave River. Other crewmen stand ashore, having taken off the freight, which was unloaded to lighten the scow while running rapids.

The Illecillewaet glacier in the western reaches of the Rockies dwarfs two workers on the Canadian Pacific Railway. This great river of ice, whose façade stretched for over 10 miles, was one of the largest of hundreds of glaciers within sight of the right-of-way along one section.

A wooden trestle straddles the gravel and mud of a glacial stream bed on the right-of-way through Rogers Pass in the Selkirk Mountains. This was one of five major bridges that helped carry the track over an 800-foot grade in 15 miles.

"Lords of the lakes, Sinbads of the wilderness"

In 1836, citified Easterners who doted on tales of adventure in exotic lands found plenty of excitement in a new book by the prolific author-traveler Washington Irving. The subject of Irving's latest work was the fur trade in the distant Northwest, and he announced it with a rousing burst of purple prose:

"While the fiery and magnificent Spaniard, inflamed with the mania for gold, has extended his discoveries and conquests over those brilliant countries scorched by the ardent sun of the tropics, the adroit and buoyant Frenchman, and the cool and calculating Briton, have pursued the less splendid, but no less lucrative, traffic in furs amidst the hyperborean regions of the Canadas, until they have advanced even within the Arctic Circle. It was the fur trade, in fact, which gave early sustenance and vitality to the great Canadian provinces."

Irving's readers knew next to nothing about the Canadian West. Indeed, Americans in 1836 knew little about their own trans-Mississippi West — virtually unpopulated except for some 35,000 countrymen in the newly established Republic of Texas. But throughout the 25 states, interest in the new Western lands was building fast. Irving had become one of the first literary boosters of the West; he published a journal of his 1832 travels with a U.S. government mission sent to visit Indian tribes in the Great Plains. And now, Irving bid fair to make a conversation piece out of the Canadian West, a wilderness larger than the American West, with even fewer civilized inhabitants.

As Irving explained in a disarming personal note, his book was the belated result of his youthful experiences with the two species of men who were the prime movers of the Canadian fur trade. Back in 1803, when Irving was a 20-year-old law clerk in New York City, he had gone on a business trip to Montreal, the bustling capital of the fur trade and the eastern terminus of "the mazy and wandering rivers that interlace the vast forests of the Canadas." This intricate network of waterways, which was both an obstacle to overland travel and a tenuous alternative to it, made the opening of the Northwest a uniquely Canadian adventure. Whereas westbound Americans would cross their open plains easily in commodious wagons, the Canadians pioneered their frontier in slender canoes, on roundabout journeys broken by arduous portages from one river to the next.

On reaching Montreal, Irving spent several days with the Scottish merchants of the North West Company, who formed "a kind of commercial aristocracy" and held "a feudal sway" over much of Western Canada. Irving was awed by those Scots, whom he showered with such flattering accolades as the "hyperborean nabobs" and "the lords of the lakes and forests." They were, to be sure, "cool and calculating" businessmen by day. But after dark, they proved to be a lusty breed with well-developed tastes for pretty Indian wenches and boisterous all-night celebrations.

As young Irving learned, a gala banquet for the Scottish fur magnates was a sumptuous feast indeed. "The tables in the great banqueting room groaned under the weight of game of all kinds; of venison from the woods, and fish from the lakes, with hunters' delicacies, such as buffaloes' tongues, and beavers' tails. There was no stint of generous wine, for it was a hard-drinking period, a time of loyal toasts, and bacchanalian songs, and brimming bumpers."

In Montreal, Irving also hobnobbed with a second dominant species of Canadian fur man — the tough and tireless French *voyageurs*. "Sinbads of the wilderness,"

After a lifetime spent stalking the Northern woods, François Gros Louis, an Indian trapper, puffs a pipe as he displays the accouterments of his trade: a steel trap, a pelt and a rifle swaddled in hide to protect it.

Irving called them, and he enthusiastically reported that they often spent more than a year at a time paddling through the woodland streams, "coasting the most remote lakes, and creating new wants and habitudes among the natives," and finally "sweeping their way down the Ottawa in full glee, their canoes laden down with packs of beaver skins."

These two very different groups of men — the enterprising Scots and the perdurable French — were the adventurers of the Canadian West. They explored and mapped the labyrinthine waterways, the rugged mountains of the Far West, the fertile south-central plains and the bleak tundra of the Arctic north. They planted the first permanent Western settlements — their crude little trading posts — and established the Canadian policy of peaceful cooperation with the Indians. They were the first rulers of Canada's West: their companies — the only form of organization on the early frontier — necessarily served as local governments. All this the fur traders accomplished long before the Americans broached their virgin West. By 1754, some two decades before Daniel Boone pushed the American frontier west to Kentucky, Canadian fur men had already reached the Rockies.

Canada survived on the fur trade through its long and difficult colonial period, when its European masters tended to consider much of the country more trouble than it was worth. Louis Joseph de Montcalm, the

This 1738 sketch by a citified Continental conceives Canada's trappers as half-naked musketeers who blazed away at humanesque beavers.

redoubtable French general, confessed that he loathed Canada—though he gave his life defending it against the British in the French and Indian Wars. And the British, having won that war in 1763 and made themselves sole rulers of Canada, were less than overjoyed by their conquest. In fact, shortsighted officials toyed with the notion of trading the whole gigantic country back to the French in exchange for the Caribbean island of Guadaloupe.

But the Canadian fur traders were men of vision, with an unshakable faith in the West's brilliant future. That great wilderness would live up to their expectations, but it would take time and enormous effort. The West would grow as a scattering of small societies, struggling to communicate and to transport necessities over the enormous stretches of beautiful but frustrating terrain.

Geographically isolated and politically disunited, the frontier communities were further handicapped by Canada's woeful shortage of manpower. With only one tenth the population of the United States, the Canadians could not keep pace with the Americans as developers of the West, nor could they prevent their aggressive neighbors from expropriating disputed territory or crossing the border in various illegal and disruptive ventures.

Clearly these many challenges could not be met until the regions of the Canadian West were knit together and linked to the East by some sort of direct, expeditious transportation. In recognition of this need, generations of fur traders had searched persistently for the fabled Northwest Passage—a waterway on which ocean-going ships could carry their furs straight through the continent to the Atlantic or the Pacific. Though no such watery shortcut existed, the Canadians would find a way to serve the same purpose. In 1885, in the climactic achievement of their pioneer epoch, they would bind their country together with a Northwest Passage made of steel—the transcontinental tracks of the Canadian Pacific Railway.

The Canadian fur trade—like Canada itself—began life as an accidental by-product of the search for the Northwest Passage. In 1535, when the French navigator Jacques Cartier discovered the broad St. Lawrence River, he thought he had found the mythical water-

way, and he sailed eagerly west, hoping to emerge in the Pacific Ocean, then to sail across it and make a fortune in the fabulous China trade. Cartier's men put ashore 550 miles upstream, visiting an Indian village on the site of the future town of Montreal. But just beyond, the St. Lawrence was blocked by formidable rapids. Undismayed by his bad luck, Cartier began trading with the local Indians, who, in their eagerness for French knives and kettles, offered him everything they possessed, including the beaver pelts off their backs.

Back in Europe, these acquisitions stirred a sensation among hatmakers, who found the skins ideal for making felt. The demand was soon so great that French traders in the New World recruited whole tribes of Indians as commercial hunters. The Indians were such excellent providers that within a few decades the supply of beaver was waning in Eastern Canada, and by the early 17th Century, the future of the fur trade had already shifted to the West.

Another French adventurer, Samuel de Champlain, saw the future clearly when he arrived in New France in 1603 expressly to trade in furs. Champlain decided to seek out merchandise instead of waiting for Indian hunters to deliver it. But he realized that the vast stretches of woods and water presented unique logistic problems and, taking a lesson from the free-roaming Indians, introduced the profession of the *voyageur*. Under his leadership, daring men from Montreal climbed into Indian canoes and paddled west on the Indians' traditional thoroughfares—the Ottawa and French rivers.

The Indian ways proved marvelously profitable and were easily adapted and refined for large-scale trade. Before long, French trading posts had been planted along the routes west, and by 1650 Frenchmen were already exploring the Great Lakes.

Meanwhile, hundreds of miles to the north, the English navigator Henry Hudson had discovered a colossal body of water that extended even farther west than the Great Lakes. The first commercial venture into Hudson Bay began in 1668, when an English combine set up Fort Charles, a trading post at the bottom of the bay. Two years later the British Crown duly issued a charter to "the Governor and Company of Adventurers of England Tradeing into Hudsons Bay."

Thus was born the Hudson's Bay Company, soon to become a powerful, indeed semiautonomous, trading

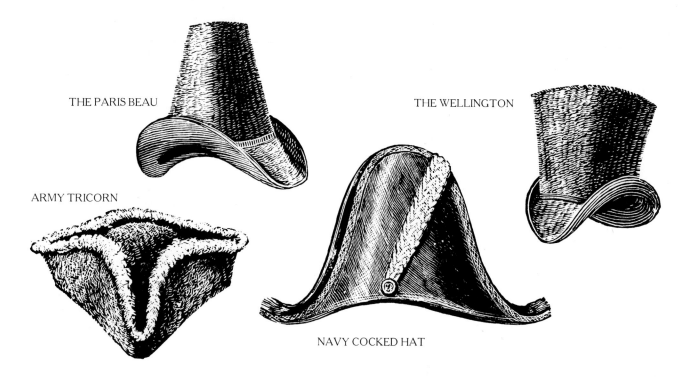

THE PARIS BEAU

THE WELLINGTON

ARMY TRICORN

NAVY COCKED HAT

and shipping firm. The royal charter awarded the company title to all the land drained by all the rivers that flowed into its namesake bay — an area of nearly 1.5 million square miles. The 18 owners of this grandiose new domain christened it Rupert's Land after the soldierly Prince Rupert, cousin to the royal family and the company's chief backer.

While the Hudson's Bay Company proprietors did their adventuring in England, resident managers conducted the fur trade with faultless British conservatism. Over the next two decades, the Englishmen built several additional "factories" — fortified trading posts — at the mouths of rivers emptying into Hudson Bay. And there they stayed put, waiting patiently until Indians came canoeing down from the interior with their harvest of pelts. The governors in charge of the posts declined to risk any inland expeditions.

The Hudson's Bay Company broke its inertia in 1689, when its first trading expedition — one Englishman and an Indian boy — traveled 200 miles inland. But by then French fur merchants, expanding west and north, had flung up trading posts on territory claimed by the Hudson's Bay Company charter, and were crowding in on Hudson Bay itself. Damning each other as invaders, the French and British traders fought a long and bitter struggle for command of the Indian trade. Several British posts on Hudson Bay changed hands repeatedly; some were destroyed, rebuilt and destroyed again.

In 1713, after four decades of sporadic skirmishing, the French traders abandoned their efforts to oust the

English from Hudson Bay, but they still controlled the interior and thus preempted the Britishers' main source of furs. It took far greater wars, fought out by England and France on two continents over five more decades, to decide the fate of Canada and its fur trade. Finally in 1763, after British armies had won smashing victories at Montreal and Quebec, the Treaty of Paris put a formal end to the French and Indian Wars, with France ceding its Canadian territory and all other continental possessions. The gentlemen of the Hudson's Bay Company assumed that they would now have an easy time taking over the whole Canadian fur trade.

On the contrary, the competition got stiffer. Most of it came from an unlikely new source — Scottish freelancers. The Scots were by no means new to Canada: for decades, numbers of Highlanders had been emigrating to the eastern maritime regions to escape despotic overlords. But not until the fall of the French colonial government was the fur trade attractive to the Scots. In the 1760s, more and more of them went to Montreal and set up little companies.

As small-time businessmen, the Scots operated the only way they could — by scrambling to survive. Adopting the French system wholesale, they hired canoemen and — to the astonishment of the sedentary English governors on Hudson Bay — led their crews in person, along the old *voyageur* routes westward to the Great Lakes and north to the edge of the fur frontier. The Scots quickly earned a reputation for daring, determination and purveying rum to the Indians, a trade in which they outdid by a wide margin the Hudson's Bay Eng-

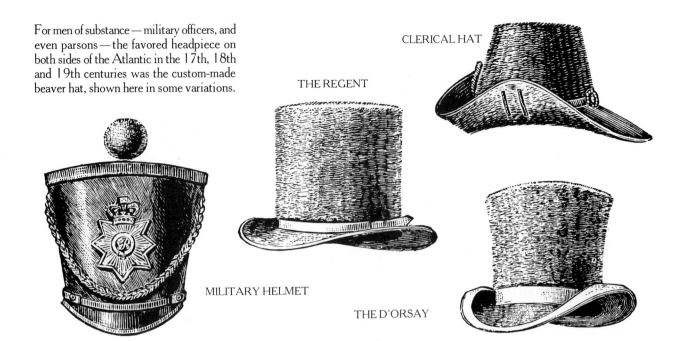

For men of substance — military officers, and even parsons — the favored headpiece on both sides of the Atlantic in the 17th, 18th and 19th centuries was the custom-made beaver hat, shown here in some variations.

THE REGENT

CLERICAL HAT

MILITARY HELMET

THE D'ORSAY

lishmen. Still, because the Scots competed with each other as strenuously as they did with everyone else, the English considered them no threat to the Hudson's Bay Company. In fact, Hudson's Bay men sneeringly referred to them as "the pedlars."

In the 1770s, however, various Scots began heeding the old truism about strength in unity. Pooling their assets and energies, several Scottish merchants formed the nucleus of the North West Company in 1775; still more partners would be drawn into the firm before it jelled a dozen years later. By then the Scots even dared to dream of crushing the Hudson's Bay Company and monopolizing the Canadian fur trade.

In 1775, the rival groups were engaged unknowingly in a race to an undiscovered region. The Scots of the North West Company, or Nor'Westers as they called themselves, were extending their trade routes northward. And the English governors on Hudson Bay, having finally been authorized to set up trading posts in the interior, were sending expeditions west in search of good sites and Indian hunters to sell them furs. Ahead of the rivals lay the Arctic watershed, an immense wilderness that no white man had ever seen, and that contained the greatest fur bonanza on the continent: incalculable quantities of beaver, marten, fisher, otter, mink, weasel, fox, lynx and wolf. The discovery of this treasure trove would usher in the heyday of the Canadian fur trade, with the greatest profits going to the merchants who got there first.

The Scottish Nor'Westers won the race in 1778, but the man who actually got there first was an Amer-

ican ally. He was Peter Pond, a strange, powerful character, driven by great dreams and dogged by a succession of fatal encounters. Colleagues acknowledged that Pond was "a trader of some celebrity in the northwest," but also thought him "odd in his manner," with "a violent temper and unprincipled character." Whatever accounted for his oftentimes baffling behavior, Pond was a frontier genius who blazed trails across half a continent and played a major role in the wilderness for more than three decades.

Pond's quixotic career began in 1756 when, at the age of 16, he left his home in Milford, Connecticut, to escape his father's shoemaking trade. He joined the British colonial army and served during the last four years of the French and Indian Wars. After various adventures abroad, Pond trekked out to a frontier area whose commerce centered on a small post called Detroit and there entered the fur trade. In his six years there, he became a supremely adept trader and — for the first time as a civilian — a killer.

As he described the fatal episode, Pond was deliberately insulted by another trader, and though he tried to be forbearing, "the abuse was too grate," and it led to a duel. "We met the next morning eairley and discharged pistels in which the pore fellowe was unfortenat." According to Pond, he reported the killing but "thare was none to prosacute me."

At the outbreak of the American Revolution in 1775, Pond crossed into Canada to set up as a trader in the Northwest country, where the finest furs were coming from. Luckily, he found a backer in Simon Mc-

WILDCAT

FISHER

WOLVERINE

RIVER OTTER

SNOWSHOE HARE

KIT FOX

BEAVER

Tavish, a shrewd, arrogant, hard-driving young merchant who was fast becoming a power among the Scottish traders. By the end of 1775, McTavish engineered the series of mergers that formed the cornerstone of the North West Company.

Pond spent a season trading successfully along the Saskatchewan River, and the rich haul of pelts he brought back was probably included in a big shipment that McTavish sold in England for £15,000. Returning the next year, Pond built a sturdy trading post on the river. But by 1777, the Hudson's Bay men had built a post farther up the Saskatchewan, and Pond set his sights on leapfrogging it to explore and trade still deeper into the Northwest.

Working toward that end, Pond got backing from several frontier traders who would soon join McTavish in the fledgling North West Company. Among his new supporters were three brothers from Yorkshire, Benjamin, Joseph and Thomas Frobisher; and the two McGill brothers, John and James (James's fur profits would, in the 1820s, help found the Montreal university named after him). In the spring of 1778, the partners found themselves with some leftover trading goods, and they voted to let Pond risk an epoch-making journey to Athabasca, a region then known only by Indian reports.

Pond's expedition — about 16 *voyageurs* in four canoes crammed with several tons of supplies — started north from Cumberland House on the lower Saskatchewan River. The outward journey, along innumerable twisting streams and across some 80 portages, took all

FOUR-LEGGED TREASURES OF THE GREAT FUR FOREST
These lithographs, based on original drawings by the noted 19th Century naturalist John James Audubon and his son John Woodhouse, depict the varied quarry of Canadian hunters and trappers. The animal upon which the fur trade was built was the beaver; its hide, sold in bulk by the pound, brought $3.50 American in 1801 prices. Furriers gladly bid $6.40 per pelt at auction for sleek and shiny otters, which they transformed into magnificent coats. The fisher's soft fur, though in less demand, fetched $1.60, while wildcat and wolverine each brought $2.40 — the latter to the delight of woodsmen, for this beast was a notorious bait stealer and trap wrecker. The handsome but small kit fox was worth only 40 cents, and at bottom was the ubiquitous snowshoe hare, valued at only pennies since it often wound up as filling for quilts.

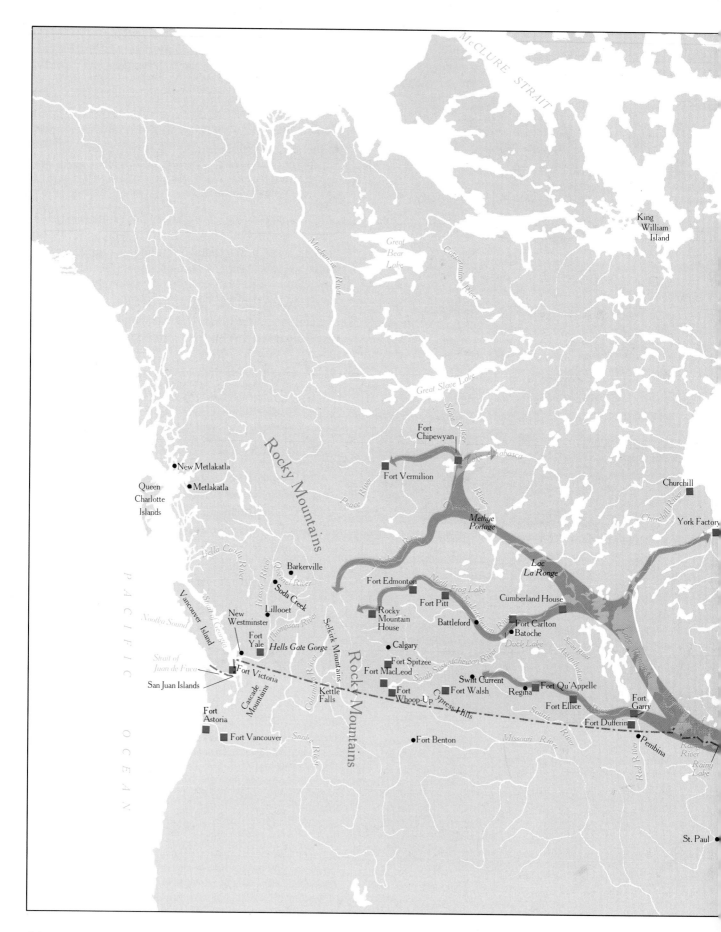

McCLURE STRAIT

King
William
Island

Great
Bear
Lake

Mackenzie River

Coppermine River

Great Slave Lake

Slave River

Churchill

Churchill River

York Factory

Fort
Chipewyan

Lake Athabasca

Fort Vermilion

Peace River

Athabasca River

*Methye
Portage*

*Lac
La Ronge*

Rocky Mountains

New Metlakatla

Queen
Charlotte
Islands

Metlakatla

Bella Coola River

Fraser River

Barkerville

Fort Edmonton

North Saskatchewan River

Fort Pitt

Frog Lake

Cumberland House

Saskatchewan River

Sturgeon River

Lake Winnipeg

Soda Creek

Quesnel River

Rocky
Mountain
House

Battleford

Fort Carlton

Batoche

Duck Lake

P
A
C
I
F
I
C

Nootka Sound

Vancouver Island

Strait of Georgia

New
Westminster

Lillooet

Thompson River

Selkirk Mountains

Calgary

Assiniboine River

Fort Yale

Hells Gate Gorge

Fort Spitzee

Fort MacLeod

Fort
Victoria

*Strait of
Juan de Fuca*

San Juan Islands

Cascade
Mountains

Columbia River

Kettle
Falls

Fort
Whoop-Up

Cypress Hills

Swift Current

Fort Walsh

Regina

Fort Qu'Appelle

Fort Ellice

Fort
Garry

Fort
Astoria

Snake River

Fort Vancouver

Fort Benton

Missouri River

Souris River

Fort Dufferin

Red River

Pembina

*Rainy
River*

*Rainy
Lake*

O
C
E
A
N

Rocky Mountains

St. Paul

26

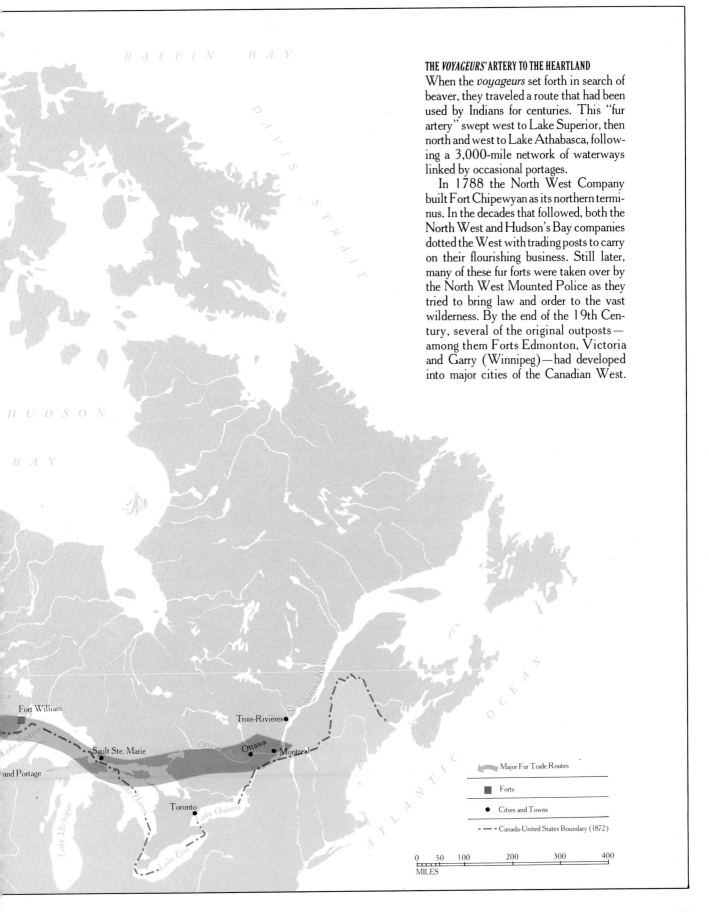

THE *VOYAGEURS'* ARTERY TO THE HEARTLAND

When the *voyageurs* set forth in search of beaver, they traveled a route that had been used by Indians for centuries. This "fur artery" swept west to Lake Superior, then north and west to Lake Athabasca, following a 3,000-mile network of waterways linked by occasional portages.

In 1788 the North West Company built Fort Chipewyan as its northern terminus. In the decades that followed, both the North West and Hudson's Bay companies dotted the West with trading posts to carry on their flourishing business. Still later, many of these fur forts were taken over by the North West Mounted Police as they tried to bring law and order to the vast wilderness. By the end of the 19th Century, several of the original outposts—among them Forts Edmonton, Victoria and Garry (Winnipeg)—had developed into major cities of the Canadian West.

Major Fur Trade Routes

Forts

Cities and Towns

Canada-United States Boundary (1872)

| 0 | 50 | 100 | 200 | 300 | 400 |
MILES

This brass trading coin, bearing likenesses of King George IV and, on the reverse, a beaver to denote its value of one pelt, has been holed at the upper edge so that Indian trappers could wear it as an ornament until ready to redeem it at the company store.

summer. Historically, Pond reached the high point of the trip one day in late August. He and his men, carrying canoes and supplies in short relays, struggled across the desolate 12 miles of the Methye Portage, which separated the Hudson Bay and Arctic watersheds, and came to rest on a cliff towering 700 feet above the Clearwater River. From where Pond stood, he could see more than 30 miles out over a dense evergreen forest. Beyond, a mighty river, soon to be named the Mackenzie, snaked northward to the remote Arctic Ocean; along with its tributaries, the Mackenzie drained a larger area than any North American river system but the Mississippi. Of more immediate importance, the enormous region fairly teemed with fur-bearing animals.

Pond's *voyageurs* hauled their canoes and gear down a narrow cliffside trail, and reembarked westward on the Clearwater. After running a series of treacherous rapids, they entered the broader, smoother waters of the Athabasca River and paddled to a good campsite 30 miles from Lake Athabasca. There the crewmen threw together crude log cabins and settled in for the bone-chilling northern winter. During the winter, Pond dealt for furs with the Chipewyan Indians, and when he left in the spring he had twice as many furs as the canoes could carry and had to cache the surplus to await his return.

When Pond came out of the wilderness with his load of superb dark pelts, the fur rush to the new Northwest was on in earnest. Thanks to Pond's bold thrust into the unknown, the Scots of the North West Company had outflanked the less aggressive Hudson's Bay men, and they quickly nailed down their advantage. Work parties found and marked the best route to Pond's trading post near Lake Athabasca, and made the traders' journey easier and safer by setting up an intermediate depot at Rainy Lake.

Pond made another successful trip back and forth to the Athabasca post in 1780, but the next year, he

and his party were caught by an early freeze and were forced to winter over at Lac La Ronge. There Pond had another deadly encounter.

Reports of the episode were vague—Pond and a clerk had supper one night with a fellow North West trader named Jean-Étienne Waden, who was later found dead. The supposition was that Pond or the clerk had shot Waden during a scuffle. Both men were subsequently tried for murder in Montreal, and were acquitted—though, as one associate put it, "their innocence was not so apparent as to extinguish the original suspicion."

Indeed, Pond and Waden had had plenty to argue about. The major members of the North West Company—principally McTavish, the Frobishers and the McGills —had appointed Pond to develop the Athabasca region over the protests of several small traders in the firm, who felt that their interests would be better protected with their friend Waden in the post. If Waden had accused Pond of favoring the McTavish group, it would have been enough to provoke that violence-prone man to action.

In any case, Pond soon had reason to regret his allegiance to the McTavish group. The big operators, shaken by Waden's death, tried to strengthen their control over the North West Company, and in the process they reapportioned shares in the firm. Pond was now invited to become a partner in the company, but was voted only a minor share because he had contributed little capital. To Pond, this was a niggardly reward for his momentous discovery of Athabasca. He spurned the offer and left Canada.

In 1785, Pond turned up in New York City, where he attempted to interest the Continental Congress in a crude map he had drawn of the Athabasca region. The map showed a clear water route north to the Arctic Ocean—suggesting a Northwest Passage. But the U.S. Congress was too busy with the problems of infant nationhood to be much interested in the distant Canadian

Northwest. Pond had no recourse but to patch up his differences with the North West Company and return to Athabasca.

All too soon, he found himself in fierce competition with a rival trader named John Ross. The predictable result was another quarrel, in which — also predictably — Ross was shot to death. Once again, Pond escaped retribution. He left Canada for good in the spring of 1790 to spend the rest of his years adventuring along the Mississippi. But before he departed, the veteran American infused his replacement in Athabasca, a young Scot named Alexander Mackenzie, with his passion for unknown lands. In the years to come, Mackenzie would perform incredible feats of discovery, winning wealth and fame as Canada's premier explorer.

In the 1790s, the Canadian fur trade came into its glory years. The North West Company rose to imperial wealth and power on pelts from Pond's fur Eldorado; Simon McTavish, now known as "the Marquis of the Montreal fur trade," ran the far-flung firm with an iron hand.

Year after year, the company functioned smoothly on a strict schedule dictated by travel time and the turn of the seasons. Operations began and ended with a summer rendezvous at the focal point of trade, Grand Portage, a large fortified depot on the northern shore of Lake Superior. In early May, when the ice broke up around Montreal, the partners who ran the business headquarters there started on their 1,000-mile journey west with great canoeloads of supplies; they traveled up the Ottawa River, down the French River into Georgian Bay and the North Channel of Lake Huron, then on across Sault Ste. Marie into Lake Superior. The partners who had spent the winter trading for furs started south and east laden with packs of pelts. The wintering partners and the Montreal men met at Grand Portage, conferred and celebrated for a month, then exchanged their cargoes and returned to their bases before their watery highways froze solid again.

The rendezvous began in late June. At Grand Portage, lookouts would spy the Montreal brigades far across the lake. There might be as many as 30 freight canoes in each brigade, and several brigades in the birchbark flotilla. Each craft, high-prowed, gaily painted and nearly 40 feet long, carried an astounding burden of four tons and was driven along by a crew of eight to 10 *voyageurs*, whose red-bladed paddles flashed and dipped rhythmically in the summer sun.

Just a little short of the trading post, the Montreal men beached their canoes to perform a brief ritual. Every *voyageur* put on his red-tasseled cap, his blue jacket and a gaudy sash. The clerk or partner in charge of each brigade, called the *bourgeois* by his men, donned the symbol of his status — a tall top hat of lustrous beaver felt. Then, with flags lettered "N.W. Co." flying on the prows of the lead canoes, and with the *voyageurs* shouting and singing, the brigades put on a last, showy burst of speed and raced into the pretty oval harbor of Grand Portage.

Of course Simon McTavish was there in his private canoe. As he clambered onto the dock, McTavish gazed with pardonable pride at his wilderness capital, which he had completed in 1784. The post, spreading out before him in a natural amphitheater of rocky hills, was surrounded by a palisade 15 feet high, reinforced with a bastion and a heavy gate. Inside the stockade stood a dozen buildings. The Great Hall, which was used for dining and business meetings, was surrounded by living quarters, shops, warehouses and a stone powder magazine. One of the shops was the *cantine salope,* or harlot's tavern, where the *voyageurs* could blow their pay on liquor and the large local complement of Indian and half-breed girls; for the men who got into drunken brawls, the post also had a sturdy lockup, known as the *pot au buerre,* or butter tub.

Before the Montreal men could settle down to serious carousing, they were obliged to tackle an onerous job. Their cargoes — sacks filled with 90 pounds of provisions and trade goods — had to be transported overland to a smaller depot on Pigeon River, the southern terminus of waterways from the west and north, where the frontier traders would arrive with their pelts and take on supplies for the return journey. The trail between the fort and Pigeon River was nine miles long, and it twisted over rocky hills and across muddy flats that fully justified the name Grand Portage. *Voyageurs* said that it was as hard to cross such portages as it was to get to heaven.

A sack, or *pièce*, was slung on the small of a man's back, and a beltlike leather tumpline was looped around his forehead, so that by thrusting out his neck he could

A fleet of sturdy boats laden with furs from the Western wilderness sails down the Saskatchewan River as a squall rolls after them. The insignia on the sail of the central boat in Paul Kane's painting is thought to be a good luck symbol painted by the Ojibwas who manned the craft.

take some of the weight off his sacroiliac. Another *pièce* was then tossed on top of the first, making a standard load of 180 pounds. Each *voyageur* was required to carry four such loads across the portage.

But the eight-sack quota was exceeded by many *voyageurs*, whose competitive instinct was sharpened by the company's offer of a Spanish peso for each additional *pièce* that a man transported. Many men carried three sacks at a time, and some occasionally handled as many as four. Five *pieces* — weighing three times more than the average canoeman — were reportedly carried on several occasions by Pierre Bonga, a giant black *voyageur*.

As soon as a *voyageur* was loaded up, he started out at a steady shuffling trot, his upper body bent forward, his neck and shoulder muscles straining against his burden. Naturally, portage trails of any length were divided into a series of *poses*, or resting places; these were spaced at intervals of 600 yards to a half mile, depending on the roughness of the terrain. The Grand Portage had 16 *poses*. Yet even with these periodic rests, the work was punishing. Acute hernia and injuries suffered in falls under the huge loads killed many *voyageurs* and disabled many others; only drowning took a higher toll.

By early July, small groups of men from the various remote outposts began arriving at the Pigeon River depot, swelling the two-way traffic on the portage trail. These *voyageurs*, who called themselves *hommes du nord* or north men, wore buckskins and looked more like Indians than Frenchmen as they stormed down the trail with their long black hair flying and their bales of pelts jouncing on their backs. They were the elite of the trade, paid more than the Montreal men for their riskier, lonelier work on the frontier, and they joyfully lorded it over the Montrealers.

The north men had no great love for their own monotonous travel diet of pemmican — dried buffalo meat and berries encased in fat — but they jeeringly called the Montrealers *mangeurs du lard* in an unkind reference to their Eastern fare of pork fat and maize, cooked to a thick mush. Worse, the north men would taunt the pork-eaters with their favorite boast, "Je suis un HOMME DU NORD!" This unmistakable aspersion led to many a furious fight. At every annual rendezvous, dozens of *voyageurs* were treated for knife wounds, gouged eyes, torn ears and bitten-off noses.

After the north men had hauled their pelts to the fort, they changed into pants and shirts and — *voilà* — they were indistinguishable from the pork-eaters. In fact, the *voyageurs* were remarkably uniform in almost every respect. With rare exceptions such as Pierre Bonga, they were French or mixed-blood descendants of French and Indian alliances. Physically, they were made by and for the brutal work of loading, paddling and carrying their canoes. They tended to be short, wiry men with deep chests and big muscular shoulders. Thomas McKenney, an American who toured the fur country, explained the *voyageur*'s physique thus: "A Canadian, if born to be a labourer, deems himself to be very unfortunate if he should chance to grow over five feet five, or six inches; — and if he shall reach five feet ten or eleven, it forever excludes him from the privilege of becoming *voyageur*. There is no room for the legs of such people, in these canoes. But if he shall stop growing at about five feet four inches, and be gifted with a good voice, and lungs that never tire, he is considered as having been born under a most favourable star."

By mid-July, the last groups of north men had arrived, and while the partners conferred, the *voyageurs* found themselves with a week or two to laze around. They would settle their accounts with the company clerks, sign up for another year, do their laundry and repair their gear. They gorged themselves on bread, butter and fresh meat at the *cantine salope,* where they spent most of their waking hours. There they also consumed more than enough fiery liquor and enjoyed the companionship of the Cree and Chippewa girls, many of whom were extremely pretty. As one Nor'Wester wrote, "They have a softness and delicacy in their countenance which rivals the charms of some of our more civilized belles."

Meanwhile, in the Great Hall, Simon McTavish, with his partners and leading traders, reviewed the past year's business and set goals for the year ahead. When the bulk of the decisions had been made, McTavish ordered his aides to start preparations for the company's annual banquet and ball.

A week later, the climactic day arrived. As dusk gathered, the little cove in the great lake twinkled with lights. Outside the fort, campfires blazed as the *voyageurs* donned their Sunday best. Inside the Great Hall, hundreds of candles shed their warm light on the banquet tables. The celebrants entered and took seats in order of rank. First came Simon McTavish and his partners, all decked out in silk vests, fawn-gray coats and dress swords; they seated themselves at a table in front of the huge fireplace. They were followed in by company officers, traders, clerks, interpreters and guides, who took places at broad plank tables to the rear of the hall. Everyone immediately pitched into a heroic repast that included quantities of beef and venison, smoked hams, baked whitefish and tender new potatoes from the fort's garden — all dished up by cooks brought from Montreal for the purpose. The men punctuated their feasting with frequent toasts — to the company, to the fur trade, to one another and "To the Mother of all the saints!" The partners were served great drafts of port and Madeira; the others went to a barrel and dipped out a powerful punch made of sugared rum and various other surplus spirits.

When everyone had eaten all he could, the tables were pushed back to make room for dancing. At this point, the doors were flung open to admit the *voyageurs* and the local Indians who had eaten outside. The canoemen crowded onto tables and benches along the walls, while the Indians hunkered down in front on bright blankets.

As the musicians tuned up their instruments, a young Scottish clerk might toss a pair of crossed swords on the floor and do an impromptu dance around them to the noisy applause of his audience. Then Simon McTavish would stride onto the floor with the daughter of a local chief, and the ball would get under way with a Highland reel.

Dancing and other such worldly frivolities were frowned upon by Daniel Harmon, a puritanical Vermonter who had signed on as a company clerk in time for the rendezvous in 1801. But in the first numbers that year, Scots and Indians swung about so sedately that even Harmon approved. He confided to his diary, "For musick we had the bag-pipe, the violin, and the flute, which added much to the interest of the occasion. At the ball there was a number of the ladies of this country; and I was surprised that they could conduct with so much propriety and dance so well."

Harmon's good report of the festivities suggests that he retired early, for he surely would have been scan-

dalized by the scenes that followed. When the Scots relinquished the dance floor, their former partners were seized and flung wildly about by the *voyageurs,* who stomped and whirled through athletic gyrations until sweat glued their shirts to their backs. The drinking increased as the evening wore on. Late at night, the merrymakers poured out of the Great Hall and roamed around the fort in drunken groups until sunrise reddened the peaceful surface of the lake.

In spite of hang-overs, the men of the North West Company commenced their new business year while the morning was young. The crews of north men headed sluggishly over the portage trail to their Pigeon River embarkation point. Their canoes were 25 feet long, about 15 feet shorter than the Montrealers' craft, and each was manned by a smaller crew of six to eight *voyageurs.* Fully loaded with a ton and a half of cargo, the north canoe drew only 18 inches of water; its relatively light weight and maneuverability were perfectly suited to travel in the narrow streams that lay ahead.

One by one, the brigades of north men shoved off into Pigeon River. Standing fore and aft in each canoe, the bowman and steersman stroked with paddles nine feet long; the men in the middle, seated none too comfortably on narrow crossboards, used paddles four feet in length. The paddles were carved of resilient basswood or red cedar, and their narrow blades and stout handles took a good deal of hard use without breaking.

The outbound brigades paddled up the Pigeon River and through a string of lakes that led off to the west and northwest. When the river became narrower and the crews could make little headway against the faster current, they stood up and propelled the canoes upriver with long metal-tipped poles. When the river bottom was too deep or too muddy for poling, everyone would jump ashore and "line" the canoe, pulling it along with a tow rope much as horses dragged barges up a canal. If all else failed, the crewmen would portage around the rough stretch, with the middle men hauling all the goods while the bowman and steersman carried the canoe on their shoulders.

In currentless lakes or smooth stretches of river, the *voyageurs* paddled tirelessly, keeping up a steady pace of about 40 strokes a minute, covering four or more miles an hour. Occasionally, the *bourgeois* would signal a rest period, which was known as a pipe because the men had just enough time to smoke a small clay pipe of strong tobacco. In the long northern twilights, many a day started at 3 o'clock in the morning and lasted until 9 o'clock at night, with only two brief breaks for breakfast and lunch. On one such day, the American visitor Thomas McKenney mercifully asked his men to call it quits after 16 hours of paddling. "They answered they were fresh yet!" McKenney reported with astonishment, noting that they finally encamped two and one half hours later, after covering 79 miles.

Whenever a brigade put ashore for the night, the crewmen overturned their canoes to serve as their shelters. While the cook heated up their dinner, making a stew of pemmican and corn or wild rice, the *voyageurs* carried torches from the fire to melt chunks of pine pitch or spruce gum, which they used to recaulk their canoes along any seam that had sprung a leak. The men would have to put ashore for recaulking several times a day when they reached the tempestuous rivers farther north.

To the *voyageurs,* the monotony of the journey was worse than the physical exertion it entailed, and they seized on every opportunity to break their routine. A welcome interruption came with the crossing of a long ridge line several days out of Grand Portage. Up to that point, the *voyageurs* had been laboring upstream on rivers that flowed in a southerly direction; beyond, they would ride downstream on rivers that twisted northward.

To mark the divide, the men staged a mock ceremony resembling the one that salt-water sailors performed on crossing the equator. Any tenderfoot making his first trip to the north country was required to kneel while someone used a cedar bough to splash him with

A HUNTER'S VIEW OF A BUSTLING TRADING POST
This detailed sketch by a frontiersman shows a day during the trading season at Rocky Mountain House — a remote outpost on the banks of the North Saskatchewan River. Most of the fort's residents — as well as Indian hunters who have set up lodges outside the palisades — are busy with chores. A few, however, line the banks to watch the departure of a brigade of freight boats and the arrival of a band of pelt-laden Blackfeet. Founded by the North West Company in 1799, Rocky Mountain House flew the Hudson's Bay flag after the companies merged in 1821.

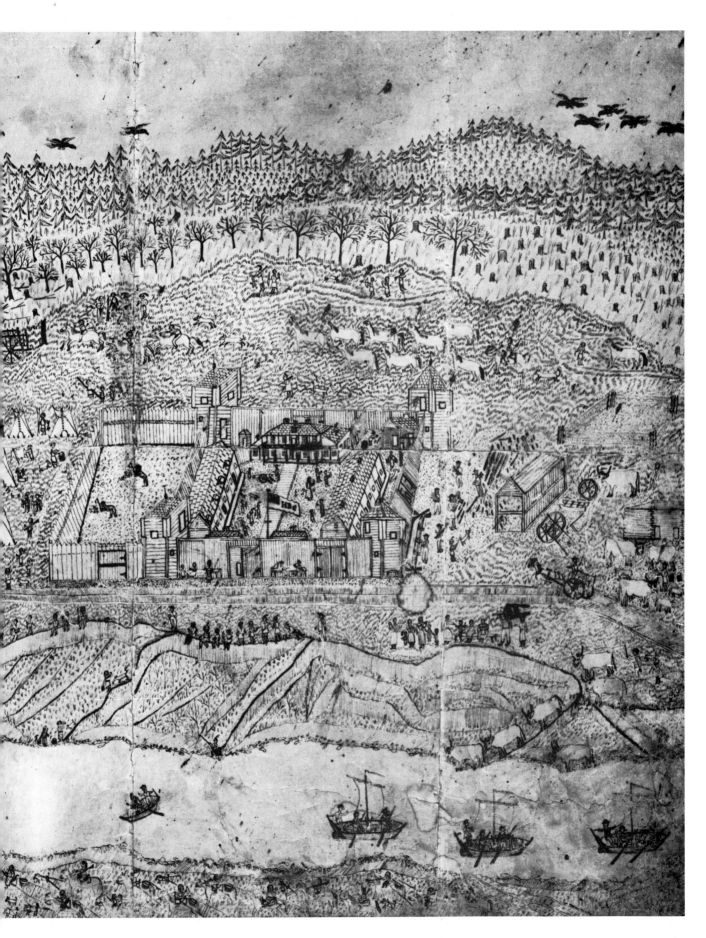

water from the north-flowing stream. Then the *bourgeois* would break out a keg of rum for a night of singing, boasting and horseplay.

Sport of quite another sort tempted the crews where a north-flowing stream descended sharply. Running dangerous rapids was strictly enjoined by company order, but the crews would gleefully disobey if the *bourgeois'* boat was out of sight. The guide would plunge his craft into the torrent, with the other canoes following him single file. In each boat, the middle men paddled furiously to hold a steady course, and the bowman and steersman flung their long paddles from side to side, shoving the craft away from menacing rocks and aiming it through the narrow chutes. All too often, the canoes were shattered on rocks or swamped by waves, and scores of foolhardy *voyageurs* ended up in picturesque graves along the worst rapids on the river road north.

From the wild white waters of Winnipeg River, the brigades paddled into Lake Winnipeg, a shallow inland sea 250 miles long and up to 65 miles wide. Here the danger was wind, which would lash the waters into steep waves that could overwhelm a loaded canoe. The superstitious *voyageurs* would speak to the wind, murmuring, "Blow softly, Old Woman, blow softly."

Most of the time they were wasting their breath, for the wind was usually strong. But on rare occasions the Old Woman relented, and gave them a mild southerly breeze. On each canoe, the crew would rig up a pole with an oilcloth sail and then relax, smoking and singing, as the craft scudded along at about eight miles per hour. The songs they sang were marvelously varied: patriotic airs, old hymns, love songs, humorous or obscene ditties. Each song, sacred or profane, would be ended with a piercing Indian yell.

The size of Lake Winnipeg made it the *voyageurs'* favorite body of water for racing. If the boatsmen of the Athabasca district happened to spy a brigade bound for a post on the Saskatchewan or Swan River, they would shout an insulting challenge across the water. The Athabasca men considered themselves the *crème de la crème* of the north men because their Fort Chipewyan was the most remote outpost. To make up for their longer journey, they carried lighter loads, and so they would win nearly every race. But for that very reason, the other brigades would eagerly accept the Ath-

abascans' challenge and struggle mightily to beat them.

Dropping their sails, the brigades would line up and start out with a rousing war whoop. The crews would step up their normal paddling beat to 50 strokes a minute, then 55 and even 60. According to Duncan McGillivray's journal, one epic contest between the Athabascans and another north-country brigade went on without a break for two days and nights, its intensity measured by the fact that an exhausted steersman fell out of his boat, was stoically ignored by two passing boats and would have drowned had not his crewmates gone back to fish him out. The race ended in a draw, noted McGillivray, when the crews "being entirely overcome with labour and fatigue, agreed to camp and cross the rest of the Lake together."

At Cumberland House, west of Lake Winnipeg, the Athabascans wound northwestward toward the Churchill River and its chain of lakes where they would run or bypass more than a hundred rapids. At length they labored across the Methye Portage, the 12-mile-long trail that Peter Pond had first traveled back in 1778. After they had descended the face of the 700-foot cliff, the canoeing was relatively easy down the Clearwater and Athabasca rivers. Some 250 miles from the portage, the northernmost north men saw their home post looming up ahead: Fort Chipewyan.

Fort Chipewyan was a scaled-down version of Grand Portage, and so was the reception it gave to the homecoming Athabascan brigades. Families and friends swarmed around the *voyageurs*, exchanging embraces and joyfully grabbing the little gifts that the men had brought back. Naturally, there was a feast and dance. These affairs, held in the *bourgeois'* house or the trading hall, were as lively as the summer ball at Grand Portage, though usually a bit cramped for space. One Nor'Wester wrote of a welcoming gala at his snug little fort: "All were merry but we were much crowded, there being present 72 men, 37 women, and 65 children, and the room being only 22 x 25 feet made it disagreeably warm."

The arrival of the canoe brigades attracted Indians from far and wide. The overtures to trade were always elaborate. As Duncan McGillivray described the Indians' arrival at Fort George on the Saskatchewan: "At a few yards distance from the gate they salute us

A party of *voyageurs* from the Hudson's Bay Company portages trade goods at a supply post along the route to the fur country.

with several discharges of their guns. On entering the house they are disarmed, treated with a few drams and a bit of tobacco, and after the pipe has been plyed about for some time they relate the news with great deliberation and ceremony relaxing from their usual taciturnity in proportion to the quantity of Rum they have swallowed, till at length their voices are drowned in a general clamour. When their lodges are erected by the women they receive a present of Rum, and the whole Band drink during 24 hours and sometimes much longer. When the drinking match has subsided they begin to trade."

The trading was done on credit; an Indian hunter was given a gun, powder, shot and other necessaries, which he swore to pay for with the returns from his winter trap lines. His debt was reckoned in terms of beaver skins, or *plus* (pronounced and often spelled "plews"). A gun had to be repaid with 14 *plus*, a blanket with six *plus*; two *plus* would settle for such small items as an ax, a shawl, a kettle, a beaver trap or a length of cloth.

The most valuable item of barter was high wine, concentrated distilled spirits, which the traders would water down to suit the tastes — and the alcohol tolerance — of the various tribes. For the veteran tipplers of the Saulteaux tribe near Grand Portage, eight or nine quarts of 180-proof spirits were mixed with enough water to fill a nine-gallon keg; for the less-experienced Western tribes, four or five quarts of spirits sufficed to make a keg of "Blackfoot rum." Whatever mixture, a keg of diluted alcohol fetched 30 *plus*.

The effect of liquor upon the Indians was a matter of deplorable record: it drove them to debauchery, fighting, occasional murders and a few sizable raids. One trader on a Red River post south of Lake Winnipeg made this grim, sardonic entry: "Indians having asked for liquor, and promised to decamp and hunt well, I gave them some. Grand Gueule stabbed Capot Rouge, Le Boeuf stabbed his young wife in the arm, Little Shell almost beat his old mother's brains out with a club, and there was terrible fighting among them. I sowed garden seeds."

Though the rum trade was at best irresponsible, it detracted but little from the constructive relations between the red men and the fur traders. In fact, this relationship was so soundly based on mutual need, and so happily free of built-in antagonisms, that it spared Western Canada the full-scale Indian wars that wracked the American territories to the south.

Unlike the more numerous Americans who went west as settlers and forced the Indians to fight for their land, the few fur men in the early Canadian Northwest were interested only in pelts, which the Indians alone could — and eagerly would — supply in great quantity in exchange for manufactured goods. Generations of amicable dealings between Scottish traders, French *voyageurs* and Indian hunters led to a robust intermingling of their various customs, traditions, social life and even bloodlines.

Besides commercial pelts, the Indians contributed corn, pemmican, wild rice, maple sugar, moccasins, buckskins and the indispensable canoe. Indians guided the traders through the maze of waterways, showed them how to fish through holes in the ice, and taught them the ways of winter travel in the north country, where the snow was too deep for walking and the cold was so intense that — as an Athabascan trader wrote — "One ought to have his Blood composed of Brandy, his Body of Brass and his Eyes of Glass."

Thanks to Indian inventions, the fur men hiked through drifted snow on snowshoes and transported supplies and pelts on sleds drawn by the natives' trained dogs, which could haul 600-pound loads a distance of 70 miles a day. The *voyageurs,* with their ingenuity and keen eye for display, decked out their dog teams with gaudy belled harnesses and embroidered saddle blankets, and they even made up sets of tiny leather boots to put on the animals' feet when the route was covered over with jagged ice. The dogs became so fond of these comfortable booties that they would sprawl on their backs, pawing the air and whining to have their footgear put on them.

As vital as the dog sled was in the lives of the fur men, an even greater Indian contribution to the trader was the woman who became his wife and the mother of his children. For Scot and Frenchman alike, it took an Indian mate to make life itself possible in the long, dark northern winters. She cooked, mended, tanned leather and fashioned it into clothing and moccasins. She stripped birch trees of their bark, stitching and gluing the pieces to the skeletons of canoes. She dressed game and hauled back the meat; made willow frames

A white captive's harsh tales of Indian life

Tanner appears as a gentleman in a portrait in the frontispiece to his narrative.

One tragic tale to come out of the Canadian frontier was that of the man in the portrait above. His name was John Tanner. In 1789, when he was nine years old, marauding Shawnees captured him near his family's cabin in what was to become Kentucky, and took him to the Great Lakes region. There he was adopted by a powerful old Indian woman, Net-no-kwa, of the Ottawa. He learned Indian skills so well that he grew into a fine hunter and, by age 20, was regarded as a leader of his band.

Like other Indians, he guided and hunted for white fur traders. Instinctively, he identified with them, and at one point became so deeply embroiled in the fierce rivalry between the North West and the Hudson's Bay Compa-

nies that he alienated his adopted tribesmen. Before long, Tanner was a complete outcast, unable to live at ease with either race. Forlornly, he made his way to Sault Ste. Marie, where he told the story of his life as a white Indian to a doctor, who published it in 1830.

The Indians whose ways Tanner chronicled were a far cry from the noble savages of 19th Century fiction. They lived with poverty, starvation, drunkenness, disease and exposure to cold. Searching for game, Tanner's band often went days without food. "Suicide is not very unfrequent among the Indians," said Tanner; sometimes it was brought on by "the alienation of mind produced by liquor." Drinking bouts lasted days, with men and women "lying by the fire in a state of absolute insensibility."

The results were often disastrous to the drinkers. "In the course of a single day," recalled Tanner, "Net-no-kwa sold one hundred and twenty beaver skins, with a large quantity of buffalo robes, dressed and smoked skins, and other articles, for rum. . . . Of all our large load of peltries, the produce of so many days of toil, of so many long and difficult journeys, one blanket, and three kegs of rum, only remained, beside the poor and almost worn-out cloathing on our bodies."

Apparently Tanner received neither fame nor fortune from his tale, for he sank into lonely degradation. In 1846, he disappeared. Several years later, in a swamp outside Sault Ste. Marie, a hunter found a skeleton thought to be Tanner's. But no one will ever know his fate for sure.

Colin Fraser, a second-generation fur man who was born and raised on trading posts, examines a black-fox skin as he sorts and grades the pelts, which he bought from trappers in the Northwest Territories. Fraser later realized a handsome profit when he marketed the batch of furs for $35,000.

and stretched raw pelts over them to cure for shipment; wove leather thongs into the supporting network for snowshoes; and gathered firewood, berries and wild rice — in addition to keeping her husband's bed warm and bringing up their energetic offspring. All this and more for a very small purchase price.

For a few blankets, an Indian father of no particular rank would gladly sell his daughter, who might be no more than 12 years old. Such deals were a venerable tradition in the north country, and few *voyageurs* had any qualms about making a buy, or reselling the chattel. A departing *voyageur* who could not find a buyer for his woman might simply abandon her.

But after several years and a couple of children, many a feckless *voyageur* discovered to his surprise that his Indian alliance had become permanent and deeply felt. Large numbers of *voyageurs* returned to their Indian mates for 20 or 30 winters, and eventually they retired to their Northwestern outposts in preference to the East. And as the fur trade spread, their descendants — known as half-breeds, mixed-bloods and Métis — became the backbone of numerous frontier settlements throughout Canada.

The Scots, being more sophisticated than the French-speaking *voyageurs,* were more cynical about acquiring Indian mates; they realized that they were forcing young women into concubinage. But the traders and clerks refused to deny themselves the amenities of the country, and the prosperous wintering partners would deal for a chief's daughter, and sometimes several, in a calculated campaign to cement relations with the local tribes. In turn a chief would demand and get a horse or two for a daughter. At any price, a chief's daughter was a bargain. She taught her Scot the language and idiosyncrasies of her tribe, and as the lady of his house, she brought her people and his together in a string of convivial social events.

Out of these alliances between dissimilar cultures came many tales that were amusing, tender and sometimes sad. In several cases, intelligent Indian girls balked at submitting to buyers whom they found unappealing. Instead, they became wilderness coquettes, using their big, black eyes and their considerable wiles to get a man of their own choosing.

Alexander Henry, an up-and-coming young trader, became the choice of one chief's daughter, and after a tipsy New Year's party at his first post on the Red River, he awakened to the sobering discovery that the girl had adopted him as her spouse. In his diary entry for January 1, 1801, Henry wrote: "Liard's daughter took possession of my room, and the devil himself could not have got her out." Henry tried to escape from her by going off on a buffalo hunt. But the girl was still there when he returned, and it was not until January 30 that Henry could write: "I got rid of my bed-fellow, who returned to her father with good grace. Fine weather." Two days later, however, "The lady returned. A terrible snowstorm."

Eventually the persistent spouse prevailed, and Henry came to refer to her fondly as "Her Ladyship." He brought her along when he took charge of Fort Vermilion on the upper Saskatchewan in 1808, and the fort's roster credited the couple with three children. Alas, Henry makes no mention of his family in his later journals, and their fate is unknown. Henry died at a Columbia River post in 1814 after a night of drinking, when a skiff in which he was riding capsized, drowning all seven occupants.

A story with a gentler ending involved Daniel Harmon, the same Vermonter who had grudgingly complimented the decorum of the Indian girls at his first Grand Portage ball in 1801.

Being a man of stern scruples, Harmon had long rejected his friends' urgings to acquire an Indian mate. But in October 1805, with another lonely winter setting in, Harmon capitulated. "This Day," he wrote soberly in his journal, "a Canadians Daughter (a Girl of about 14 years of age) was offered me, and after mature consideration concerning the step I ought to take I finally concluded it would be best to accept of her. In case we can live in harmony together, my intentions now are to keep her as long as I remain in this uncivilized part of the world, but when I return to my native land shall endeavour to place her into the hands of some good honest Man, with whom she can pass the remainder of her Days."

Harmon's mate, the daughter of a Cree Indian and a *voyageur,* was named Elizabeth Duval, and his life with her exceeded his hopes for mere harmony. When the North West Company dispatched him to the fresh fur grounds of New Caledonia beyond the Rockies, he took his Elizabeth with him, and they together served at several posts.

After 19 years in the fur trade, Harmon decided to return to the United States and he grimly faced up to the problem of disposing of Elizabeth. After much soul-searching, he concluded that he could not part with his wilderness wife. In a heartfelt diary entry, totally unlike his prim, cold notes of the early days, Harmon explained: "The union which has been formed between us, in the providence of God, has not only been cemented by a long and mutual performance of kind offices, but, also, by a more sacred consideration. We have wept together over the early departure of several children, and especially, over the death of a beloved son. We have children still living, who are equally dear to us both. How could I spend my days in the civilized world, and leave my beloved children in the wilderness? How could I tear them from a mother's love, and leave her to mourn over their absence, to the day of her death?"

Harmon could not and did not abandon his family. In the summer of 1819, he married his Elizabeth in a church ceremony and set out for the East with her and their daughters Sally and Polly. They made their way to a small town in Vermont. And there Daniel and Elizabeth Harmon raised several more children.

The North West Company reached the peak of its power around the turn of the 19th Century and stayed on top for 15 imperial years. The roster of Nor'Westers reached 2,000 traders, clerks and other employees, and schooners flying the "N.W. Co." flag plied the Great Lakes. The partners lived like kings on 15-year proceeds estimated at £1,185,000. Almost all of the company's profits were distributed in annual dividends, and sums of £400 per share were not uncommon.

Eventually, however, the Scots' munificence cost them dearly. The prudent owners of the Hudson's Bay Company, content with annual dividends of only 4 per cent, left much more working capital in the business, and thus the English traders had the resources to compete ever more successfully with the North West Company after 1810. By 1818, both of the companies were suffering unacceptably heavy losses in their fierce rivalry, which often featured armed clashes in the wilderness and costly lawsuits in London. To save the fur trade from ruin, the British Crown stepped in and pressed for a merger. When the rivals finally made peace and joined ranks in 1821, it was under the name and control of the Hudson's Bay Company.

Yet the merger produced no great change for anyone but the partners of the North West Company. Most of the Scottish traders and clerks went on with their work as Hudson's Bay employees. The *voyageurs* continued their annual rounds; new bosses could hardly alter the rhythm of the seasons. If anything changed for the canoemen, it was that expanding fur trade provided them with more jobs and sometimes with better pay.

One beneficiary, a retired *voyageur* well over 70 years old, looked back with satisfaction on his long career under Scottish and English traders. In a stirring monologue, he declared: "I have been 24 years a canoeman and 41 years in service; no portage was ever too long for me. Fifty songs could I sing. I have saved the lives of 10 voyageurs. Have had 12 wives and six running dogs. I spent all my money in pleasure. Were I young again, I should spend my life the same way over. There is no life so happy as a voyageur's life!"

An Indian trapper family, clad in traditional buckskin and trading-post cloth, gathers for a smoke in a lodge near Fort Garry in the 1820s.

A trio of canoes, with artist Frances Ann Hopkins amid the *voyageurs* in the nearest craft, slides out into the mists over a still lake.

The arduous life of "the happiest people in existence"

The lot of the fur-trading *voyageurs* was one of extreme hardship. "They shivered on the sunless trails deep in the woods, fought colds and insects and dysentery, cried out at night from the pain of knotted muscles and lamed backs," observed one writer. Their food was most often corn-meal mush and tallow-like pemmican flavored with hair, sticks, bark and sand. In winter, they built hearths of green logs and slept with their feet virtually in the fire; the heat would melt a watery pit in the snow, and sometimes they slid into it in the night.

Yet for all the discomfort, these hardy French-Canadian canoemen struck another observer as "the happiest people in existence." As they pushed their fragile birchbark vessels thousands of miles west, they made the wilds ring with their cheers, laughter and lusty songs. They took a special joy in caring for the occasional passengers in their midst, even to the point of carrying them piggyback through icy waters to and from the canoes. And if a lady was along, the *voyageurs* tenderly gathered wild roses to brighten her breakfast.

One such guest in the 1860s was Frances Ann Hopkins, the wife of a Hudson's Bay Company official. Mrs. Hopkins kept no journal. She did not have to. Her impressions were recorded in a sketchbook, and later, upon her return to civilization she turned them into a series of paintings that magnificently evoke the rugged *voyageurs* and the wilderness life they led.

The artist and her husband admire a water lily as eight colorfully garbed *voyageurs* propel a goods-laden canoe along a waterway.

Courtesy Public Archives of Canada, Ottawa

Bow- and sternmen keep the bow of a canoe pointed carefully upstream, as crewmen ashore track or haul the vessel through a rapid.

In the evening, a damaged canoe is diligently mended with a bark patch sewn onto the hull and then sealed with melted pitch.

2 | Odyssey to the Pacific

On the maps of the world in the mid-1700s, the sprawling interior of the Pacific Northwest was terra incognita. This mysterious territory beckoned a generation of explorers led by Captain James Cook, George Vancouver and, most notably, one Alexander Mackenzie. A fearless young Scot, Mackenzie mounted two heroic expeditions that made him the first white man to travel overland from Canada's interior to the Pacific coast.

What fired Mackenzie's imagination in 1787 was one of the day's more fanciful maps. It was drawn by a fellow explorer named Peter Pond, whose consuming dream of a Northwest Passage connecting the Atlantic and Pacific appears on the work, a copy of which is reproduced at right.

Starting with coastal charts made in 1778 by Cook, Pond seized on an inlet and expanded it until it reached hundreds of miles inland. To this he all but connected a mythical western outlet of Great Slave Lake, thus indicating a navigable route to the coast. Other features of his map, such as Lake Clair, did in fact exist but were inaccurately located.

The problem with this and other maps was not latitude, or north-south position, which could be calculated with reasonable ease from the sun by use of a sextant and an almanac. The difficulty was the east-west line, or longitude. To determine longitude, a man had to know the correct time in Greenwich, England (the prime meridian), and the exact time at his location, and he had to check them both against the position of Jupiter's satellites. Then, by referring to astronomical tables, he could determine his distance from Greenwich, or longitude.

Untrained in mathematics and carrying fallible instruments, Pond always assumed that the Pacific coast was a brief canoe trip away. It was not. But that was for Mackenzie to prove.

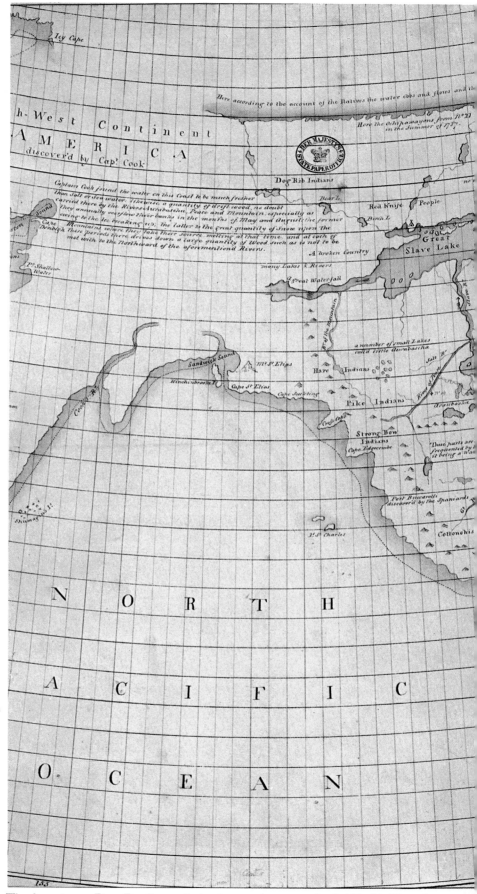

The deception on Peter Pond's map is the short gap between a fancied Cook's River (*upper*

52

left) and the body labeled A Great Waterfall. The error was based partly on a tale of Indians Pond thought had traveled the waterway.

The epic discoveries of a fearless Scot

At 7 o'clock on the evening of May 9, 1793, a tiny band of explorers stood on the bank of the Peace River in what is now northwestern Alberta. They were about to embark on a journey that would become an epic of Canadian history. Six — Joseph Landry, Charles Ducette, François Beaulieux, Baptiste Bisson, François Courtois and Jacques Beauchamp — were *voyageurs,* seasoned veterans of the North West Company's back-country trade. Two were Indians, signed on to serve as interpreters and hunters. One was the expedition's second-in-command, a young company clerk named Alexander McKay. The leader was another young Scot, Alexander Mackenzie, an intense, curly-headed blond equipped with a few crude navigational instruments and a singular purpose.

Below the little log fort they had built and wintered in, the men loaded a 25-foot canoe with the last of their baggage: pemmican, beans and flour, arms, ammunition, rum and a supply of presents with which they hoped to win the assistance of Indian tribes they might meet along the way. All told, 3,000 pounds of cargo nestled in the bottom of their slender birchbark vessel. For a moment they stood bareheaded and silent; the two men appointed to remain at the fort, Mackenzie noted in his journal, "shed tears on the reflection of those dangers which we might encounter in our expedition, while my own people offered up their prayers that we might return safely from it."

Then the 10 men — and a large, friendly dog someone had thought to bring along — climbed carefully into their fragile craft and began paddling upstream toward the sunset. Somehow they were going to breach the awesome barrier of the Rocky Mountains and become the first white men to find a route across the northern mass of the continent to the Pacific Ocean — in a canoe.

As he embarked on this improbable voyage, Alexander Mackenzie, at 29, already had behind him 14 years of experience in Canada's rugged fur trade. He had made one previous attempt to reach the Pacific in 1789. That first attempt had failed. But it had been invaluable preparation for the ordeal ahead.

Born on the Isle of Lewis in the Outer Hebrides, Mackenzie had emigrated to New York with his widowed father at the age of 11 when the family, like so many other Scots, had been forced off their lands by a succession of poor crops and rising rents. A few months after their arrival in 1775 the American Revolution broke out, and the elder Mackenzie joined a Royalist regiment, leaving young Alexander in the care of two aunts who sought safety, first in New York's upper Mohawk Valley and later in Canada. There the boy continued his schooling until, at 15, he quit to become an apprentice in the fur-trading concern of Finlay, Gregory & Company.

Mackenzie served his profession well in various posts from Detroit to Ile-à-la-Crosse, rising rapidly to a partnership at 20 when his firm was merged with the young and aggressive North West Company. During the winter of 1788, he was assigned to the company's so-called Athabasca department as second-in-command to Peter Pond, the onetime Connecticut Yankee who had built the region's first post on the Athabasca River 30 miles south of the lake. More importantly, Pond proved to be the catalyst in Mackenzie's career.

At 47, Pond was an old man by fur-trade standards, and he had long harbored a vision of discovering a Northwest Passage. The maps he had drawn as a part of his dream fueled the fires of ambition in the young Scot. One map in particular fascinated Mac-

Alexander Mackenzie, knighted by King George III for his incredible journey across Canada to the Pacific Ocean, sat for this proud portrait in London around 1800.

55

kenzie. Prepared in the summer of 1787, it showed the Great Slave Lake north of Lake Athabasca drained by a mighty river that flowed due west, directly toward the inlet at the present-day site of Anchorage.

Pond was convinced that the Anchorage inlet, or "Cook's River" as he called it, after the famous British mariner, must be the mouth of a great "River of the West" rumored to exist since early times. The Rocky Mountains, Pond reasoned, must end around lat. 62° 30' N. to allow the river to flow westward to the Pacific, north of them. Moreover, he believed the distance to the ocean from the mountains must be relatively short — a week's travel or less. Contributing to this fantasy, in the days when longitude was not easy to establish accurately, was Pond's blithe placement of key features, such as Lake Athabasca, a good 700 miles west of where they actually were.

All through the winter of 1788-1789, Pond and his young successor spent long evenings poring over the maps, for Pond's vision became Mackenzie's own peculiar ambition.

And on the 3rd of June 1789, Mackenzie left Fort Chipewyan, headed — he hoped — for the Pacific, in three canoes with five *voyageurs* and six Indians. In a later account of this first exploration westward, Mackenzie stated that it was "performed by the order of the N.W. Company." But the likelihood is that the project was Mackenzie's own, and that his partners knew little or nothing about it.

The first leg of their journey was down the Slave River. The weather was wretchedly cold and blustery, and one canoe was wrecked by rapids, its cargo ruined. Reaching Great Slave Lake, they spent two weeks probing the ice along the shore before they located a passage. The river was broad and strong, and for nearly 300 miles they followed it westward, excitement rising. Then, just as they glimpsed the Rockies ahead, the stream veered dismayingly north.

Nevertheless, Mackenzie pushed doggedly downstream, paddling from three in the morning to nine at night, and making as much as 100 miles a day. By July 10, he found himself in the maze of a vast delta system, threading among countless islands with the snow-clad Rockies still looming as a solid wall to the west. Climbing to the highest point of one final island, Mackenzie saw stretching to the northern horizon noth-

ing but a bleak, unbroken landscape of pack ice. His "River of Disappointment," as he now sadly called it, had led not to the warm waves of the Pacific, but to a frozen "Hyperborean Sea" without hope of passage.

Mackenzie lingered for another day or two to take navigational sightings and observe the salt-water tides, but the outward voyage was obviously at an end. He and his men must turn back quickly, so as to reach Fort Chipewyan before winter. He gave the name of Whale Island to the treeless mound where he and his men had camped, and set up a marker post on which he inscribed his name, the latitude and the date.

Then began the arduous return trip against the river's fierce current, a labor at which they still managed a herculean 30 miles or more a day. On Saturday, September 12, with the first snows of autumn already dusting the land, they sailed on a favorable wind across Lake Athabasca to the fort.

In 102 days Mackenzie had traveled 2,060 miles to the mouth of Canada's largest river and back. Henceforth that river would bear his name. He had staked a British claim to the western Arctic seaboard and a fresh-water drainage basin behind it larger than all of Europe west of the Rhine. Unhappily, he had also demonstrated that Cook's Inlet did *not* push into the North American interior, that there was no Northwest Passage through the continent in those latitudes, and that a passage was probably impracticable at a higher latitude — "the Sea," as he noted, "being eternally covered with Ice."

At the annual gathering of fur traders in Grand Portage, at the western end of Lake Superior, in the spring of 1790, Mackenzie's partners did not seem particularly impressed by his feat. "My expedition is hardly spoken of, but this is what I expected," he wrote his cousin Roderic at Fort Chipewyan. After all, the men in the company, who called themselves Nor'westers, were practical fur men, and the expedition had not secured for them a trading route to the Pacific. Still, the partners were not entirely unappreciative of Mackenzie; in the new agreement drawn up that summer, he was awarded two of the 20 shares in place of the one he had held before.

Possibly the partners meant it less as a salute to an intrepid explorer than as an inducement for their young

Captain Cook's fateful voyage to the Northwest

James Cook consults his charts in this portrait made just before his last voyage.

By February of 1776, Captain James Cook, at 47 the best known explorer of his century, had already charted the coasts of Australia and New Zealand on one voyage, and circumnavigated Antarctica on a second. The British Board of Admiralty, not wishing him to risk further peril, only wanted his advice on an upcoming voyage: whom should it assign to reach the western shoulder of North America, and there-

in find a passage to the Atlantic?

Naturally, Cook volunteered. In two vessels, the 462-ton *Resolution* and the 300-ton *Discovery,* Cook and a crew of 191 sailed three quarters of the way around the world before sighting the Northwest Coast on March 7, 1778. Putting in at Nootka Sound on Vancouver Island, the expedition was met by Indians who, Cook observed, were eager to swap

the luxuriant pelts of sea otters for cheap iron goods, such as flat blades and chisels.

"Nothing would go down with our visitors but metal," Cook wrote after a few days, "and brass had by this time supplanted iron, being so eagerly sought after that hardly a bit of it was left in the ships."

His holds filled with furs, Cook pressed north on the larger task of finding the passage. He was following a rather fanciful Russian map that showed Alaska as an island separated from North America by a broad passage leading north to the polar sea, which was then thought navigable.

All summer long Cook probed the coast, looking for the elusive waterway. As the shoreline turned west, so went Cook until, in late August, having negotiated the Bering Strait, the explorers were repulsed by polar ice.

Bitterly disappointed, Cook termed his Russian chart "a map that the most illiterate of seafaring men would have been ashamed to put his name to." He sailed for the Sandwich Islands, intending "farther search of a passage the ensuing summer."

He never did search farther. In an affray on shore with hostile Sandwich Islanders — Hawaiians — on the 14th of February 1779, Cook was stabbed to death. But most of his crew escaped back to the ship, sailed to China where they sold their furs for fabulous prices, and then returned to England. There, the news of the fur fortune, together with Cook's maps and journals, published posthumously in 1784, touched off the frenzied race for the Northwest fur trade.

colleague to stay home and help tend the growing trade. If they did, it was a wasted suggestion. Mackenzie's first failure had only heightened his zeal to find a passage to the Pacific. He spent the winter analyzing his first expedition, and decided that his navigation had been faulty. His most grievous failing, he believed, had been his inability to determine longitude properly.

With that, he boldly asked his partners for a year's leave and in the fall of 1791, sailed off to London, where for the better part of a year he immersed himself in the arcane science of astronomy and navigation. By September 1792, he was back at Fort Chipewyan, ready to strike out again. This time he would travel west and south.

Alexander Mackenzie's account of his second journey, like that of his first, was a working document, crammed with measurements and directions, navigational fixes and miscellaneous information that might be useful to those who followed. He was not a "candidate for literary fame," he wrote. Yet his journal is filled with vivid glimpses of the wildness and beauty of the country the men traversed, the incredible hardships they endured and the dangers they overcame.

On the evening of May 9, Mackenzie and his nine companions, plus their dog, departed the small log fort in which they had spent the winter and started paddling west up the Peace River. They went only a few miles to check canoe and equipment before camping for the night. The next day the expedition embarked in high spirits, and Mackenzie allowed himself a moment to describe the prairies and foothills through which they were passing. "This magnificent theater of nature has all the decorations which the trees and animals of the country can afford it," he wrote. "Groves of poplar in every shape vary the scene; and their intervals are enlivened with vast herds of elks and buffaloes." And he added: "The whole country displayed an exuberant verdure; the trees that bear a blossom were advancing fast to that delightful appearance, and the velvet rind of their branches reflecting the oblique rays of a rising or setting sun, added a splendid gaiety to the scene."

Not a candidate for literary fame, indeed.

On May 17, less than a week out on the Peace River—and sooner than expected—the Rocky Mountains hove into view, "a very agreeable object," as Mackenzie observed, with their summits decked in glis-

tening snow. Game was still abundant, but Mackenzie feared that gunfire would scare off Indians, who might be helpful sources of information. So they sent the dog bounding after a herd of buffalo, and shortly a plump calf had been rounded up for the evening meal. The men feasted and relaxed around the campfire with their *regale* of rum.

Over the next few days the expedition pressed swiftly upstream. Then the river narrowed and quickened, and Mackenzie confronted his first obstacle: the roaring Canyon of the Peace, which snaked through the hills for 20 turbulent miles. For one entire week he and his men fought their way up rapids and cascades beneath vertical cliffs, from which, he reported, boulders plummeted down in terrifying barrages.

In one two-mile stretch alone, they were forced to unload and carry their cargo over four separate portages, towing the partly manned canoe through violent eddies and whirlpools. Mackenzie wrote that they almost met disaster when "a wave striking the bow broke the line and filled us with inexpressible dismay, as it appeared impossible that the vessel could escape being dashed to pieces, and those who were in her from perishing." At the last moment another wave providentially lifted her ashore. The men were shaken enough to start grumbling about returning home. Mackenzie thought it prudent to call a halt for the night—"particularly," he noted, "as the river above us, as far as we could see, was one white sheet of foaming water."

On Tuesday, May 21, a scouting party reported that the water route was totally impassable for the next nine miles. The men took to the woods with their axes, hacking a trail through the brush and trees of a mountainside. The cargo was backpacked and the canoe was hauled up the steep path by passing a towline around a succession of stumps. It was brutal work, and all the more so for a strange cactus-like plant about nine feet tall, armed with "small prickles which caught our trousers, and working through them, sometimes found their way to the flesh." Mackenzie called it the devil's club, or *bois picant*.

At length they reached the end of the canyon. Here the waters of the Peace were more placid. But now there were snow-covered mountains on all sides, and the men shivered inside their blanket coats. On May 29, a storm broke and they were forced to stay in camp. Mackenzie busied himself writing a first account of their progress and hardships so far; he then carefully rolled it up, inserted it in the bunghole of an empty rum keg and "consigned this epistolatory cargo to the mercy of the current." History does not record its fate.

On May 31, after pushing up yet another churning staircase of rapids, Mackenzie's party was confronted by a fork in the river, where a wall of rock split the Peace into two tributaries, one climbing northward, the other south. The first was temptingly broad. But an old Indian, whom Mackenzie had met near his base camp, had warned him that the northern branch soon lost itself among the mountains. The southerly branch, though narrower and more perilous, would eventually lead to a carrying place—and thence to a "great river."

How reliable was the old man's advice? Mackenzie's disgruntled Indian interpreters urged him to take the northerly route, and so did his crew. But Mackenzie bet on the old Indian, and almost immediately regretted it, for the expedition spent the afternoon struggling barely three miles upstream. "A very tardy and mortifying progress," Mackenzie noted sourly.

Days, then weeks, passed as the group pushed up the river, later named the Parsnip for the wild sprouts that grew along its banks. Increasingly, Mackenzie felt misgivings, and desperately hoped to make contact with local Indians, who could guide him through the mountains. At last, on June 9, rounding a bend, the men smelled smoke and heard sounds of running. Suddenly, two Indians burst from cover, "brandishing their spears, displaying their bows and arrows, and accompanying their hostile gestures with loud vociferations."

Through his interpreters Mackenzie assured the warriors that he meant no harm. Then, in a bold move, he went ashore and took each Indian by the hand. "One of them," he observed, "but with a very tremulous action, drew his knife from his sleeve, and presented it to me as a mark of submission to my will and pleasure."

The Indians were Sekanis, "people of the rocks," and they hardly presented a threat to the explorers. The entire ragged, ill-fed band consisted of three men and their wives and eight children. They had heard of white men, they said, but had never seen any before. Occasionally, however, they obtained bits of iron from other tribes that went down to the sea—Stinking Lake, they called it—to trade with fair-skinned people who came there in "vessels as big as islands."

Eager for more information, Mackenzie passed out beads and other trinkets, as well as some of his precious pemmican. But the Sekanis said that the trading tribes had to go by overland trails; they knew of no great River of the West.

Mackenzie once again was in a quandary. Should he plunge ahead? Should he return to the Peace and try the north fork? Should he abandon his canoe and try to find the overland trails? Or, as his men urged him, should he simply quit? To Mackenzie, the last was unthinkable. "To return unsuccessful, after all our labors, sufferings and dangers," he wrote in his log, "was an idea too painful to indulge." Perhaps the Sekanis had not told all they knew; perhaps, too, his own interpreters were not reporting everything they heard. Mackenzie continued his overtures to the tiny Sekani band, giving the children sugar as a special treat.

Next morning, "at 9 o'clock," the precise Mackenzie recorded, he overheard one of the Sekanis say something about a great river, a phrase whose Sekani equivalent Mackenzie knew himself by now. Confronting the Indian, he had the man sketch its location with a piece of charcoal on a strip of bark. He mapped a route that went up the stream they were following, across a series of little lakes and carrying places, then down a small river; this would lead them to a great river, where there were many warlike people who lived in houses built on islands.

Taking one of the Sekanis as a guide, Mackenzie set out with rekindled hope. Within two days, they were crossing the first of the little lakes. Its entrance was choked with driftwood and its waters were so high from the melting snows that, Mackenzie remarked, "the country was entirely overflowed, and we passed with the canoe among the branches of trees." At the far end, an Indian trail led up through a narrow defile and over a low ridge. Stopping to survey the scene, Mackenzie suddenly grasped the significance of the spot.

The small lake he had just traversed—Arctic Lake, as it was subsequently named—was the highest and southernmost source of a single, vast water system that flowed northeastward down from the Rockies. The system traced its path east through the Parsnip and the Peace, then north through Athabasca and Great Slave lakes, gathering other rivers on the way until, as a mighty river, it debouched into the "Frozen Ocean," which Mackenzie had reached four years before.

The low ridge over which they had just portaged their canoe and cargo—exactly 817 paces by Mackenzie's count—was the Continental Divide. They were the first white men to cross it north of the Spanish territories in the far Southwest.

Descending on the far side of the ridge, the men now saw spreading out to the west the beginnings of a whole new watershed. Two small streams flowed down to the blue waters of another pond—Pacific Lake, as it was later named. On its banks, Indians had left a few canoes; they had hung baskets containing articles for later use from the trees. Mackenzie helped himself to a few items that might come in handy—a net, fishing hooks, a goat's horn and a wooden trap—and took great care to leave in exchange a knife, some firesteels, beads and awls.

Mackenzie was exultant: for the first time since setting out a month before, they were going downstream. But the going was as hazardous as ever. Two men sent ahead to reconnoiter the lake's outlet brought back news of "a fearful detail of rapid currents, fallen trees and large stones," wrote Mackenzie, and he named the place Bad River.

He was not a superstitious man. Had he been, he would have sworn that the gods were conspiring against him, for the next day, June 13, was an almost fatally unlucky one. To lighten their heavily laden craft, Mackenzie and a few others decided to get out and walk. "But those in the boat," he noted dryly, "with great earnestness requested me to re-embark, declaring, at the same time, that if they perished, I should perish with them."

They had scarcely gotten underway on a stretch of white water when the canoe slammed into a rock, turned sideways in the current and fetched up with a sickening crunch on a gravel bar. The men refloated her, but were helpless in the maelstrom. In moments the stern shattered on a boulder, sending the steersman sprawling to the bottom of the canoe. The force of the impact drove the craft to the opposite shore, where the bow too was smashed in. Desperately, the bowman made a grab for the branches of a small tree in hopes of holding the boat ashore, but the tree bent like a catapult, snatching him from his seat and shooting him

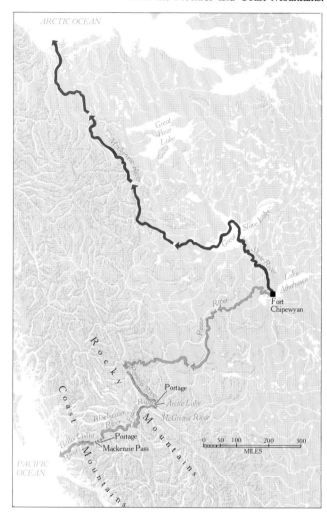

On his first journey of exploration in 1789, Mackenzie failed to reach the Pacific, but did blaze a trail to the Arctic Ocean. When he finally achieved his goal in 1793, it was by a treacherous route across the Rockies and Coast Mountains.

into the woods "with a degree of violence that threatened his destruction," wrote Mackenzie.

The canoe, meanwhile, was careering over another cascade that ripped open its bottom and broke away the thwarts. The *voyageurs* tumbled out into the torrent with the panic-stricken steersman screaming, "Every man for himself!" Mackenzie's bellowed counterorder to hang onto the broken hull probably saved their lives. The men obeyed, and after several hundred yards, they and their leader were mercifully carried into an eddy of calm water.

The men were so dazed by the beating, and so numbed by the icy water, that minutes passed before anyone could stand. Mackenzie's two Indian interpreters and the Sekani were so shaken by the experience that they wept uncontrollably. But no one had been se-

60

riously injured—though precious cargo had been lost, including the entire supply of musket balls. The 80 pounds of gunpowder they were carrying was intact but soaked. Like everything else, it had to be spread out to dry—and that necessity almost brought an emphatic end to the expedition. On his way to bed that evening, one of the *voyageurs* mindlessly strolled across the drying gunpowder puffing on a lighted pipe. Mackenzie indignantly wrote that the fellow had very nearly "put a period to all my anxiety and ambition."

Next morning, they made emergency repairs to the canoe with patches of birchbark, pieces of oilskin and a great deal of melted pitch. The canoe had become so heavy from repeated waterlogging and patching that on portages four men instead of the usual two were needed to carry her on their shoulders, as they stumbled through mud, roots and fallen trees. By now their Sekani guide was thoroughly disenchanted, and one night he simply vanished. Mackenzie cursed and pushed on without him. At last, on June 17, he and his exhausted *voyageurs* had the "inexpressible satisfaction of finding ourselves on the bank of a navigable river, on the West side of the great range of mountains."

The river, which came to be called the McGregor, was 200 yards wide. It soon carried them on its ample current to a fork, then down a still broader and more turbulent river—the Fraser—beneath lofty firs, wide-spreading cedars and high white cliffs crowned with pinnacles in grotesque shapes.

Sweeping around a bend, they suddenly came upon the first of the warlike peoples the Sekanis had warned them about. A handful of Indians appeared on the bank and loosed a shower of arrows, which happily fell short. A few miles on, Mackenzie and his men landed to examine a deserted lodge 30 feet long and 20 feet wide constructed of cedar and divided into apartments for three families. One noteworthy feature of the camp was a large cylindrical contraption made of wooden slats obviously intended for catching fish. It was the work of the Carrier Indians, then a major tribe on the west slope of the Rockies. They built seasonal dwellings to use when salmon came upstream to spawn. Neither fish nor game were in evidence now, however, and as a precaution against starvation on his return, Mackenzie ordered the first of several caches. The men buried a 90-pound bag of pemmican deep in a hole

and made their campfire over it to mask the spot.

Farther down the Fraser, the explorers surprised a larger encampment of Carrier Indians, and again were greeted by volleys of arrows. As he had with the Sekanis, Mackenzie decided on an "adventurous project" and coolly stepped ashore alone, holding up "looking glasses, beads, and other alluring trinkets." As insurance, however, he stuffed a brace of pistols in his belt and ordered one of the Indian interpreters to carry two muskets and shadow him out of sight in the woods.

After repeated entreaties Mackenzie finally persuaded the Carriers, seven families including 18 men in all, to sit with him and talk about the route ahead. As usual, the reports were disheartening: the river they were on, the tribesmen said, was very long, and it ran south, not west. It was altogether impassable in three places, where falls and rapids thundered between cliffs much higher and more fearsome than any they had yet encountered. Added to the perils, the downstream people were exceedingly savage and would almost surely kill the intruders on sight.

Once more Mackenzie faced a crucial decision. He believed that he must be at last on the great River of the West. But he was mistaken. That river indeed existed, but it lay far to the south, flowing through what is now Washington and Oregon. Unbeknownst to Mackenzie it had been named the Columbia by an American captain charting the Pacific Coast the summer before. The river the Canadians were struggling down reached the sea more than 200 miles north of the Columbia, at the site of present-day Vancouver, British Columbia. And as the man for whom it was to be named, Simon Fraser, was to rediscover a decade later, it was no natural trade route, but one of North America's most violent major watercourses.

Mackenzie could not know any of this. But he had already seen enough of the Fraser's swift current to be cautious, and the tales of the Carriers about conditions downstream added to his apprehensions. Moreover, he had only 30 days' worth of rations remaining—not enough to follow this long, angry, southward-flowing river to its mouth and return.

After an uneasy night, Mackenzie made his decision. He would abandon this river and strike due west overland across the mountains by the paths the Indians took. It was his only chance of reaching the sea. ◉

Death and disappointment in the high Arctic

During the time that Alexander Mackenzie and George Vancouver were looking for a Northwest Passage in the lower latitudes, other explorers seeking the elusive waterway headed straight north to the ice-packed Arctic. The men who went on these expeditions often came back scurvy-ridden and half-mad — if they came back at all.

The first white man to brave the barren tundra was Samuel Hearne, a trapper sent by the Hudson's Bay Company to find the passage. Hearne traveled from Churchill on Hudson Bay to the Arctic coast before giving up in 1771. "Once, upward of seven days," he wrote, "we tasted not a mouthful of anything except a few cranberries, scraps of old leather, and burnt bones."

After Hearne's trip, there was a hiatus of 50 years in the search for the passage; then a British government prize of £20,000 lured a series of gentlemen-explorers. Perhaps the best known was Sir John Franklin, a doughty adventurer who led three expeditions to the frozen frontier. The first two — in 1819-1821 and 1825-1827 — retraced Hearne's path overland to the Arctic Ocean; there, Franklin's crews surveyed more than 1,800 miles of icy coast from canoes, and proved that no land barrier prevented ocean passage across the western half of Canada's Arctic coast.

In 1845 Franklin volunteered for a sailing expedition to find a clear channel across the top of the continent. With two ships and supplies for three years, the 59-year-old commander sailed from England into the Davis Strait and Baffin Bay. Not one of the 129 men who set out with him was ever seen again. But an expedition mounted for the purpose of searching for him — one of 40 in the 14 years after his disappearance — found grim evidence of his fate: a small boat off King William Island near Cape Crozier, containing two skeletons and a pathetic baggage of silk handkerchiefs and silver teaspoons engraved with Franklin's crest.

Another of the parties seeking Franklin did find a way across the top of the continent, but it was a route no one would ever again attempt for commerce. In 1851 Captain Robert McClure entered the Arctic Ocean from the Pacific, sailed on an easterly track for 1,000 miles — and then became icebound for more than two years in the strait that now bears his name. On April 19, 1853, he and his crew went on foot to Dealy Islet, with conclusive evidence that although a Northwest Passage existed, not even during the summer would it be navigable.

One of Franklin's camps huddles on a high sandstone bluff overlooking the Coppermine River,

SAMUEL HEARNE

SIR JOHN FRANKLIN

ROBERT McCLURE

about nine miles from the Arctic Ocean. This drawing is by artist George Back, who accompanied Franklin on his first and second expeditions.

Franklin's men and dogs draw sledge-mounted canoes over an Arctic lake in Back's drawing. It was June 1821, and the ice was "honeycombed by the recent rains," Franklin wrote, and "lacerated the feet at every step. The poor dogs, too, marked their path with their blood."

Back shows two dories avoiding ice floes in Beaufort Bay. "The boats were exposed to no little danger of being broken between the masses of ice from which larger pieces frequently fell," wrote Franklin.

An unknown artist depicted the fate of two crewmen after their discovery in 1857. Surmised a rescuer: "These two, not being able to keep pace, were left with such provisions as could be spared."

Captain Robert McClure's bark, *Investigator,* lies ice-bound near the missing leg of the Northwest Passage in this water color by a member of the 1851 expedition. The crew finally abandoned ship and walked 160 miles across the ice to finish the first transit of the "Passage."

The trek began on July 4. The men buried a cache of pemmican, corn and gunpowder, and built a platform on which they inverted their canoe. The rest of their provisions they slung on their backs, the Canadian *voyageurs* carrying 90 pounds each, Mackenzie and MacKay 70 pounds. Their two Indian interpreters had packs of 45 pounds each — and objected to carrying anything at all.

Their route lay along a well-marked trail, through heavily wooded ridge country. The first evening a friendly older Carrier Indian with three companions joined the camp, and agreed to act as guide for part of the journey. Mackenzie was interested to see that one of the new arrivals carried a European halberd, obviously obtained in coastal trade, and another a pelt of sea otter that he exchanged for some beads and a brass cross. As the men lay down that night, they were lulled to sleep by the natives singing in soft, plaintive tones that reminded them of their own church music.

At a Carrier encampment the next day, farther along the trail, there was fresh evidence that the sea could not be far off. Dangling as ornaments from the ears of some children were two types of coins, Mackenzie observed, "one of his present Majesty, and the other of the State of Massachusetts Bay, coined in 1787." That night, fearful lest his chain of local guides might break, Mackenzie insisted on taking an Indian into his bed. "My companion's hair being greased with fish oil, and his body smeared with red earth," he related, "my sense of smelling threatened to interrupt my rest; but these inconveniences yielded to my fatigue, and I passed a night of sound repose."

For several more days, the explorers marched westward, negotiating for new guides as the old ones departed, and stopping on occasion to cache provisions.

In camp one evening, the Canadians watched with fascination while two of their Indian companions hunkered down to play a favorite game. Each had a bundle of about 50 small polished sticks, some marked with red lines around them. "As many of these as one of the players might find convenient were curiously rolled up in dry grass," Mackenzie noted, "and according to the judgment of his antagonist respecting their number of marks, he lost or won." Somewhat less appealing were the fish roe the natives offered as a delicacy; they were boiled and seasoned with a powerful, rancid oil, and the smell was enough to sicken Mackenzie, though the extreme hunger of his companions "surmounted the nauseous meal."

By now the Canadians had reached the landward slopes of the coastal range, and they began the long climb with their heavy packs. Hour after lung-searing hour they toiled upward and finally emerged above treeline in a narrow pass through which howled a tempest of alternating hail, snow and rain. When the storm cleared, one of the Indian hunters brought down a small mountain deer. The ravenous men gulped down their first fresh meat in weeks, and with rising spirits washed their filthy clothing and shaved off their matted beards.

As they descended to the brink of a precipice on the trail that evening, the whole stunning panorama of the coastal mountains and fjords suddenly opened up to view. Immediately they could sense the change in climate. Here, warmed and watered by Pacific winds, grew cedar trees lofty and thick beyond imagination — some were as big as 24 feet around — as well as stately hemlocks, pines and spruce. Far below in the valley their guides pointed to the gleaming ribbon of a river, and to a little village nestled in its bank. The exhausted men wanted to stop where they were for the night. Mackenzie insisted on pushing on.

It was pitch dark when they reached the edge of the woods near the village. Mackenzie went on alone, groping through the gigantic trees. Finding several families cooking a meal of fish outside their huts, he walked up "without the least ceremony, threw down my burden and after shaking hands with some of the people, sat down upon it." The villagers, Bella Coolas, must have heard news of the white man's coming, for they received him warmly and without surprise, making signs that he should go up to the great house of the chief.

The lodge, bigger than any Indian dwelling Mackenzie had ever seen, was built high above the ground on massive posts, apparently to raise it above the river's floodwaters. A broad, sloping timber into which steps had been hewn reached up to the door. "By this curious ladder," Mackenzie wrote, "I entered the house at one end; and having passed three fires, at equal distances in the middle of the building, I was received by several people, sitting upon a very wide board. I shook hands with them, and seated myself beside a man, the dignity of whose countenance induced me to give him

that preference. In a short time my people arrived, and placed themselves near me, when the man by whom I sat immediately rose, and fetched, from behind a plank four feet wide, a quantity of roasted salmon. He then directed a mat to be placed before me and Mr. MacKay. When this ceremony was performed, he brought a salmon for each of us, and half a one to each of my men."

The chief seemed to be signaling that the white men were welcome to stay overnight in the great house. But Mackenzie could not be certain and decided to sleep outside. The chief ordered a fire prepared, and boards placed about so the visitors would not have to lie on the ground. He also presented them with a large dish of salmon roe pounded into a sort of cream, and another dish of roe, with berries and herbs, that Mackenzie found quite agreeable. "Having been regaled with these delicacies," he wrote, "we laid ourselves down to rest with no other canopy than the sky; but I never enjoyed a more sound and refreshing rest, though I had a board for my bed, and a billet for my pillow."

At five the next morning, the men awoke to find that their Indian friends had lighted a fresh fire for them and were ready with a meal of salmon and the plumpest, juiciest gooseberries and raspberries they had ever seen. After breakfast Mackenzie inspected the village and its inhabitants, whom he found a well-fed and handsome lot. Their dress was a single robe tied about the shoulders and falling almost to the ground in back, made of cedar bark prepared into a fine hemp and interwoven with lustrous sea-otter skins or embroidered with designs in red and yellow threads. The women, Mackenzie noted, wore their hair short so that it required little care, while the men wore theirs long in plaits and smeared it with oil and red earth, carrying, instead of a comb, "a small stick hanging by a string from one of the locks, which they employ to alleviate any itching or irritation of the scalp."

Mackenzie was equally impressed with the industry of the Bella Coolas. They subsisted almost entirely on salmon and had built a large weir across the river, named for the tribe, in which they caught great quantities of the fish. He noticed, however, that the villagers motioned him back when he attempted to have a closer look. Later, when one of his men casually tossed a venison bone into the river, an Indian immediately plunged in to retrieve it, throwing it on a nearby fire and washing his hands. At length the reason behind these actions became clear: the Indians believed that the smell of animal meat, or anyone who had touched or eaten animal meat, might drive away the fish on which the tribe depended so completely for survival, leaving them to starve.

Mackenzie quickly disposed of their remaining venison and by 1 o'clock that afternoon they were off again. They left Friendly Village, as they called it, in two borrowed canoes stoutly built of cedar, with seven Bella Coolas to paddle them on their way. When they came to another fish weir across the river, the Indians put their passengers ashore temporarily. Then, in a stunning display of bravura canoemanship, the Indians approached the weir and, in Mackenzie's words, "shot up over it without taking a drop of water."

After a few hours' travel downstream, their guides brought them to another, still larger village. If anything, the chief there was even more effusive than the one at Friendly Village. He hugged Mackenzie to him, then snapped the neckstring of a magnificent sea-otter robe he was wearing and draped it over the white man's shoulders. He invited the Canadians to a Gargantuan, three-hour feast of roasted salmon and a special delicacy, square cakes made from the tender inner bark of the hemlock, pounded to a paste and sweetened with salmon oil. Mackenzie repaid the hospitality as best he could by giving the chief a pair of scissors. This strange instrument, he explained, was for the purpose of clipping the old man's beard, which was very long. The chief was entranced and instantly put his new treasure to enthusiastic use.

Mackenzie estimated the population of Great Village, as he called it, at perhaps 200 men, women and children. They lived in four massive lodges erected on posts 12 feet above the riverbank, each at least 100 feet long and 40 feet wide. Inside these lodges were communal hearths and living areas flanked by low partitions that formed smaller sleeping compartments about seven feet square. In each apartment Mackenzie noticed beautifully made chests of cedar, and rows of poles from which hung an abundance of cured salmon.

Down by the riverbank Mackenzie studied with great interest a splendid canoe of cedar, 45 feet long and four feet wide, painted black and decorated with white figures of fish. Along the gunwales, fore and aft, were embedded rows of gleaming white objects that resembled nothing so much as human teeth; they were actually those of sea otters, the chief explained. Ten winters ago, he indicated, he and 40 of his people had voyaged in this vessel down to the ocean, where they had encountered two large ships full of fair-skinned men who had treated them kindly. Mackenzie recalled with a start that he had read of canoes adorned with "human" teeth. It was in the journals of Captain Cook, who had cruised this coast on his last voyage of discovery in 1778.

After spending a night at the village, Mackenzie prepared to journey on in a borrowed canoe with four paddler guides, including the chief's son. But just as they were about to set out, there was an embarrassing incident: one of the *voyageurs* reported an ax missing. A small thing, perhaps. But to the explorers axes were as vital as pemmican or muskets. Mackenzie immediately demanded its return and remained insistent until it was finally produced—from under the chief's own canoe. Also missing was the expedition's faithful dog, which had somehow wandered off and could not be found. Sadly, the men went on without him.

Some miles downriver, Mackenzie and his companions arrived at a third village, which they found largely unoccupied, the inhabitants evidently off somewhere to trade or fish. To their elation, from the porch of a lodge where they elected to sleep, they could at long last see their goal: a long, narrow arm of the Pacific Ocean, reaching in toward the river's mouth.

That night they slept peacefully, and at dawn launched a canoe into the fjord, whose seaweed-laden banks widened as the men paddled outward. Sea otters and seals appeared in increasing numbers; the men shot at them, but the animals plunged agilely into the water unharmed. At two in the afternoon, strong winds and mounting swells finally forced them to land in a cove, where the chief's son secured a large porcupine for the evening meal.

But at this point, a change came over their Indian companions. To Mackenzie they anxiously indicated that they were loath to continue farther. And next morning, the reason became all too clear. No sooner had the party paddled out from shore than three canoes packed with menacing warriors swooped down on them. These were the Bella Bellas, more warlike than

The indomitable map maker who rowed 10,000 miles

When Alexander Mackenzie paddled down the Bella Coola River to the Pacific tidewater and painted his name on a boulder, he was asserting rights to an area that another Briton had already claimed for king and country. In June 1793, barely a month ahead of Mackenzie, Captain George Vancouver, also seeking a Northwest Passage, had entered the mouth of the same river at a place he named Restoration Cove.

At the time, Vancouver was in the second of three summers of arduous exploration. The Pacific Coast's broad outline had been set down by Captain James Cook in 1778. The 33-year-old Vancouver, who had been a midshipman with Cook, took up the task of detailed charting by following every inlet to its head.

With 100 men, Vancouver left Falmouth, England, on April 1, 1791, in command of two vessels, *Discovery* and *Chatham*. It took a full year to sail 20,000 circuitous miles to the starting point for his survey, just north of San Francisco Bay. Before tracing a single line on a chart, the captain took 85 lunar observations to establish his location with absolute precision.

Whenever weather and water permitted, Vancouver surveyed directly from *Discovery* and *Chatham*, rarely covering more than five miles a day. Where the water was shallow or the coast fogbound, the vessels stood offshore and the work proceeded from small cutters and dories. Once, during the second summer, the hard-driving Vancouver and his lieutenants rowed 700 miles into and out of fjords — but

Captain George Vancouver

advanced the survey only 60 miles in a direct line.

Vancouver spent the winters in Hawaii, and made the first accurate survey of the island chain. In spring, he returned to charting the continent.

The task ended at Port Conclusion, just north of today's Canadian-Alaskan border, in August 1794. Vancouver reached England in October of the following year, having covered an estimated 65,000 miles by sail, and another 10,000 under oar. He had pushed his men unrelentingly. One seaman wrote, "His salutation I can never forget, his language I will never forgive." Yet in his four-and-a-half-year voyage, Vancouver had mapped 1,700 miles of shore line, circumnavigated the 250-mile-long island that bears his name and proven again that there was no navigable link to the Atlantic. For his efforts, England raised his pay from six shillings, sixpence to eight shillings a day.

An Indian village clings precariously to the face

of a steep rock at the entrance to Bute's Canal in this detailed engraving from Vancouver's account of his lengthy map-making travels.

their upriver neighbors — and more experienced with the often-avaricious whites who had sailed up the coast in search of treasure. With a great show of disdain the Indians scrutinized the newcomers. Through the Bella Coola guides, an arrogant warrior made Mackenzie understand "that a large canoe had lately been in this bay, with people in her like me, and that one of them, whom he called Macubah, had fired on him and his friends, and that Bensins had struck him on the back with the flat of his sword."

Though Mackenzie was at a loss as to their identity, Macubah was undoubtedly George Vancouver, who had put into this very fjord on his coastwise explorations some six weeks before. Bensins was almost surely Archibald Menzies, the botanist assigned to the expedition. (Vancouver's account of the voyage referred to an encounter with natives in Dean Channel on June 3, 1793, but mentioned no dispute.)

Whatever the case, in telling his tale the warrior had brazenly boarded the white men's canoe and made free use of Mackenzie's gun and sword to dramatize his complaints. He now returned to his own craft and ordered Mackenzie to follow him back to the village.

Outnumbered and fearful, Mackenzie and his men instead raced to shore and scrambled to the top of a massive rock. More Bella Bellas arrived until there were 10 canoes with scores of warriors yelling and gesticulating for the Canadians to climb down and surrender. Mackenzie steadfastly refused, and his men thrust their muskets forward. The confrontation continued until sunset. And then the Bella Bellas suddenly departed, leaving the little party atop their fortress rock to warm themselves by a small fire and scrape together a meal out of what rations they had remaining. That night, under a bright summer moon, Mackenzie doubled the guard, keeping two men constantly on watch until dawn.

The Bella Bellas reappeared at first light — two large, heavily manned canoes coming from the direction of the village, apparently forerunners of a war party. The Canadians' young Bella Coola guide pleaded with Mackenzie to flee before they all were slaughtered. The youth's agitation was so great, Mackenzie noted, that he literally foamed at the mouth.

With great deliberation, Mackenzie took a fresh sighting to confirm their position. And then, before departing, he mixed some vermilion coloring with grease and smeared in large characters on the face of their rock redoubt: "Alexander Mackenzie, from Canada by land, the 22nd of July, 1793."

The return trip was marked by haste, confusion and great good luck. By dint of some furious paddling, Mackenzie and his crew managed to outrun the rascally Bella Bellas, whom they gradually left behind in a race back up the mouth of the river. But when the explorers reached the Great Village of the Bella Coola, they found the formerly hospitable chief in a frenzy of worry that his son might have been killed by these strange white men. Though the youth returned safe and sound, Mackenzie had to part with most of his remaining presents to regain a semblance of good will. Even as they left, there was a noisy debate among the Indians as to whether the disruptive white men should be allowed to go in peace.

After leaving, the tiny party of eight white men and their original two Indian guides stumbled along, expecting attack at any moment. Fortunately, it never came. Three days into the return journey, they were delighted and astonished to come across their long lost friend and mascot, the dog. The poor creature was reduced almost to a skeleton, and ran wildly back and forth without seeming to recognize its masters. Only by dropping bits of their precious food along the path, could they get him to follow along and, as Mackenzie fondly put it, "recover his former sagacity."

Struggling back across the coastal range, the men were so weak and wracked with colds that they scarcely had the strength to gather firewood at their evening camps. Mackenzie was afflicted with painfully swollen ankles, and one of the Indians was so sick they had to carry him in their arms. But at the base of the mountains, they found their cache of food in good condition and their canoe untouched. On August 6, they started up the Fraser and McGregor, over the little lakes and portages that marked the Great Divide, and down the welcoming current of the Parsnip and the Peace.

Emerging below the turbulent Canyon of the Peace, the party found the weather strangely but pleasantly hot, and the foothills and plains teeming with buffalo and elk, on whose roasted meat they thankfully gorged themselves. On Saturday, August 24, just 107 days after they had first set out, Mackenzie concluded his log: "At length, as we rounded a point and came in view of the Fort, we threw out our flag, and accompanied it with a general discharge of fire-arms; while the men were in such spirits, and made such active use of their paddles, that we arrived before the two men we had left here in the spring could recover their senses to answer us. Thus we landed at four in the afternoon, at the place we left on the ninth of May."

Even more than his first voyage to the Arctic, Mackenzie's dash to the Pacific stands as a testament to his resourcefulness and fortitude. In 74 days, he and his men had covered more than 1,200 miles over the most rugged portion of the continent's backbone. On the 33-day return, stretched almost beyond human endurance, they had averaged an incredible 36 miles a day. Mackenzie could scarcely comprehend how they had managed it.

Even for a resilient young Scot, steel-tempered by years of wilderness life, such an odyssey was bound to take its toll. All that winter at Fort Chipewyan, Mackenzie found himself disturbingly tired and depressed. When he attempted to transcribe his notes into a proper journal he could not concentrate, his dark moods adding to the usual burdens of solitude and short rations that characterized life at a winter post. By summer, however, he seemed to have recovered. He had also vowed to quit the north country, and to devote himself to the broader implications of his travels, and to the future strategy of the fur trade.

At Grand Portage, and later in Montreal and London, Mackenzie struggled to convince his partners and government officials that trade should be extended to the Pacific as swiftly as possible, and that a truce with the rival Hudson's Bay Company was imperative to allow common access to the heart of the continent. More than that, he argued passionately that a merger of the two into a single powerful, crown-chartered and -supported company was the only way to assure British-Canadian domination of commerce in the face of an increasingly aggressive United States.

His business partners rewarded his efforts with an additional share in the company. But high-level indifference to his schemes, and a growing rivalry with the most powerful of the partners, Marquis McTavish, persuaded him to seek a change. When his contract ex- pired in 1799 he did not renew it, but moved to England, where he helped organize the XY Company, a vigorous concern that gave the two older giants of the fur trade a run for their money for a few years until it was merged into the North West Company.

More importantly for history, Mackenzie was now wealthy enough to do what he chose. And with the help of a writer named William Combe, he committed his voyages and visions to print. In December of 1801, in London, there appeared an imposing volume bearing an imposing title: *Voyages from Montreal on the River St. Laurence through the Continent of North America to the Frozen and Pacific Oceans; in the Years, 1789 and 1793. With a Preliminary Account of the Rise, Progress, and Present State of the Fur Trade of That Country. Illustrated with Maps.*

Mackenzie's *Voyages* was an instant success, and helped earn its author a knighthood from King George III. Among the work's interested readers was Napoleon Bonaparte, who obtained a translation for its military value. At the time he was entertaining notions of furthering his campaigns against the English by means of a diversionary attack on Canada up the Mississippi Valley and in through the northern rivers and lakes. A notable purchaser of an American edition in 1803 was President Thomas Jefferson. He was completing arrangements for the Lewis and Clark expedition to the Pacific Coast, and he made sure a copy went along.

Mackenzie was now almost 40, and the flames of ambition that sent him on his two incredible journeys were burning lower. Though he continued his efforts to merge the fur trade and continually urged the British government to take possession of the entire Pacific Coast, he was increasingly content to remain off stage. In 1812 he married Geddes Mackenzie, a beautiful young kinswoman, and settled down to the life of a Scottish laird on his estate bordering Moray Firth; there the couple had a daughter and two sons.

In 1820, returning from a trip to Edinburgh, Mackenzie died unexpectedly of kidney disease. He was 56. He had not lived to see his dreams of an amalgamated fur empire realized. But the very next year, his partners in the North West Company at last joined with the gentlemen of Hudson's Bay to build an empire stretching all the way from Montreal to the Columbia River, the Oregon Territory and the Western Sea.

Totem poles rise above a Haida village, Skidegate, on Graham Island in the Queen Charlotte Islands.

The munificent bequest of the great god Raven

"In the beginning, Raven made us, and everything, and totem poles too." With these words, the elders of the seven prosperous coastal tribes recited the story of creation. And their listeners had every reason to believe that Raven was a generous spirit.

Mountains rising out of the Pacific formed a spectacular coastline of craggy islands and fjords. Majestic forests of firs, cedars and redwoods grew on the slopes. The warm Japan Current kept the climate mild even in winter. Salmon swam up rivers in such numbers during spawning season that a few weeks' work supplied food for several months.

Thus blessed, the Northwest nations had the leisure to create one of the great native civilizations in the New World. This culture reached its highest tangible expression in woodworking. Magnificently carved totem poles, turned out by such tribes as the Haida, Kwakiutl and Bella Coola, reflected a complex social structure and rich mythology: animal deities, like the guardian-spirit Thunderbird, were intertwined with people and various objects. The result was a combined coat of arms and family tree that depicted a person's real and fabled lineage, as well as his inherited and acquired ranks.

The talented artisans who carved these poles, some as high as 50 feet, were impressive housebuilders and shipwrights too. They built gabled lodges that covered more than 3,000 square feet, and seagoing canoes that held up to 50 men.

In this earthly paradise, the measure of social status became a display of wealth. An eldest son's initiation into manhood or a new chief's elevation was the occasion for a potlatch — a ceremony at which a chief demonstrated his inexhaustible riches by lavishing the most expensive gifts (*overleaf*) he could afford on his rivals. In turn, each recipient hosted his own potlatch at which he sought to provide gifts of still greater value. Potlatches degenerated into such fiercely competitive matches of wastefulness that the Canadian government outlawed them in 1884.

Kwakiutl tribesmen prepare for a gift-giving potlatch ceremony with towering stacks of goods — mostly Hudson's Bay blankets. At the greatest potlatches, a chief might distribute as many as 30,000 blankets. One chief who favored jewelry gave out close to 10,000 silver and brass bracelets.

77

A Kwakiutl family is dwarfed by the carved interior posts of a lodge being built on Gilford Island. After visiting a coastal Indian dwelling in 1788, the English trader John Meares wrote: "The trees which supported the roof would render the mast of a first-rate man of war diminutive."

At the start of wedding festivities, a Kwakiutl dancer, dressed in a feathered costume and a beaked mask to represent the Thunderbird, performs a wing-flapping ritual in the bow of a canoe approaching the bride's village. The locale is the northeastern coast of Vancouver Island.

At the coming-of-age ceremony of a Kwakiutl male, dancers represent creatures in the myth of Baxbakualanu X siwae, the Cannibal-at-the-north-end-of-the-world. One of his attendants was Hohok, a fabulous long-beaked bird-monster portrayed by the two performers in the foreground.

83.

On Gilford Island, the freshly painted visage of a sea monster glares from the housefront of a ranking chief. A sheathing of loose planks made the lodges *(left)* look ramshackle, but served a purpose: the boards were shifted to create smoke vents and openings for air and light.

Large statues of a Thunderbird and two funerary figures guard the grave of a Mamalilikulla chief on Village Island. Even in death, an aristocrat's wealth was honored. The chevron-shaped symbols on the tall pole at left represent the many canoes given away by the chief at potlatches.

3 | From a city of stumps to a gem of empire

"Imagine a bank of the river densely wooded with immense pines, maples, cedars, firs, and upon this bank a few acres of land where the trees, instead of being upright, are lying on the ground half rotten, half burnt, with huge stumps and roots some 10 or 11 feet in diameter, thickly scattered among the few wooden houses which have sprung up since about a year. This is New Westminster — a perfect chaos." This first impression of the re-cently founded capital of the fledgling colony of British Columbia was written in 1860 by metallurgist Francis Claudet, who was later credited with recording the scene in the photograph shown here. The Royal Mint in London had sent Claudet, 23, to be the colony's official assayer — an important post, for British Columbia was in the midst of a gold rush.

Ten years before Claudet's arrival, the southern tip of Vancouver Island and the mountainous wilderness on the mainland were the exclusive preserve of a handful of Hudson's Bay traders. But the lure of quick riches brought thousands. By 1871, when the boom had subsided and most of the restless prospectors had moved on, the area could boast of towns, roads and a permanent population of 36,000. The remote, stump-ridden outpost of empire had been transformed into a thriving center of the budding dominion.

An Indian in his dugout glides past British Columbia's capital, named New Westminster but referred to by residents as Stumpville.

A princely gift from a trio of province builders

In the long view of history, the West Coast wilderness that Alexander Mackenzie explored in 1793 did for Canada what California did for the United States. Like California's gold fields, the remote fir forests that lay west of the Canadian Rockies attracted adventurous men long before the immense interior was settled. Like the Californians, the Canadians who put down roots on the Pacific shores forced their Eastern countrymen to grapple with the thorny problems of setting up long-distance communication, military defense, legal and political ties. In the end, for Canada as well as for the United States, it was the early establishment of a West Coast foothold that ensured the growth of a nation that stretched all the way across the continent.

Yet in the beginning, it seemed that the explorations of Alexander Mackenzie in 1793 would be a long, long time bearing fruit — and that possibly the land would be denied to Canada entirely. A decade after his momentous trek, the Far Northwest was a magnificent limbo, claimed but unoccupied by England, Spain, Russia and the United States. Occasionally, the ships of those nations arrived to trade with the Indians along the coast. But overland commerce showed no signs of developing; at the turn of the century, the North West Company and the Hudson's Bay Company were still too busy competing for the Canadian heartland to send pathfinders and fur buyers across the Rockies. Even more discouraging, the contentious Eastern colonies of Ontario, Quebec, Nova Scotia and New Brunswick could not suppress their local animosities, much less

agree on what to do about the remote, mysterious land fronting on the Pacific.

It took a serious international threat to produce action of any sort. In 1803, the United States Congress voted an appropriation for a Corps of Discovery to explore the West, and later that year Meriwether Lewis and William Clark led 42 frontiersmen from Missouri to blaze a practicable route to the Pacific. While London and the colonial capital at Ottawa pondered this new development, Canadian fur men and a few thoughtful merchants understood its significance instantly. They realized that American traders and fur trappers would follow Lewis and Clark into the region known as Oregon, and that a fierce competition for trade and territory would soon ensue. Clearly the Canadian fur companies would first have to occupy and exploit the Far West before they settled their own power struggle.

The North West Company took the initial step in 1805. A party of traders and *voyageurs* traced Mackenzie's footsteps to the banks of the Peace River, where they built a fort called Rocky Mountain House. Then they followed the Peace and Parsnip rivers to the juncture of the Pack River at McLeod's Lake. There they built the very first post west of the Rockies. The McLeod's Lake depot was a small beginning, but it committed the Canadians to their epic task of settling the Far West and joining it to the East.

The first small parties of men who pressed the bold venture were frontier veterans, accustomed to the hazards of exploration and the lonely life of the wilderness. But their past experience merely suggested the rigors they would face in the remote Far West, barricaded from the East by the massive Rockies and 15,000 miles from England by sea, with help and supplies at least three months away. Here it would take a special breed of pioneers, endowed with enormous will power,

Sir James Douglas, first governor of British Columbia, displays the lordly bearing that served him so well in the early days, when his word was law. His stiffness earned him the nickname Old Squaretoes.

dedication and self-reliance, to brave the protracted isolation of the Far West.

Among these remarkable men, three were outstanding: an explorer, a governor and a judge. They vaulted the prairies and mountains to establish themselves on the shores of the Western ocean. Separately and together, they explored the wilds, established relations with suspicious Indians, dealt with the overwhelming turmoil of an international gold rush, bridged great chasms and hung highways on the face of impossible precipices. Above all, they laid the foundation for a new society and stamped it indelibly with the English way of doing things. The pioneer period lasted six decades, after which the empire builders were able to turn over to the embryonic Dominion of Canada a rich new province that would serve as its western bulwark and window on the Pacific. Appropriately, the name of their province combined Old World ties with New World topography: British Columbia.

The first of these province builders was David Thompson, a pathfinder of supreme tenacity and skill, whose great contribution was to find the source of the Columbia River and chart a broad waterway over which would pass the fur wealth of the Northwest. Like Mackenzie, Thompson had been preparing for his destiny since his early teens. But unlike Mackenzie, he began as a Hudson's Bay man. That company had taken him in 1784 from London's Grey Coat School, a charitable institution for orphans, and apprenticed him for seven years in the New World fur trade.

Thompson was then 14, short in stature but strong, with broad Welsh features and an equally broad Welsh accent. He was bright, and in the company's care, he learned prodigiously — from the traders for whom he worked at York Factory on Hudson Bay, from an old Cree Indian chief on the Bow River and from Philip Turnor, the company's chief surveyor. Turnor taught him the uses of sextant, chronometer, compass and telescope. Ever after, Thompson made a fetish of knowing his position, and he became the most trusted scout and mapmaker of the high Western fur country.

After his apprenticeship in 1791, Thompson served six years as clerk, trader and surveyor before leaving Hudson's Bay for the more aggressive coalition of Montreal traders known as the North West Company.

Philip Turnor, Thompson's old mentor, once said with sarcastic exaggeration that Hudson's Bay lost some of its best men to North West not only because a North West trader was paid more, but also because of his perks: on the trail he had "his feather bed carried in the canoe, his tent pitched for him, his bed made and he and his girl carried in and out of the canoe, and, when in the canoe, he never touches a paddle unless for his own pleasure." The truth was that the younger, more venturesome Nor'Westers attracted like-minded men.

For the next 14 years Thompson roamed thousands of miles in the Canadian Northwest, traveling by canoe, horse, dog sled or snowshoes as the season and terrain demanded. His marriage in 1799 to Charlotte Small, the half-breed daughter of a trader, interfered not at all with his explorations. On one long trip up the Saskatchewan River, Charlotte went along, leading two small children by the hand and packing a baby on her back, papoose style.

Working principally from the Nor'Westers' main depot at Fort William on the north shore of Lake Superior, Thompson probed west into the Rockies, north to Lake Athabasca, and south to the Missouri in what one day would be North Dakota. On his surveys, he lost no opportunity to trade for furs, and he established strings of new trading posts along his routes. In one respect at least he departed radically from the fur-business norm: he detested alcohol, and refused to deal in it. Once, overruled by superiors, he was compelled to add two kegs of liquor to his trade goods. "When we came to the defiles on the mountains," he later wrote, "I placed the two kegs of alcohol on a vicious horse, and by noon the kegs were empty and in pieces."

Thompson was 40, with 26 years of experience behind him, when he received the climactic assignment of his career. In 1810, his superiors in the North West Company sent him to renew the search for the headwaters of the Columbia River, whose broad estuary had been known to the British since the American Captain Robert Gray discovered it in 1792. The Nor'-Westers, hoping to use the river as a fur highway to the sea, had been searching in vain for its inland origins since Mackenzie's expedition of 1793. Meanwhile, new developments had made the quest more urgent.

In the first place, Thompson's colleague Simon Fraser had failed in his efforts to find a more northerly water route to the sea. In 1808, Fraser led a party to the river later named after him and began canoeing downstream. But it soon became obvious that the stream was fraught with peril; the explorers seldom paddled south for more than a day without having to make a dangerous portage across dizzying rock walls to avoid thunderous rapids. Though Fraser finally reached the mouth of this stream after five arduous weeks, he wrote it off as unnavigable except for the first 100 miles.

Then, as the Nor'Westers refocused their interest on the Columbia, they learned to their alarm that John Jacob Astor, their American rival, had dispatched a ship around Cape Horn to found his own fur empire in the vast drainage basin of the Columbia. If Astor was to be beaten to the punch, Thompson had no time to waste on exploring by trial and error. He had to find the Columbia's upper reaches almost at once.

Thompson had been trying to do just that since 1807. On two occasions of supreme irony, he had stumbled on the stream without recognizing it — which was easy to do, for the river's way out of the Rockies was tortuous. The first time, in 1807, he came on the river as he emerged from a canyon leading west from the north fork of the Saskatchewan. Though this new

stream was sizable, he never thought it might be the Columbia because it ran in the wrong direction: north-northwest, instead of southwesterly, as he believed it should. He did not learn until much later that the Columbia flowed north for over 200 miles before taking a hairpin turn and setting out directly for the Pacific.

Thompson's second unknowing encounter with the Columbia came in the winter of 1811. He and his party of 13 men were 5,000 feet up in the Rockies near Athabasca Pass when they spotted a major river twisting through the valley below. Thompson led his men down the mountain and camped at the edge of the river. They stayed there through March, hunting and reprovisioning and building a big canoe. At last, the craft was completed. But Thompson, still bedeviled by that cantankerous stream, could not believe that his direction lay anywhere but to the south. So he launched upstream and southward. Had he gone downstream and north, he would soon have negotiated the 180° bend and found himself headed toward the sea.

As it was, by canoe and then afoot, Thompson led his men in a great loop south into what would become Montana and thence west across the panhandle of future Idaho to a point somewhere near the present site

Fort Astoria, a small enclosure in this early engraving, was taken over by the British in 1813, giving them control of the Columbia's mouth.

This 1846 cartoon, published in the satirical British journal *Punch*, was inspired by American claims to Oregon Territory. In the caption, a bemused John Bull cries to upstart America, "What? You young Yankee-noodle, strike your own father!"

of Spokane, Washington. This detour covered at least 600 miles and consumed eight weeks. But he finally got on the right track. Obtaining horses, he moved northward about 100 miles until he came to the cataract of Kettle Falls. This, he decided, was the real Columbia—and at last he was right.

On July 3, in a newly built, cedar-planked canoe, Thompson started downstream, noting that he intended to "explore this river in order to open out a passage for the interior trade with the Pacific." At the mouth of the Snake River he paused to erect a pole claiming the region as British and to palaver with Indians about the advantages of trade with his company.

A day or so later, Indians advised him that an American ship had arrived at the mouth of the river. Thompson hurried his crew along. On July 14, seeing seals playing in the river, he knew he was near salt water. The next day, he glimpsed the sea and broke out a British ensign at the canoe's stern.

Rounding a point of land, he saw a complex of four log huts flying the Stars and Stripes. The cabins were the nucleus of the brand-new Fort Astoria, which Astor's men were building as their headquarters on the Pacific. And so the race was lost. But Thompson betrayed no disappointment and enjoyed a cordial visit with the Americans. It is possible that he really was not overly worried by the Astorians' prior arrival in this wide new land. After all, he had behind him years of Nor'Wester confidence built up in successful competition with the Hudson's Bay people.

After a week, Thompson turned upstream again, mapping, exploring along the banks, talking trade with Indians he met. Although he left the Columbia after 300 miles to follow the Snake to his supply base, he had blazed one of the great fur highways: over it, for the next half a century, would pass the peltry wealth of Northwest America. Even more than Mackenzie, he had opened English eyes to the gleam of the Pacific. And significant affairs would follow in his path.

Events soon proved that David Thompson was right in wasting little concern over the Astorians. Within 18 months after Thompson headed back up the Columbia, the War of 1812 exposed Fort Astoria and the Pacific Fur Company's Cape Horn shipping route to British raiders. John Jacob Astor was a pragmatic man, and he sold out to the North West Company.

Thereafter, the Nor'Westers dominated the Pacific Coast fur trade. The treaty ending the war specified the return of all captured territory, and the United States demanded return of Astoria, which the Nor'Westers had renamed Fort George. The British maintained, with some truth, that the post had changed hands by purchase, not conquest. But nobody really lusted for a new war over a few isolated log huts. So the nations effected a Solomonic compromise. The Union Jack came down and the Stars and Stripes went up—but the North West Company retained ownership under U.S. sovereignty and continued to trap. And the glossy harvest of furs continued to move over Thompson's watery highway.

In 1821 the merger of the North West Company and the Hudson's Bay Company (under the latter's name) served to cement the British-Canadian fur men's grip on the Northwest. Working in concert, the joint corporation's fur trappers and traders ranged as far south as San Francisco Bay and eastward as far as latter-day Ogden, Utah. Their purpose was to trap the Northwest so clean that the pushy Americans would never come back.

But now a new development arose to worry the traders and governors of Hudson's Bay. In the past, competition in the Northwest had been purely commercial—fur man against fur man. Recently, however, the mother countries had been taking an increasingly active interest, and the possibility of conflict was strong.

The origin of the problem was an 1818 treaty between London and Washington fixing the Canadian-U.S. border. The treaty makers had extended the international border from Lake Superior along the 49th parallel to the eastward face of the Rocky Mountains. But there, unaccountably, they quit. Everything west of the mountains—from the Spanish holdings that ended at 42° N. to Russian Alaska, which began at about 55°—was open to anybody.

Though the Hudson's Bay men had long believed that the westernmost sector of the international boundary would surely be fixed at 46° N.—which coincided with the line of the Columbia's westward flow—by 1825 that proposition no longer seemed so probable. In the United States, the great westward movement of population was underway. Obviously the land-hungry

The sternwheeler *Onward* docks on the Lower Fraser River in 1868. Flat-bottomed, wood-burning steamers, which drew barely a foot of water while carrying 100 tons of cargo, were perfectly suited to travel on this shallow river, whose channel was a labyrinth of sandbars.

pioneers were going to be tempted by the empty wilderness west of the Rockies. In anticipation of a flood of Americans, Hudson's Bay's chief factor on the coast, Dr. John McLoughlin, abandoned Fort George at the mouth of the Columbia and moved to what he hoped would be a more secure site 80 miles upriver on the north bank. It was named Fort Vancouver.

Then, in 1842, in an even more significant move, Dr. McLoughlin summoned his chief accountant, James Douglas, and sent him off to secure a new company refuge likely to remain forever above the Yankee tide. Douglas found what he was looking for at the head of a lovely harbor at the southern end of Vancouver Island, just outside Puget Sound. The next year he there founded Fort Victoria, which, in time, became a brilliant gem on that queen's diadem of empire.

Like Mackenzie and Thompson, James Douglas was enlisted in the fur trade as a youth and trained on the job. He had been born in South America to a Creole woman and a British colonial officer. In 1819, the 16-year-old Douglas was in boarding school in the British Isles when the wanderlust struck him. He packed his textbooks along with his clothing and signed on as a junior clerk with the North West Company. He did not see Britain again for 45 years. But in that time he had more effect on British-Canadian interests in the Far Northwest than any man before or after him.

He was serious and studious, a purist with the English tongue, offended by slang or sloppy usage. He once returned a daughter's letter, commenting that it had been "pruned of redundancies, as a study. Observe how it is improved by the process." Like Thompson, he married a half-breed "according to the custom of the country," that is, without benefit of clergy. Years later, he married her properly when the sanctimonious wife of an English chaplain snubbed Amelia Douglas as an unwed mother and concubine.

Unlike Thompson, Douglas was a giant, well above six feet. As a young man he had a quick temper, "furiously violent when roused," as Sir George Simpson, a Hudson's Bay Company governor, put it. Douglas once invaded an Indian village singlehanded after a murderer, found his man and — according to one version — "blew out his brains, in the centre of his tribe."

In later years, Douglas not only learned to suppress his tendency to explode but cultivated an air of great dignity. He believed absolutely in the uprightness of the British cause, British justice, British invincibility and British decency. It was well that he held his faith so firmly. For that faith was almost all he had to bolster him in his task of building and ruling two enormous colonies full of savage Indians and rowdy prospectors, mostly American.

At first there was little hint of the forthcoming extent of Douglas' domain, or of the turbulence with which it would be afflicted. The outpost of empire that Douglas began building on Vancouver Island in the early 1840s quickly evolved into an English village as staid as a hamlet in Kent. The rude original stockade was expanded into a spacious compound guarded by two bastions mounting nine-pounder cannon and enclosing more than a dozen capacious buildings. Beyond the walls grew up clusters of cabins of erstwhile traders who were turning to the more tranquil pursuits of farmer and dairyman. Gardens of imported hollyhock, wallflower and mignonette bloomed in the dooryards.

Life under the stern eye of Chief Factor Douglas followed a serene and orderly course. In the evenings the company officers dined in considerable style, their table set with silver and clean linen. Douglas recited grace before meals and firmly guided the conversation to topics of politics, science and matters of culture. Idle chatter and levity were not encouraged.

For a time in late 1844 this corner of empire seemed threatened when James Knox Polk campaigned for the United States Presidency on the expansionist slogan, "Fifty-four forty or Fight!" This seemed to mean that if Britain did not cede all Far Western lands below lat. 54°, the U.S. under President Polk would seize them by force. But after the election, Polk the Chief Executive proved less bellicose — at least toward Canada — than Polk the candidate. In 1846, little Victoria achieved sovereign legitimacy of a sort when the 49th parallel boundary was extended all the way from the Rockies to the sea with a slight accommodating jog at the end to leave Vancouver Island British.

By 1849, Douglas felt secure enough at Victoria to remove the company's headquarters there from Fort Vancouver on the Columbia. He made the move with a staff "composed of one Sandwich Islander with an invalid sailor who instead of helping was required to be waited on. With that numerous and respectable train I

A San Juan islander at the northern end of
the island tends crops under the protection
of a British garrison sent to keep peace in
1859 after the escalation of a spat with
American settlers over, of all things, a pig.

had to guard our collected treasure — 636 lb. of gold-
dust and twenty packs of otters, worth altogether about
£30,000, a noble prize for a gang of thieves."

That same year the British Colonial Office in London cemented the British title to land above the 49th
parallel by declaring Vancouver Island a Crown colony. Two years later Douglas was made governor,
while keeping his job as chief company officer.

Douglas never explained the source of the gold he
had carried to his new capital. Probably it had been collected in trade with Indian prospectors on the mainland. In any case the company's accumulation of gold
was to be the cause of a frantic invasion of Victoria.

By 1858, the colony's hoard of gold had grown so
large that Douglas, concerned at having all that precious dust on hand, sent off 800 ounces to the U.S.
mint in San Francisco. And there was much more
where that came from: a major gold strike had just

been reported up the Fraser River on the mainland.
When word of Douglas' shipment, backed by news of
the Fraser River bonanza, got round San Francisco,
things began to happen in a big way.

On Sunday morning, April 25, 1858, Victorians
had just emerged from church to stroll homeward when
they were confronted with a startling apparition. An
American paddlewheeler was entering the harbor, its
rails thronged with cheering, gesticulating men. The villagers watched uneasily as *Commodore,* out of San
Francisco, docked and disgorged 450 rough, red-
shirted miners carrying packs, blankets, spades, pans
and pickaxes — and most of them Bowie knives and revolvers as well. About 60 were fellow Britons, an
equal number were white Americans, 35 were blacks
and the rest Germans, French, Italians and others.

Commodore's passenger list more than doubled Victoria's population in the space of a morning. Shortly

thereafter, the sidewheeler *Sierra Nevada* arrived with 1,900 gold-crazy passengers; then came *Orizaba* and *Cortez* with 2,800 prospectors and camp followers. By midsummer, Victoria was bursting with 30,000 people and had become the staging base for one of the wildest gold rushes of all time. Douglas was sharply aware that he held no mandate on the mainland across Georgia Strait. But he was equally aware that it was claimed for Britain, and that to make the claim stick, somebody would have to police it. So he issued a proclamation declaring all mainland mines Crown property and setting out regulations for the issue of licenses "to dig, search for, or remove gold."

On Vancouver Island, Victoria was almost submerged under the weight of her guests. Hard on the heels of the miners came those who lived off miners — "fishermen, French cooks, jobbers, speculators, land agents, auctioneers, hangers on at auctions, bummers,

bankrupts and brokers of every description," as one resident listed them. Victoria's hillsides were stripped of timber for firewood and building material as a tent and shanty town swiftly arose. The price of building lots jumped from $50 to $3,000. On the waterfront hundreds of boats were building for the 40-mile voyage across Georgia Strait to the gold fields. No town in the American West experienced a more volcanic boom.

In the center of the turmoil stood Douglas, a tower of assurance. When a crowd of miners buttonholed him in the street, he delivered an impromptu, slightly ungrammatical welcome. "Now I know, men, you wish me to say that there are lots of gold in Fraser's River, but that I will not say, because I am not certain of the fact myself. But I think the country is full of gold. I have told our glorious Queen so, and now I tell you so, and if I mistake not, you are the very men who can prove whether my opinion be right or wrong." ◉

From cannibalism to capitalism: the triumph of Reverend Duncan

In the early 1850s, the Tsimshian Indians of coastal British Columbia were regarded with fear and loathing by whites and fellow Indians alike. Only 2,500 in number, the Tsimshians made up in savagery what they lacked in population. Bands of Tsimshians mercilessly attacked other tribes in the Nass River region, slaughtering and enslaving their neighbors. Their own villages were scenes of murder, rape, thievery, drunkenness and debauchery of every sort. Worst of all, the Tsimshians practiced ritual cannibalism, and ghastly tales were told of orgies in which they feasted on human flesh.

Such was the state of affairs in 1857 when an English lay preacher named William Duncan arrived in British Columbia to teach the Scriptures. His introduction to the Tsimshians could hardly have been grimmer. In horror he reported seeing "a poor slave woman being murdered in cold blood, thrown on the beach and then torn to pieces and eaten by two naked savages." Wrote Duncan: "O dreadful, dreadful to see one's fellow creatures like this when the blessed Gospel has been 1800 years in the world."

Forthwith, Duncan set out to redeem the benighted Tsimshians. As a beginning, he spent nine months mastering their tongue and tribal lore. He then sallied forth from his base at Fort Simpson to visit Tsimshian villages, giving sermons and relating the story of Noah's Ark in terms of a great flood that was a part of their tribal legend.

Before long, Duncan was teaching reading, writing and arithmetic, as well as the Scriptures, to both children and adults. By 1862, four of the nine principal chiefs had forsworn their evil ways, and hundreds of tribesmen were following Duncan's teachings.

That year, to insulate his flock from heathen influences — not the least being whiskey and guns peddled at Fort Simpson — Duncan moved 600 Tsim-

Duncan sits for a portrait about 1855

shians 20 miles north to an abandoned Indian village named Metlakatla. They consecrated it by building one of the largest churches north of San Francisco. Twenty-five years later, the tribe moved north again to found New Metlakatla on Annette Island in Alaska. The new settlements hummed with industry as Duncan taught the Tsimshians spinning, soapmaking, blacksmithing and carpentry — and how to make money by selling the fruits of their labor. And, since all work and no play would never do, he gave them music lessons, the better to provide themselves and visitors with entertainment.

Duncan presided over all this as a benevolent despot, tending the sick, settling disputes, performing marriages and baptisms, and eulogizing the dead at funerals. By 1900, Metlakatla was a thriving industrial town centered on a salmon cannery and sawmill. The once fearsome Tsimshians were now capitalist entrepreneurs whose children began their school day singing, "Guide me, O Thou great Jehovah." And when Duncan died in 1918, at 85, the desolated Tsimshians insisted on burying him in Metlakatla near the community church.

In Sunday hats and suits, Tsimshian Indian converts prepare for a brass-band concert in front of Metlakatla's church. Under the aegis of preacher William Duncan, who was a skilled musician, the band greeted visitors with a repertory that included "God Save the Queen."

Outfitted with uniforms, bats and gloves, members of the New Metlakatla baseball team await another season of rivalry against nearby Alaskan teams. Duncan also taught his charges gymnastics and football.

Eight Tsimshian Indian girls sit by the spinning wheels that Duncan taught them to use. A visiting English lord pronounced the maidens "as well dressed as any clergyman's daughter in an English parish."

A row of well-kept clapboard houses overlooks Metlakatla's salmon cannery, a major business that Duncan built out of native fishing skills. A portion of the stock was owned by Indians who worked there.

Duncan works on his books at home in Alaska in his later years. Wooden cases like those on the floor were a profitable cannery sideline; villagers built them for export with or without salmon inside.

Though Douglas hoped this gold rush would bring prosperity to his colony, he knew that the Queen's men were few and without real power. Maintaining order would have to be more a matter of presence and implied retribution. And so he warned the freewheeling gold seekers that "the law of the land will do its work without fear and without favor."

In a lesser man this warning would have been bluster; in Douglas' case, by the solemn act of asserting that there was law and authority, he created both.

When, months later, London heard what he had done, the Colonial Office placed its stamp of approval upon him, saying he deserved "much credit for acting as he has always done—with promptitude and intelligence." The Crown decided to give him wider scope and some real muscle: the crown colony of British Columbia was created, and 165 Royal Engineers and a judge were sent to administer the law Douglas had invented out of hand. Naturally, Douglas was made governor of the new colony as well as Vancouver Island.

Never the man to wait for official sanction, Douglas had already set out on his own to see how the miners were faring on the mainland. At Hill's Bar, site of a significant strike about 100 miles upriver from the Fraser's mouth, he ran head-on into a major test of his authority. A band of Indians who, as he put it, were "naturally annoyed at the large quantities of gold taken out of their country by the white miners," were "mustered under arms in a tumultuous manner" and threatening to "make a clean sweep of the whole body of miners." In turn, the miners had armed themselves, and a violent confrontation seemed imminent.

Douglas went at the problem in the dual role of stern parent and adroit politician. He first lectured the Indians severely on keeping the peace—and then bestowed a small government sinecure upon their leader. The grateful chief responded by assuring Douglas of his unswerving loyalty, and led his braves back to their village. Douglas next turned to the gathering of miners and sharply advised them they were present "merely on sufferance, that no abuses would be tolerated and that the laws would protect the rights of the Indian, no less than those of the white man." The miners listened to this imposing man, then peaceably dispersed.

Back in Victoria, Douglas took steps to ease the lot of miners for whom adequate supplies, if at all available, could be had only for ruinous prices. To get the supplies 100 miles up the Fraser to the head of navigation at Fort Yale, Douglas relaxed a ban on American vessels in the river and pressed the Hudson's Bay Company's two steamers into service as well.

Some captains took to racing, piling on fuel and tying down the safety valve. In so doing, the captain of a steamer named *Fort Yale* set a new upriver speed record. And in trying to do even better, he blew her up. The explosion of her boiler was so emphatic that one 90-pound chunk was found a quarter mile away. The captain died in the blast, along with four white miners and an uncounted number of Indians and Chinese. Other skippers and passengers were undeterred by the disaster. For there was much gold up that river —in the ground for the miners, and in freighting for the captains. A single vessel, *Surprise*, reaped revenues of $250,000 for the 1858 season alone.

As always in gold fields, there was not enough good ground to go around. And by late summer the majority of the miners had departed downriver. But a few thousand diehards remained and began to push up the Fraser's formidable canyon with its Hells Gate Gorge.

No boat could live in those churning, rock-strewn rapids, and so the miners resorted to a terrifying thread of a pathway along the canyon. One traveler wrote: "Two or three places we descended, although almost perpendicular, by the aid of one or two trees which had been partially cut so as to hang down—deuced dangerous. I caught hold of a piece of rock to save myself —it gave way and I saw it bound down an immense height into the river—happy I was I did not follow it."

Well aware of the canyon's perils, Governor Douglas went into action again. He knew of another, roundabout route to the upper Fraser. With considerable labor it could be made passable, and it was much safer. So he offered the miners a hard Scottish bargain. If they would agree to work for nothing, and put up $25 personal bonds for good behavior to boot, he would show them where to build their own road, and furnish transportation and grub while they were working on it. Close to 500 men accepted. Thus, between August and late December 1858, the Harrison Trail, named for the first major lake it traversed, was laid out to bypass the Fraser's defile. The 150-mile route required eight loadings and off-loadings for ferry trips on lakes until it reached a place called Lillooet, about 40 miles above the Fraser's junction with the Thompson River.

In November 1858, James Douglas finally received his formal commission as governor of British Columbia as well as Vancouver Island. The next month, the means of enforcement arrived: the promised Royal Engineers and the judge. The officer in command of the Engineers was Colonel Richard Clement Moody and the judge was Matthew Baillie Begbie. No overworked centurion of empire in dire need of some competent help was ever better served.

Colonel Moody was the first to demonstrate his worth. Shortly after Douglas had sworn Begbie into office, word came downriver that a California desperado named Ned McGowan was leading a rebellion against the Crown at Hill's Bar. With 22 of his Engineers and Justice Begbie, the colonel set out for the scene.

Landing at Fort Yale, the party was met at the dock by an armed and sullen band of miners. Moody left his troops and the judge in the background. "Soldiers," he later said, "should be considered the very last dire necessity—their presence also often exasperates." The miners met his audacious approach with "a salute, firing off their loaded revolvers over my head. If it was to try my nerves, they must have forgotten my profession. I stood up, and raised my cap and thanked them in the Queen's name for their loyal reception."

If Moody's gesture was a bluff, it was a bolder one than McGowan could think of. He surrendered and was tried before Justice Begbie. In this, his first case, Begbie contented himself with a dressing down and a stiff fine. The verdict satisfied Moody, who observed that the Americans saw that "in the Queen's dominions an infringement of the law was really a serious matter, and not a sort of joke as in California."

Begbie's quick and personal method of disposing of this first case set a style he would follow for many years as he presided over the administration of justice in British Columbia and Vancouver Island. As a jurist, he knew little formal law, and he did not like law books, complaining that they were both confused and confusing. He had been an indifferent student at Cambridge, much preferring the more stimulating pursuits of rowing, boxing, tennis, singing, acting, card-playing, traveling and the company of females. But if he lacked book learning, he had something better suited to the rough mining camps: a commanding presence, a powerfully developed morality and a bold willingness to act on his convictions. He was as tall as or taller than Governor Douglas, bearded, handsome, with a voice that rose incongruously high when he was angry—as was often the case. In addition, he owned a lively sense of dignity regarding a queen's court. He had with him at all times a wig and judicial robes, and never held court without donning them, whether in a miner's cabin, a barn, a saloon or on horseback in an open field.

He left little doubt where he stood on all matters. On one occasion, when the jury acquitted a man of assault in a barroom battle, his honor coldly addressed the accused, "Prisoner at the bar, the jury have said you are not guilty. You can go, and I devoutly hope the next man you sandbag will be one of the jury."

Being naturally endowed with the temperament for it, Begbie accumulated enemies more readily than most men. Few of his ill-wishers, however, wanted to take him on face to face. For one thing, his size was intimidating. For another, it was known that he had once knocked out a saloon brawler with a single punch.

In general, the judge looked down on his detractors with lofty disdain. One day, taking his ease on the balcony of a mining-town hotel, he overheard men in the street below discussing a plan to ambush him as he rode out of town. The judge listened, then went to his room and got his full chamber pot, which he emptied on the plotters' heads, thereafter resuming his reverie.

His sentences were most often severe, for he held that when a crime of violence was committed the malefactor ought to suffer for it. Once, in response to complaints that he had sentenced men to be whipped, he wrote Douglas: "My idea is that if a man insists on behaving like a brute, after fair warning, and won't quit the Colony; treat him like a brute and flog him."

But he was not capricious in his judgments, and he probably did not deserve the sobriquet, "Hanging Judge," applied to him by his enemies. There is little to indicate that he sent many men to the gallows and, indeed, ample evidence that he felt a deep repugnance against taking life. Once, having sentenced an Indian to death for murder after a lengthy trial, he wrote Douglas and asked the governor to commute the sentence he had felt forced to impose. "I am not at all convinced that his execution is necessary, although I am sure it would have been just. It is scarcely right to keep a poor fellow on the tenterhooks for so long & hang him at last."

Whatever his unorthodoxies, Justice Begbie was exactly what Governor Douglas needed to impose order on a disorderly population. He rode his circuit diligently, ably appointed and administered a group of local magistrates and directed a tiny corps of 15 underpaid but doggedly loyal constables in an area of thousands of square miles. After three years on the job he was pleased to report to Douglas: "It is clear that the inhabitants almost universally respect and obey the laws, and voluntarily prefer good order and peaceful industry to the violence and bloodshed to which other Gold mining regions have been subjected."

Despite this growing strength, the colony's rulers were slow to lose their basic fear that an aggressive American government would follow the swarming miners with an out-and-out takeover. And in the summer of 1859 all Victoria was on edge over a bizarre international incident that almost triggered a war. The 1846 British-American border treaty had been vague about the western extremity of the boundary, where the line jogged south of Vancouver Island through the Strait of Juan de Fuca. No one was quite sure just which of the channels between the islands in the strait the border actually followed.

Naturally, both sides laid claim to the islands. On the most westerly, San Juan, Douglas had sought to assert British sovereignty in 1850 by establishing a Hudson's Bay Company farm. The Americans, in turn, had attempted to collect U.S. taxes and, failing, had confiscated some livestock. There the issue rested. For almost a decade, the Hudson's Bay Company farmers and a handful of American settlers who had also established themselves on San Juan went about their affairs in peace.

Then one fateful day in June 1859, a Canadian-owned pig got loose and began rooting around in an American settler's garden. The indignant American summarily shot the porker — at which the equally outraged Hudson's Bay Company agent demanded compensation. The incident escalated until eventually it came to the Olympian attention of General William S. Harney, Commander of the U.S. Army in the Pa-

Citizens of Barkerville, B.C., gather along the elevated wooden sidewalk to watch a cattle drive go down Main Street — which was barely 18 feet wide due to a tipsy surveyor's error. Booze also brought the boomtown's abrupt demise in 1868, when a drunken miner chasing a dance-hall girl knocked over a stove and Barkerville went up in flames.

cific Northwest. Harney, something of a hothead to begin with, saw a splendid opportunity to enhance American holdings — not to mention his own reputation as a go-getter. Forthwith he landed on San Juan, allegedly to protect American settlers, a detachment of 60 soldiers under an intrepid young captain named George Pickett (who in four years would win immortality with his charge at Gettysburg).

Across the strait, Victoria seethed with patriotic fury. Douglas, who among his hats wore that of Vice Admiral of Vancouver Island, dispatched three vessels bristling with Royal Engineers. As the little fleet stood offshore, awaiting further orders, a debate ensued between Douglas, the colony's House of Assembly and one Rear Admiral R. L. Baynes, who had just arrived in port as commander of Her Majesty's Pacific Squadron — thus outranking Douglas. The legislators were howling for action. Decrying the American occupation as "clandestine, dishonest and dishonorable," Speaker J. S. Helmcken thundered, "We must defend ourselves, for the position we occupy today would make the iron monument of Wellington weep and the stony statue of Nelson bend his brow!"

Douglas was feeling equally bellicose. The only cool head in the crowd belonged to the Royal Navy's Baynes; he refused to land so much as a rowboat on San Juan without the direct concurrence of London. The ships returned to port, and the explosive matter of what had now been dubbed the Pig War was left to the diplomats to resolve. In Washington, D.C., Lord Lyons, the British Minister to the United States, took up the incident with the U.S. State Department. After months of delicate negotiation, it was finally agreed that the saber-rattling Harney should be relieved by Washington, and that, pending a final decision, the islands should be jointly occupied by British and American troops.

In 1860, two garrisons set up friendly encampments on the island. The arrangement remained in force for more than a decade. The main competition among the troopers was over who would cut the most dashing figure at their lively social functions, which invariably attracted boatloads of Victoria's prettiest belles. The fun ended in 1872, when ownership of the San Juan Islands was finally submitted to the sole arbitration of Germany's Kaiser Wilhelm. As Douglas had feared, the Kaiser awarded the islands to the United States.

No gold field lasted forever, and the regions where gold was found in the West generally declined into torpor and depression after the stuff petered out — at least until they discovered some more solid economic base. But in British Columbia in the early 1860s, it almost seemed that providence had decreed the precious yellow metal a renewable resource.

By late 1859 the sandbars of the Fraser had been pretty thoroughly cleaned out all the way to Lillooet, more than 200 miles upriver. Most of the prospectors had drifted away and in Victoria merchants had little to do, as one observed in disgust, but "stand by their doors and project idle spittle into the streets."

Then in the late autumn of 1860 the electrifying news came down from the high mountain interior once again. From the western foothills of the Cariboo Mountains, near the headwaters of a Fraser River tributary called the Quesnel, word arrived that gold was to be found thereabouts by the ton.

Two prospectors, "Doc" Keithley and George Weaver, had made the strike. At first they had turned up modest but encouraging traces on a nearby creek they named in honor of Doc. They pursued the lead with two others, John Rose and Sandy MacDonald. At the head of Keithley Creek, they crossed a low divide and descended to another creek bed they later named "Antler." And there, in the afternoon sun they saw gravel so shot through with gold that they hardly needed to pan for it. Nuggets up to a quarter-pound in weight lay glimmering in the shallows.

While the sunlight lasted they shoveled and panned and stuffed their lean pokes. In the morning they awoke to a classic miner's dilemma. There was snow on the blankets: winter was at hand and it was time to hole up until spring. The question was, should they leave the trove unguarded and trust to luck that nobody else would stumble on it, or stick with it through winter?

They stuck. Two of the quartet hiked cross-country to get provisions from a trading post on Cariboo Lake while the other two began felling logs for a cabin. They had hoped to keep the strike quiet until spring, so as to be able to explore and stake out the best ground in privacy. But secrecy was next to impossible where gold was concerned. The two shoppers made the tactical error of buying heavily under the curious gaze of other prospectors, who themselves had been ready to call it quits for the winter. When the two men started back, they were followed. Word spread, and all winter prospectors struggled through the snow to reach Antler Creek. Before spring 400 men had come in, many existing in burrows in the snow.

When the ice broke up on the Fraser and the Cariboo in the spring of 1861, the prospectors who had gone away as the Fraser sandbars played out surged back again—from California, from New York, from Liverpool. Victoria flourished again as a supply base.

The Cariboo strike differed from others before and after it in a couple of significant ways. The gold had been deposited in incredibly rich concentrations and, since every creek in the region appeared to be seeded with the metal, for once there seemed to be enough to go around. By the fall of 1861, Governor Douglas' Gold Commissioners had recorded $2.5 million taken out of the Cariboo region and they believed that miners had probably panned as much again without bothering to report it.

One gold seeker by the name of William "Dutch Bill" Dietz discovered gold in a stream called Williams Creek, so the story goes, by stumbling and falling into it. When he got up dripping he remembered the prospector's dictum: test the gravel wherever you are.

Cariboo miners use a windlass to raise ore from a shaft on Williams Creek. Some claims produced nearly a million dollars for their owners.

Cariboo Road, the so-called highway to British Columbia's gold fields, leads along a narrow ledge blasted into the side of the otherwise impassable Hells Gate section of Fraser River gorge. Stagecoaches rumbled through at a rate of 60 miles a day, compelling slower mule-drawn wagons to pull over to the edge of this precipice to let them through.

It proved so rich that before long 4,000 miners were working seven miles of the stream bed. Ironically, Dietz's claim proved one of the poorest on a creek that was to be among the world's richest. One J. C. Bryant took an unbelievable 96 ounces of metal, worth $1,543, out of a single pan of gravel. A claim called the Caledonia yielded $750,000 and another named Aurora bettered it by $100,000.

A latecomer to Williams Creek, Henry Fuller Davis, at first thought himself shut out, the stream bed was so solidly staked. But, being an observant sort, he noticed that one claim seemed wider than the 100-foot legal limit. Measuring confirmed his guess. The claim was actually 112 feet in width; Fuller instantly claimed the excess and took $15,000 out of it. Ever after he was known as Twelve Foot Davis, a confusing sobriquet for a man five feet two.

Like Twelve Foot, a Cornish sailor named Billy Barker, having jumped ship in Victoria, arrived after the best pickings seemed exhausted. Finding nothing more promising, he and some equally inexperienced partners began digging into a bank of gravel, to the vast amusement of more knowledgeable colleagues. At 52 feet, they hit a deposit that yielded $600,000.

Like every other back-country gold-strike region, the Cariboo country spawned a boomtown, swiftly built, ramshackle, lusty and ruinously expensive. This one was named Barkerville, after Billy the sailor. In its heyday in the early 1860s, Barkerville boasted a population of 10,000 and claimed to be the biggest town west of Chicago and north of San Francisco. It was able to provide all the necessary services and diver-

THE STAGECOACH TYCOON OF THE CARIBOO ROAD

At the start of the Cariboo Road near Yale, B.C., a freight wagon drawn by a team of eight mules of the celebrated Barnard's Express line prepares for the journey to mining towns up to 400 miles away. The line was started in 1863 by Frank Barnard *(inset),* who pioneered the route on foot, profitably backpacking letters for two dollars each and newspapers for one. By the time the wagon road was completed in 1865, he was sending 14-passenger coaches on 800-mile round trips, charging travelers a staggering $130 a head. Even after the boom days of the gold rush faded, Barnard's Express, popularly known as the BX, continued to serve the frontier for a half century, until the Canadian Pacific railroad had completed its main line and a network of feeders.

sions: provision stores, laundries, barbershops, blacksmiths, churches, three breweries, 13 saloons. The prices were as outrageous as any ever conceived below the 49th parallel. Flour went for $300 a barrel, boots for $50 a pair and the hurdy-gurdy girls in the theater saloons charged $10 a dance. That item had scarcely ever exceeded a dollar a dance in the woolliest gold camp on the United States frontier.

In fairness it must be said that Barkerville had excuses for the cost of living and playing. The Cariboo digs were 500 miles from the coast, more than 350 miles beyond the first Fraser strike. In the beginning the only way to reach the new gold fields was via a hastily hacked-out extension of the famed Harrison Trail. Sent to inspect the route to the fabulous new strike, Lieutenant Palmer of the Royal Engineers reported: "It is difficult to find language to express in adequate terms the utter vileness of the trails of Cariboo—slippery, precipitous ascents and descents, fallen logs, overhanging branches, roots, rocks, swamps, turbid pools and miles of deep mud."

In Victoria, James Douglas reached a momentous decision: he would build a 400-mile 18-foot Queen's Highway all the way from the head of navigation at Fort Yale to the diggings, hanging it where necessary on the awesome flanks of the Fraser River Canyon.

Here was a concept to give the boldest man pause. The engineering challenge was stupefying enough. More than that, such highways cost vast sums of money, and the colony had little public revenue beyond license fees from miners and saloonkeepers. But Douglas knew that sooner or later such a road would have to be built if the country was to be opened up for settlement. He also understood that Britain would never consent to finance his highway. So he floated a loan from the Bank of British Columbia with its gold-fattened depositories, and planned to make parts of the road pay for themselves by granting contractors toll privileges on bridges and sections of roadway.

For its time and the state of the art, the Cariboo Road was an achievement of the highest magnitude. In May 1862, engineers started work on the most difficult parts—six miles of sheer walls in the Fraser Canyon just north of Fort Yale, and a nine-mile stretch of cliff along the tributary Thompson River. In some places, they blasted the shelf of the road out of the

solid rock; in others, they built a foundation up the cliffs from the river edge—massive structures of timber cribwork filled with rock ballast.

At a point where it was necessary to cross the river, a contractor named Joseph Trutch was commissioned to erect the first suspension bridge in western North America. Since it was impossible to haul bulky steel cable to the scene over existing trails, Trutch imported spools of light wire on muleback and twisted them into wire rope on the spot. Finally the homemade cables, draped over timber towers anchored in rock masonry, supported a roadway spanning the 300-foot chasm. Then he mounted a four-horse wagon carrying three tons of freight and rolled onto the bridge. It held.

By September 1863, the road ran 300 miles north beyond Fort Yale. There travelers had to switch to a sternwheel steamer whose component parts had come over the road as it advanced. The last part of the route remained no more than a trail until 1865, when at last the road was extended for the final 63 miles from Quesnel to Barkerville.

Riding out at one point to inspect the road under construction, Governor Douglas expressed satisfaction with the highway's "smoothness and solidity" and registered approval that the former "passes of ominous fame have lost their terrors. They now exist only in name, being alike safe and pleasant by the broad and graceful windings of the Queen's Highway."

Perhaps so, but then Douglas had been trained on more demanding trails. The Cariboo Road could still extract a chill from tenderfeet like Lord Milton and Dr. W. G. Cheadle, the first tourists to travel it. Riding in an express wagon, they reported with a shiver that "the road is very narrow, the mountainside terrifically steep. We rattled down at a fearful pace—a wheel coming off, the brake giving way, or a restive horse being almost certain death."

The pride of the Cariboo Road was Barnard's Express & Stage Line, known locally as the BX, which eventually ran 400 miles from Fort Yale into the heart of the mining area. F. J. Barnard had prudently retired from a career as a sailor after surviving a steamboat explosion. His BX grew from a pony express mail service to an imposing fleet of six-horse Concord stages, bright red with yellow running gear, which carried mail and passengers between Fort Yale and Soda Creek in

52 hours despite stops every 18 miles for rest and a change of teams.

Overnight accommodations at the wayside houses were on the primitive side at first, with travelers sleeping on top of, and under, tables and benches. But as more and larger hostelries were erected, the beds markedly improved and the meals grew positively sumptuous. For 50 cents, a passenger could enjoy a breakfast of thick porridge and cream, beefsteak, fried potatoes, hot cakes, coffee and fresh-baked pie.

A woman, of no matter what description, was accorded the strictest priority, getting the best seat on the coach. At night she received the most comfortable quarters, and at meals took the place of honor at the right of the driver, who always sat at the head of the table and made sure his passengers were taken care of properly. Although the Barnard coaches at times carried as much as $600,000 in gold, they were seldom held up, partly because of Judge Begbie's unforgiving attitude toward miscreants, partly because Barnard's drivers were known to be prideful and touchy men, apt to take extreme umbrage at any interference.

By the late 1860s, after about $100 million had been taken out of the Cariboo region, the great bonanza began to play out. The traffic over the Cariboo Road carried fewer fortune hunters. But in their place came families bound for permanent homesteads in the farming and grazing country of the high intermontane plateaus. The highway that gold built was serving Douglas' ultimate purpose, civilizing the province.

By then, Victoria had become a stable seaport capital, whose 6,000 people made a good living in lumber, fishing and shipping. The streets were now paved and gaslit, and lined with substantial homes, banks, hotels, churches, schools and parks.

Victoria had something else to be proud of. Determined to turn his town into a proper capital city, Douglas had erected a complex of official buildings to house a government grown both sizable and important. As always, finances had been a problem. Douglas knew that the Colonial Office in London would not willingly pay for the project. But he also remembered that under the terms of an 1849 Royal Grant, London had agreed to reimburse the Hudson's Bay Company for its colonizing expenses on Vancouver Island. After some wrangling, Douglas persuaded the company to set aside land for his government compound and advance the money for construction. If housing the government suitably was not a colonizing expense, he told himself, then what was?

When the Colonial Office heard of the plan, it howled its displeasure, but by that time the buildings were all but finished. For their airy design and flaring roof lines, Victorians fondly dubbed the new buildings "The Birdcages," and they served their function handsomely for many years.

Douglas' official rule as governor ended in April 1864, when he somewhat reluctantly retired and went off to visit England and Scotland. Opponents on both sides of Georgia Strait had been agitating for years to get him out of office. The cause of their discontent was precisely the qualities on which Douglas had drawn to build both colonies to stability and prosperity. They said he was autocratic and he was. They accused him of practicing nepotism and he did; the husbands of two of his five daughters were given employment with the colonial government. The critics demanded democracy, a proposition in which Douglas had not the slightest faith.

Douglas returned home to Victoria in June 1865, and spent the rest of his days, until his death of a heart attack in August 1877, as British Columbia's honored and much-consulted elder statesman. He was 74 when he died, and in one capacity or another had served his adopted land for more than half a century. It was only fitting that he lived to see his last and greatest goals achieved.

In 1866, Vancouver and the mainland colony of British Columbia merged. And by 1870, the legislature of the new province was debating whether to remain under the Crown, join the newly confederated Dominion of Canada — or as a few new residents darkly suggested, become a part of the United States. The dominion won, largely because of a grandiose promise to build a transcontinental railway across the empty plains. At midnight on July 19, 1871, the Victorians assembled in the streets to hear the bells rung and to hark to the thud of the saluting cannon. British Columbia was now part of Canada, a princely gift to the new dominion from the hands of such men as David Thompson, Matthew Begbie and James Douglas.

Victoria's colonial office and other government buildings, dubbed "Bird Cages" for their pagoda-like shapes, are reflected in the harbor.

A bit of England in the wilds

The voyage halfway around the world from Old England to Vancouver Island was a six-month trial, with seasickness, smallpox and the prospect of shipwreck as ever-present companions. But the surviving colonists might well have wondered on arrival just how far they had come after all.

To be sure, the scenery was different. James Douglas, who had established Fort Victoria in 1843, declared the site "a perfect Eden" because of its majestic trees and view of the Olympic Mountains. Yet the weather was remarkably like that in the British Isles. And so thoroughly transplanted were English customs that settlers immediately felt at ease.

After 20 years, Fort Victoria had six churches, one synagogue and several elegant hotels. A cricket club was founded and horse racing became popular. There was a Masonic Lodge, a Philharmonic Society, and the theater company performed *Othello* with gusto. And when a dress ball took place in May 1859, the *Gazette* reported that it was "attended by the beauty and fashion of the town"—the ladies in "silks and ribbons direct from Paris."

Members of the New Westminster and Victoria cricket clubs laze on the lawn of Beacon Hill Park in 1865. By then cricket matches were a regular feature of colonial life; among Victoria's players were a future governor of the colony, a lawyer, a judge and a gold commissioner.

Boatloads of colonial ladies and gentlemen and their bonneted babies enjoy an outing in one of the coves rimming Victoria Harbor. To celebrate Queen Victoria's birthday on May 24, Victorians staged a grand regatta of small craft.

Handsomely supplied with baskets of food, china and linen napery, picnickers take their ease at the Gorge, a narrow arm of Victoria Harbor, in 1884. The site was a favorite with the colonists; local boosters claimed: "The Gorge is to Victoria what Hampstead Heath is to London."

Patrons meet for five-cent ales in the bar of the St. Charles Hotel, which was a popular watering hole not only for Victoria residents but for transient loggers and gold miners. Governor Douglas shrewdly fattened the public coffers by imposing a tax on alcohol in 1853.

Mourners watch the funeral cortege of Sir James Douglas pass down the picket-fenced road to the Reformed Episcopal Church of Our Lord in Victoria in August 1877. The doughty Douglas had died of a heart attack at age 74, after having governed the colony for 21 years.

Fire rages across the land and casts light on watching Indians. Paul Kane painted the "awful scene" near Fort Edmonton in 1846.

4 | Settlers on an awesome ocean of grass

As late as the 1850s, Canadians seriously doubted that the awesome expanse of steppe rising from the Red River of the North westward to the Rocky Mountains could ever be extensively settled.

The plains seemed inherently hostile to civilization. Captain John Palliser, sent to explore in 1857, reported that wide sections of treeless prairie could never support a large population because of the lack of firewood. Yet there was no dearth of fires. The Great Lone Land seemed incessantly aflame with grass blazes, some set by lightning, some by man; artist Paul Kane quailed from the "fiery embrace" that left the night horizon glowing balefully red.

The immense, barren prairie presented other drawbacks to settlement as well — paralyzing cold in winter, ruinous floods in spring and insect plagues in summer.

Nevertheless, Indians and buffalo had managed to thrive there, and in the mid-1860s, white civilization began actively to covet this "ocean of grass." In 1867, Canada became a dominion of four Eastern provinces and was eager to push westward to the Pacific, where settlers and gold-seekers had already established a thriving colony. At the same time, the United States was throbbing with annexationist ambitions, while north of the border gangs of American freebooters were callously

debauching the Canadian Indians.

Caught in this torment was a small pocket of settlement centered at the fork of the Assiniboine and Red River of the North. Of the colony's 12,000 souls, the majority were Métis — descendants of fur-trading *voyageurs* and Indian women. The clash of the Western Métis, who spoke French and practiced Roman Catholicism, with the English-speaking Protestants of Eastern Canada, was a cruel and tragic chapter in the settlement of the Canadian West. Yet out of this conflict was born the fifth province in the growing Dominion of Canada, Manitoba, which became a populous and prosperous center of agriculture and commerce.

The Métis: a proud nation of "scorched wood"

The Bishop of St. Boniface bestowed his blessing on the caravan departing the Red River hamlet, and then removed himself from the scene as promptly as dignity would permit. For the cacophony of shrieks and howls that ensued as the expedition got underway might have arisen from the pit of the damned. The unearthly din emanated from the ox-drawn conveyances, two-wheeled affairs known as Red River carts. There were hundreds upon hundreds of them, and the agonizing wail of all those wooden hubs turning on ungreased axles fashioned from oak logs was described by one desolated chronicler as "a thousand fingernails drawn across a thousand panes of glass." Perhaps in sympathy, perhaps in protest, an immense pack of camp-following dogs raised an insane obbligato of barks and yelps to accompany the screeching axles.

Yet to the members of the caravan, these sounds were as the sweetest of music. They bespoke the most thrilling and satisfying event to punctuate life on the Canadian plains: the great semiannual buffalo hunts in which people from hundreds of miles around met to trek south into what would become North Dakota and harvest the seemingly endless bounty of huge, shaggy beasts. On this occasion, in June 1840, the troop comprised over 400 hunters, dressed in buckskin or blue woolen capotes, sashed in scarlet, armed with muzzle-loading rifles and mounted on splendid horses. Another 200 men saw to the spare stock and herded the draft animals, while 1,000 women and children walked, or rode with the camping gear in the carts.

These men and women were dark of skin — *bois brulé*, or scorched wood, they were sometimes called

— but they were not Indian. Neither were they white. They were the people of mixed blood. In the 1840s, these half-breeds, some 5,000 strong, outnumbered whites by more than 10 to 1 in Canada's Great Lone Land, that ocean of prairie stretching from Lake Superior and the Precambrian shield above it a thousand miles west to the Rockies. They were described by an admiring British lord as "a fine race, tall, straight, well proportioned, lightly formed and extremely active and enduring. Their chests, shoulders and waists are of that symmetrical shape so seldom found among the broad-waisted, short-necked English or the flat chested, long necked Scotch."

They were a proud people. Those of partly French extraction, known as the Métis, were devoutly Catholic — "priest ridden," their detractors said. The Métis and their compatriots, who had fathers and grandfathers of Scottish or English ancestry, held among them a powerful sense of separateness and identity, almost of nationality. Being proud, they were also brave and honest. The Métis were much given to song and merriment, generous hospitality and night-long dancing, caring for this day's joys and letting tomorrow go hang.

There had been Métis in Canada as early as the 1650s, descendants of Champlain's men who founded Quebec in 1608. As a French ethnologist once observed, Métis were inevitable, after an initial lag of an appropriate number of months, whenever white men impacted on a new savage community.

The Métis had for generations been conscious of their uniqueness. They had taken the blood of diametrically dissimilar races and cultures and rendered them into something more than the sum of its parts. They were a race apart, in most ways admirable.

But now in the West, through a set of baneful circumstances, that sense of self was about to be tested as though in a crucible. The Métis would rise gallantly to

Typically clad, three Métis sit for a tintype in the 1870s. Mixing white and Indian garb, they wore fur hats, vests buttoned at the top, moccasins and sashes.

the challenge. Supreme individualists, they would under stress submit themselves to a democratic need for disciplined, common action. They would find a leader among their own, a revered "messiah," they came to call him, and they would obey him. He was young, a zealot, impetuous, intolerant of criticism, quick-tempered, a dreamer, and probably unsure of himself, but for all his frailties he proved himself to be more of a statesman than the sophisticated white politicians who in the end betrayed him. Under him the Métis would create their own government and rule themselves, until they were disastrously defeated by white bad faith.

The tragedy of the Métis was a drama of national politics. It was their ill fortune to stand in the way of

the Canadians' eagerness to fill the void between Ontario and the thriving new colonies on the Pacific Coast. Yet the agony of the Métis had a great deal to do with the creation of a unified Dominion of Canada. And the unrelated though corollary passions and disorders that came to afflict their land were responsible for the creation of a unique and famous institution, the North West Mounted Police.

In the spring of 1840 these tribulations still lay in the future. The noisy cavalcade wending southwestward from the Red River may have looked warlike but its purpose was economic — and sporting. For the Métis, the year's two buffalo hunts, in June and September,

were honored rituals, and in them they made use of that gift for disciplined democratic action they later displayed in creating and running a government.

The buffalo hunt followed a precise pattern. It began with the initial rendezvous at St. Boniface on the Red River, and a 75-mile march south to Pembina, where still more Métis swelled the expedition. At Pembina, the Métis erected a town of tents ringed around with their carts as a barricade of sorts against the Sioux who were habitually hostile toward their mixed-blood cousins. This stopover was an interim of general reunion and rejoicing while the hunters settled down to the serious business of officering the hunt. An overall chief of the hunt was elected, along with 10 captains

to share command. In time, each captain chose 10 sturdy men to act as soldiers and one superior individual to serve as a guide. For the length of the campaign, which might last a month or longer, the guides took daily turns directing the course of the hunt. Each morning a flag was hoisted on a cart belonging to the captain whose guide would lead the hunt that day. While the flag flew the guide was in charge; when it was lowered, captains and soldiers took over, directing the arrangement of the camp, policing its borders and enforcing the rules of the hunt.

These rules were democratically adopted, and clear beyond possibility of misunderstanding. The rules for the 1840 hunt stipulated:

135

1. No buffalo to be run on the Sabbath.
2. No party to fork off, lag behind or go before without permission.
3. No person or party to run buffalo before the general order.
4. Every captain with his men, in turn, to patrol the camp and keep guard.
5. For a first offence against these laws, offender to have his saddle and bridle cut up.
6. For the second offence, the coat to be taken off the offender's back and be cut up.
7. For the third offence, the offender to be flogged.
8. Any person convicted of theft, even to the value of a sinew, to be brought to the middle of the camp and the crier to call out his or her name three times, adding the word, "Thief!" at each time.

Every morning at dawn the Métis loaded up and took a course generally westward, fanning out into staggered rows of carts a mile or more across. This broad front was a defensive measure against the clouds of yellow dust, which was more offensive to Métis nostrils than the ululating of ungreased cart wheels was to Métis ears. In any event the flaws of the cart were unimportant compared with its assets. Indeed, it was the *sine qua non* of Métis economic life, so much so that the Indians called the Métis "wagon men" and devised a sign to describe them, circling forefingers to signify wheels. The cart was a marvel of utility: its light wooden body would support 900 pounds, and its dished-out wheels gave it so wide a stance that it was almost impossible to capsize. "A curious looking vehicle," the artist Paul Kane reported in the 1840s, "made by themselves with their own axes, and fastened together with wooden pins and leather strings. The tire of the wheel is made of buffalo hide and put on wet; when it becomes dry it shrinks, and is so tight that it never falls off and lasts as long as the cart holds together."

In these carts, along with their other burdens on the hunt of June 1840, went 740 firearms, 1,300 pounds of shot, 150 gallons of gunpowder plus 6,240 spare flints for the firelocks of the muskets. This arsenal was not all intended for buffalo; a sizable portion of it was reserved for use in case of attack by marauding Sioux.

For a time on that hunt, the Métis might have won-

dered if they would get a chance to use any powder at all. The caravan was 20 days out and 250 miles southwest of Pembina before the guide of the day brought them, at sundown, within sight of a huge herd of the great animals they sought. The camp bedded down in tense anticipation of the next day's business.

It began at dawn with the blessing of the traveling chaplain assigned by the Bishop of St. Boniface. The 400 horsemen mounted and reined up in ranks, awaiting the command of the chief of the hunt. This official surveyed the herd, calmly grazing a mile and a half distant upwind. He flung out his arm and shouted, "Commencez!" and the men urged their horses forward.

At this signal, wrote a Scotsman named Alexander Ross who witnessed the 1840 hunt, "the whole cavalcade broke ground and made for the buffalo, first at a slow trot, then at a gallop and lastly at full speed. They had approached within four or five hundred yards before the bulls curved their tails or pawed the ground. In a moment more, the whole herd took flight and horses and riders were presently seen bursting in among them; shots are heard and all is smoke, dust and hurry."

To a Métis, the buffalo run was more than a mere slaughter; it was the sport supreme. The Métis hunted with as much abandon as did their Indian cousins. The horses plunged through the stampeding buffalo, guided only by the pressure of their riders' knees. With both hands free, the hunters fired, reloaded and fired on the dead run. Each man carried spare musket balls in his mouth; after firing, he shook a fresh charge into the muzzle from a powder flask, spat a ball down the barrel, then stamped the gunstock on his saddle to seat the ball in its moist wadding of spittle.

It was hot work and hazardous, for the prize targets were the cows with their tender meat and more pliable hides. But the cows, being lighter and faster, were at the head of the herd, running in front of a wall of tough old bulls. To get next to a cow, within 10 feet, set for a heart shot just behind and below the left shoulder, the hunter had to thread his way through that awesome barricade of thundering hoofs and tossing horns.

At the end of the run, as the riders returned and claimed their kills, the observer, Ross, toted up the score. "The surface was rough and full of badger holes," he reported. "Twenty-three horses and riders were at one moment all sprawling on the ground. One horse gored by a bull was killed on the spot; two more were disabled by falls. One rider broke his shoulder blade and another burst his gun and lost three fingers by the accident and a third was struck on the knee by an exhausted ball. These accidents will not be thought overnumerous considering the result, for in the evening no less than 1,375 tongues were brought into camp."

The June 1840 hunt continued until all the carts were filled to overflowing. Ross noted that the hunters brought back more than a million pounds of meat — most of it quickly dried in the hot prairie sun — the equivalent of 225 pounds for every man, woman and child in the Red River settlements. Meat and hides sold to the Hudson's Bay Company fetched more sterling than all the farms — mostly worked by English- and Scottish-descended half-breeds — produced from their crops.

The Métis had been celebrating the bloody ceremony of the hunt for decades before the 1840 excursion witnessed by Ross. They would continue to do so for another 30 years. And the hunt, and their use of its proceeds, would become one of the contributing elements of the troubles that finally engulfed them.

At Red River the Métis were first forced into close association with whites in 1812. From the start the relationship was abrasive, though it began with the most benign of intentions. The year before, the 40-year-old Earl of Selkirk, a major stockholder in the Hudson's Bay Company and a patrician with a philanthropic turn of mind, had persuaded his reluctant fellow directors to sell him, for a token 10 shillings, 116,000 square miles of central British America. This was part of the sweep of steppe, swamp and rock between Lake Superior and the Rockies, called Rupert's Land to honor a cousin of King Charles II. Selkirk had in mind founding an agricultural colony and peopling it with Scottish peasants dispossessed by the Highland Clearances, in which the ruling lairds had evicted their sharecroppers in order to get land for sheep pastures.

The first 23 settlers arrived in the summer of 1812 under a governor named Miles Macdonnell, and Macdonnell immediately began making mistakes. Fearing that his greenhorn settlers would not have enough food, Macdonnell put the Métis on notice that they would no longer be permitted to sell their pemmican, fruit of the hunt, to whomever they wished; his settlers were

to have first call. He then compounded this unfortunate error by forbidding the Métis to run the buffalo on horseback. The outraged Métis scorned both edicts and continued as before.

The unpleasantness swiftly grew. The directors of the Hudson's Bay Company had been doubtful about Selkirk's colony, holding to the axiom that farming and the fur business did not mix. The men of the archrival North West Company felt even more strongly about the matter and now deliberately undertook to drive the settlers out. The Nor'Westers made the Métis their tools and incited them to a program of intimidation and harassment — tearing down fences, driving off sheep and cattle, trampling and burning crops.

Nevertheless, the Selkirk colony slowly grew, reinforced by fresh cadres of Scotch and English immigrants. As the colony increased, so did the tension. The blowup came in 1816.

On June 19 a party of Métis raiders on their way to the settlers' lots along the Red River was spotted by the lookout at Fort Douglas in the Selkirk colony. The colony's new governor, Robert Semple, armed 26 men and sent them out to confront the Métis. Shouting and insults commenced. Semple, furious at the verbal abuse, seized the Métis spokesman's bridle. Both colonists and Métis began firing. Semple went down with a bullet in one thigh. A man beside him fell dead. Then a killing frenzy seized some of the Métis and they turned to butchery, first killing, then mutilating the bodies. Only three colonists crawled back to the stockade alive.

The incident was beyond explaining. It was the one time in all the history of Métis-white hostility when the mixed-bloods gave way to savagery. Thereafter, under the leadership of a father and his son, they remained self-restrained to the point of foolhardiness.

The father was Louis Riel, by his compatriots known as "the miller of the Seine." He had with his own hands dug a nine-mile channel from the Red River to increase the flow of water over his mill wheel on a creek named, not for the great river of Paris, but for the Métis practice of seining fish there. Riel was ambitious, and he dreamed of establishing a woolen factory in the region. But the Hudson's Bay Company frowned on all industry, and he encountered only discouragement. Consequently he became an anticompany man and a leader of Métis discontent. The company had re-entered the picture in the mid-1830s, after its merger with the Nor'Westers. By then, the Selkirk colony was foundering for lack of leadership in a harsh land plagued by execrable weather and periodic insect devastations. Lord Selkirk had died in 1820, and his heirs had no taste for pouring treasure into a struggling agricultural domain half a world away. In 1836, they quietly transferred the territory back to the Hudson's Bay Company; thereafter fur, not farming, was the dominant interest in Rupert's Land.

The company appointed governors and gave the territory, in the words of Scotsman Alexander Ross, "the cool and languid care of a stepmother," which is to say almost no care at all. Many of the farmers drifted back east or south to the United States and the Métis reclaimed the land. A census of 1840 counted 4,369 inhabitants in the Red River settlements, the majority of them Métis.

By rights, the Métis and Hudson's Bay Company should have been well content with each other, for the Métis wanted nothing so much as to be left alone. However, the monopolistic company set out rules and regulations that seemed designed solely to restrict what the half-breeds regarded as their natural rights. One of these rules forbade trading with the Americans south of the 49th parallel in the new and bumptious city of St. Paul. In May 1849, the company's directors brought a Métis named Guillaume Sayer to trial for smuggling. With that, Louis Riel acted. Angered beyond endurance, he surrounded the courthouse with 300 armed followers. Inside, a nervous jury found Sayer guilty but, so vehemently as to amount to a command upon the court, recommended mercy. The court took heed and released the accused; among the Métis a cry was raised, "Le commerce est libre! Vive la liberté!"

And the commerce did remain reasonably free. By 1858 the caravans of Red River carts squealing and complaining back and forth over the trail to St. Paul were running to 600 a year. So matters stood for almost a decade, with the trade in kettles, stoves, farm implements, alcohol and all the other necessities and joys of life growing year after year. By 1867 the number of caravans topped 2,000.

In that year the beginnings of deep trouble emerged with the federation of the four British provinces in

138

A tent city rises on the plain as the great clan of Métis gathers for the premier event in their lives: the semiannual buffalo hunt. Artist Paul Kane noted that after the "intense excitement" of the chase the camp was moved directly into the carnage to speed the collection of meat.

North America (New Brunswick, Nova Scotia, Ontario and Quebec) into the Dominion of Canada. With dominion status came ambition, coupled with apprehension about the expansion-minded Americans to the south. Ottawa almost unwillingly began to be conscious of the growing settlements far out where the Assiniboine met the Red River of the North.

Sir John Macdonald, Canada's first Prime Minister, was a politician of deliberate mien, so exceedingly slow in decision that his colleagues called him Old Tomorrow. He delivered himself of a classic opinion on that vast in-between out there. "I would be quite willing," he said, "to leave that whole country a wilderness for the next half century, but I fear that if Englishmen do not go there, Yankees will."

Old Tomorrow was, for once, abreast of the times. Secretary of State William Seward had just purchased Alaska, and American politicians throughout the Upper Midwest burned to annex Rupert's Land and make the United States of America the biggest country in the world.

There was another reason for Canada to hasten its possession of Rupert's Land. Eight hundred thousand American soldiers had been left unemployed by the close of the Civil War. And in that out-of-work army, there were plenty of unruly spirits who would be only too willing to make a grab at territory above the 49th parallel. Among the wildest were the Fenians, a band of Irish-Americans fired by the novel idea of pressuring England into freeing Ireland by harassing British America. Already there had been Fenian incursions into Eastern Canada. In June 1866, a rabble of 1,000 men, most of them Civil War veterans, defeated a force of Canadian volunteers to capture Fort Erie, Ontario. Only when the United States government intervened did the invaders withdraw. It seemed entirely likely that a similar incident might occur farther west.

On March 9, 1869, a bargain was struck between the new Dominion of Canada and the Hudson's Bay Company by which the nation would buy Rupert's Land from the company for the price of £300,000. Under the terms of the sale, Hudson's Bay would retain six million of the 120 million acres of the so-called Fertile Belt, which lay in an arc stretching from Fort Garry to the border of British Columbia. The company also kept 50,000 acres around existing Hudson's Bay Company posts. The Crown agreed to lend Ottawa the money.

The one trouble with the deal was that the people most involved were largely ignored. By now almost 10,000 half-breeds, divided into 6,000 French- and 4,000 English-speaking mixed-bloods, along with 1,600 white settlers, were living in the area. No one had told them what was going on. Not even the company's governor on the spot, old and sick William Mactavish in Fort Garry, was kept informed about the negotiations. Once, in despair, he told a Métis friend, "I can guarantee nothing. Times are changing. I myself know nothing. Am I still the governor? It seems that everything gets settled in London, but they don't tell me anything."

For the Métis, the distant ferment between the Hudson's Bay Company, London and Ottawa brought feelings of deep foreboding. To make matters worse, the Métis were now leaderless. Louis Riel, organizer of the courthouse rebellion, had died in 1864, and no one had come forward immediately to take his place. But such a leader would soon appear, and he would electrify the Métis as no one could have imagined.

When Louis Riel organized the courthouse rebellion in 1849, he had a first-born namesake, then less than five years old. The boy was a Métis but just barely; he was just one eighth Chippewa Indian.

Louis the father was not a rich man, but he was a substantial citizen and a lifelong militant for Métis rights. His son grew up in that atmosphere and when the elder Louis died while the younger was away at school, the 20-year-old boy wrote his mother a heartbroken letter that said in part, "Papa always acted with wisdom; he will therefore be glorified."

In those days, while most Métis were illiterate, they included a modest sprinkling of educated men, some of whom had even been sent abroad to study. A few, in the years after trade strictures with St. Paul had been relaxed, had accumulated substantial means and built good permanent houses, sometimes of stone. Young Louis Riel's family fell somewhere along the middle of the economic scale, and his parents had no intention of letting him grow up unlettered. He was a bright youngster, and for 10 years an only child who could monopolize his parents' attention. His first teacher was

his mother who, before he was seven, had taught him something of arithmetic, grammar and history, and had imparted a devout adherence to the Catholic faith.

At seven he was sent to study under the Grey Sisters of St. Boniface parish in the colony. That year a new bishop of the Western territories, Monsignor Alexander Taché, brought in lay brothers from Montreal and established a school in the parish library. In the spring of 1858, the bishop decided that four of his charges, all Métis, were so bright that they deserved to be educated in Montreal. Louis, not yet 14, was one of the four.

At that time the road from the Red River colony to Montreal was circuitous, to say the least. It led down the trade route to St. Paul, thence via Mississippi riverboat south to Prairie du Chien, where it proceeded east by train to Chicago and Detroit, back into Canada by way of Hamilton and Toronto and finally to the destination, Montreal.

There young Riel received a scholarship in the seminary of the Gentlemen of St. Sulpice, a venerable in-

stitution dating from 1683. He turned into one of the school's star students in Latin, Greek, French, the sciences and math. By the time he was 19, he was studying the philosophers, writing poetry and seriously considering the priesthood.

But the next year, for no known reason, very possibly agonized by his father's death, he began to lose both his vocation for the church and his grip on himself. He became moody, abstracted and occasionally quarrelsome. Knowing he was bright, he could not abide criticism and would not brook contradiction. These were lasting traits, which in later years sometimes marred his performance in the career he was destined for—the "messiah of the Métis."

Riel's formal education ended abruptly in March 1865 when he walked out of the seminary shortly before the close of the term. By this time he was rambling, nervous, talking uncertainly of a career in politics. His final revulsion against life in Montreal was the result of a disastrous love affair; his girl's parents refused to let her marry a Métis. Disconsolate, insulted and disillusioned, he left Montreal in June 1866. It took him more than two years to reach Red River, an interlude filled with vague and not very productive occupations in Chicago and St. Paul. He reached home at the end of July 1868.

Before 12 months had passed Louis Riel struck his first blow for the rights and dignities of the Métis. That process continued intermittently until it brought him to his death on the gallows in 1885.

With their own eyes the Métis could foresee the portents of anguish in the annexation of their prairie homeland by the Dominion of Canada. All through the decade of the 1860s a small but increasing trickle of white British Canadians from Ontario had been moving into the Red River region.

These men were Protestant Orangemen and everything they stood for was antithetical to the easygoing, French-speaking, Roman Catholic Métis. Moreover, the strangers seemed brutal, bigoted, overbearing and greedy. With whiskey for currency they were buying land from Indians who had no right to sell and no titles to convey. The new intruders called themselves Canada Firsters or, alternately, the Canada Party. They were contemptuous of all half-breeds and particularly of the Métis. They boasted openly that they were going to take over.

Their leader was a man named Dr. John Christian Schultz. Schultz had trained in medicine, but he had arrived from Ontario in 1860 not to practice but to set himself up as a merchant and to publish a newspaper, *The Nor'Wester*, that called stridently for annexation to Canada. "The wise and prudent," proclaimed one editorial, "will be prepared to receive and benefit by the changes Ottawa would make whilst the indolent and careless, like the native tribes of the country, will fall back before the march of a superior intelligence."

It was possible for white Ontarians to wax even more scornful of Métis pride. In a letter that later became public, a crony of Dr. Schultz, a man named Charles Mair, wrote, "Many wealthy people here are married to half-breed women who, having no coat of arms but a 'totem' to look back to, make up for this deficiency by biting at the backs of their white sisters." If the region was going to fill up with such men and be governed by them, no "superior intelligence" was need-

ed to predict what was apt to happen to the Métis.

In 1869, Prime Minister Macdonald seemed almost deliberately to pull the trigger. He sent a party of technicians from Ottawa to survey the region of the Red River. The surveyors' instructions were to outline a system of square townships, somewhat like the American plan but made up of sections of 800 acres rather than 640. Nothing could have been calculated to rouse the Métis to greater anger and apprehension.

For longer than anybody could remember, Métis and their forebears had farmed what they called River, or Quebec, lots. These were long, thin strips that led from the bank of a river or stream, the source of the farm's water, and ran back through woodlands, source of fuel, and out through fertile fields to the drier prairie held in common with neighbors and called the "hay privilege." Thus, all farmers shared more or less equally in the features of the land, and none was cut off from the essentials of life.

But now, on October 11, 1869, a survey party led by a Captain Adam Clark Webb appeared and began to lay a chain across the hay privilege of a Métis named André Nault, who demanded to know what they were doing. Soon it became apparent that Nault's French was not making any headway against Webb's English, so Nault began to yell. Then he had a better idea and sent for his cousin, Louis Riel. In short order Riel appeared, leading 15 other Métis. He addressed Webb in English, which, in this community, took the Canadian officer by surprise. Riel asked what Webb was doing; Webb said he was running the government's survey. Riel put his foot on the chain and said, "You go no farther!"

Captain Webb, sizing up Riel's band of stern-faced Métis, sensibly withdrew to seek the advice of his superiors. Three officials, William Cowan, the magistrate at Fort Garry, a half-breed council member named Roger Goulet, and Governor William Mactavish were all unable to budge Riel. "The Canadian government," said the Métis leader, "had no right to make surveys in the Territory without the express permission of the people of the settlement." The surveyors did not return.

Riel's next confrontation with Ottawa's minions was on a considerably higher level, and out of it he emerged an indisputable winner. Seeking to assert au-

thority, Prime Minister Macdonald had dispatched a governor to Red River — and blundered egregiously by sending precisely the wrong man.

He was William McDougall, a longtime bureaucrat described by contemporaries as cold, inflexible, dogmatic and impatient. He had been a member of Parliament and Minister of Public Works, and throughout his career he had been an ardent annexationist. Now, in October 1869, as Riel was facing down the surveyors, McDougall was on his way to Red River, coming up through Minnesota with a retinue that included his military aide and, carried in the baggage wagons, 300 rifles.

Led by Riel, the Métis organized a *Comité National des Métis* and dispatched a messenger to meet McDougall at the border and warn him not to cross the line without permission. To give the message force, they erected a barricade across the road and manned it with 40 armed Métis. And to make the point stronger still, Riel assembled a force of 400 men at Red River, and without firing a single shot, took over Fort Garry, the Hudson's Bay Company's central establishment

in the region, from the aging Governor Mactavish.

Enraged and thinking to assert himself, Governor McDougall moved his party to an abandoned Hudson's Bay Company post just north of the border. Riel sent his chief aide, Ambroise Lépine, a famous and gigantic buffalo hunter, to call on the Canadian and advise him sternly to return to the United States. Grumbling, but in no position to resist the well-armed and determined Métis, McDougall packed his wagons and rolled back across the border.

Throughout November Riel held a series of meetings at Fort Garry, seeking to strengthen his following and clarify the Métis goals. In essence, their desires were both simple and reasonable. If they were to become part of Canada, they wanted certain things guaranteed by the Canadian government and confirmed by the Parliament in London.

The most important of the demands presented by the Métis included prior consultation, a democratic voice in their government, and protection of Métis rights to their land, religion and language. These demands, a total of 18 items in all, were embodied in a

Louis Riel *(right)* was almost a portrait of his father. The two Métis leaders had the same level stare, set mouth and prominent nose.

CANADIAN ILLUSTRATED NEWS

VOL. 1.—No 25.]   MONTREAL, SATURDAY, APRIL 23, 1870.   [SINGLE COPIES, TEN CENTS. $4 PER YEAR IN ADVANCE.

Métis rebels deliver the *coup de grâce* to Canadian Thomas Scott at Fort Garry in 1870. Scott was killed for threatening Louis Riel.

formal declaration, which was called the List of Rights.

Thus far the movement had been confined almost entirely to the 6,000 French-speaking half-breeds. Riel strove diligently to enlist his 4,000 British-descended compatriots but they remained doubtful. The English-speaking half-breeds objected to the seizure of Fort Garry and the ouster of McDougall as illegal. Although they agreed with the List of Rights and they were cool to the Canadian cause, they felt the French-speaking Métis had gone too far and they preferred to sit on the sidelines. Infuriated, Riel was scathing: "Go, return peacefully to your farms. Stay in the arms of your wives. Give this example to your children. But watch us act. We are going ahead to work and obtain the guarantee of our rights and yours. You will come to share in them in the end."

Meanwhile, McDougall was cooling his heels just across the border, and sending blizzards of messages home demanding that Ottawa act. But Prime Minister Macdonald was in no rush to bring matters to a head. And on this point, Old Tomorrow's instincts were correct. A few observant Englishmen had long suspected that the Métis when aroused would be difficult to manage. One, a Colonel Crofton, had warned: "The half breed hunters with their splendid organization when on the prairies, their matchless power of providing for themselves, their perfect knowledge of the country, would render them a very formidable enemy. White men not accustomed to such a life would soon become powerless against them."

So advised, Macdonald was content to let matters ride for a while. But Governor McDougall, who was seething with fury, finally decided to take matters into his own hands. On December 2, he ordered his aide, Lieutenant Colonel John Stoughton Dennis, to raise a military force, arm them with the 300 rifles in his baggage, and put down the Métis.

The effort became a cumulative disaster. A number of white settlers, notably Dr. Schultz and his Canada Firsters, rushed at once to McDougall's banner. But they could muster only about 60 able-bodied men. This little force took over and fortified an abandoned Hudson's Bay post called the Stone Fort, 20 miles below Fort Garry. Dennis also recruited a few Saulteaux Indians who were delighted to get free rifles. And there the effort bogged down. For his main

strength Governor McDougall had counted on the region's English-speaking mixed-bloods. But when Dennis approached them they refused, as one of their leaders put it, to fight against "those who have been born and brought up among us, ate with us, slept with us, hunted with us, traded with us and are our own flesh and blood."

Dennis issued a proclamation advising "the loyal party in the Northwest Territory to cease further action" and went back to Pembina, where McDougall still waited.

Schultz and some 70 Canadians meanwhile had gone back to Winnipeg. There they assembled in Schultz's storehouse, which was well stocked with pork and other provisions laid in for road and survey crews, and awaited the Métis. Ignoring Dennis' order to return to Kildonan, a nearby Scotch settlement, Schultz and his men stayed put until December 7, when Louis Riel, with 200 men surrounding the structure and a small cannon trained on the gate, demanded unconditional surrender. With a lopsided fight the only alternative, the Canadians surrendered and were marched to Fort Garry. Among them was a loud-mouthed Irish-born bully from Ontario named Thomas Scott. This man was to lead ultimately to the ruination of Louis Riel and the wreckage of his movement. On December 18 Governor McDougall left Pembina for the long journey back to Ottawa.

In the Red River settlement Riel moved to consolidate his position. The *Comité National des Métis* proclaimed itself to be a provisional government and raised its flag above Fort Garry. Appropriately, this device bore a French *fleur de lis* on a white field as its central emblem.

By late December, Ottawa had begun to take the Métis seriously enough to realize that some sort of conciliation was imperative. But the idea rankled Prime Minister Macdonald. "These impulsive half-breeds have got spoiled," he complained sourly, "and must be kept down by a strong hand until they are swamped by the influx of settlers." Yet Macdonald could see the wisdom of a velvet glove on the strong hand, so he sent a persuasive Hudson's Bay Company official, Donald Smith, to assure the Métis that Canada's intentions toward them were benevolent. Twice Smith addressed assemblages of 1,000 Métis, assuring them that his

146

Government forces begin one of 47 portages on the expedition to Red River in 1870. In this painting by the contemporary artist Frances Hopkins, boats and canoes are gathered at the foot of a corduroy log causeway over which they will be carried by *voyageurs* around the impassable falls.

sole object was "to bring about peaceably union and entire accord among all the classes of people of this land."

Smith's mission had no authority to commit Ottawa to anything. Yet his assurances of good faith were believed. And in a curious way, they served Riel's purpose by uniting the French- and English-speaking mixed-bloods, 10,000 strong, in a common cause.

Out of the Smith visit, Riel was able to organize a formal half-breed convention. A committee of delegates went to the ailing Mactavish for advice and was told, "Form a government for God's sake and restore peace and order in the settlement."

It was done. On February 9, 1870, by act of the convention representing all of Red River's settlers, whites as well as half-breeds, Louis Riel, age 25, was elected president. His first step, in an atmosphere of good feeling, was to release the imprisoned Canada Firsters as quickly as they would swear allegiance to the new regime. But trouble was brewing.

A few of the prisoners had escaped Fort Garry before the Riel government began its formal amnesties.

Among the escapees was Thomas Scott, the roughneck Irishman from Ontario, and Dr. Schultz himself. Schultz had got away by using a knife smuggled in by his wife to cut up a buffalo robe and splice it into a rope, which he used to climb down from a window on the second floor of the fort. Scott and 11 others had escaped by taking advantage of growing boredom and heavy drinking among their Métis guards.

At Portage la Prairie, a settlement about 60 miles from Fort Garry, Scott and a handful of intransigent Canada Firsters immediately began putting together another counterrevolution. On February 17, they marched off toward Fort Garry. They were intercepted in the snowdrifts outside Garry by the buffalo hunter Ambroise Lépine, and taken prisoner again. Jailed for the second time, Scott became violently abusive, attacking a guard and vowing to kill Riel at the first opportunity. Riel, hoping to quiet the man, visited his cell. It has never been clear whether Scott actually attempted to assault the Métis leader. But something caused the Métis to lose all patience with the Irish rebel. He was placed on trial, charged with bearing arms against the state. On March 3 a jury of seven men, presided over by Ambroise Lépine, sentenced him to death, and the next day a firing squad executed him in the courtyard of the fort. Riel had been one of three prosecution witnesses.

To Riel, Scott's execution was a necessary show of determination: "We must make Canada respect us," he said. Not surprisingly, the effect was just the reverse. In Ontario, Scott, the obscure, foul-mouthed lout, became a martyr, the symbol of every white man's prejudice against those haughty, troublemaking half-breeds. Dr. Schultz, making his way eastward, passed through Ontario like a flaming cross, declaring that Scott had been unspeakably tortured, and whipping up cries for vengeance.

In Ottawa Prime Minister Macdonald's government did its best to walk the tightrope between public passions and the obvious necessity of dealing with the new Métis government. When the Red River government's delegates reached Ontario in mid-April they were arrested on a murder warrant sworn out by Scott's brother. But they were quickly released, and Macdonald received them more or less cordially when they called to present their conditions for joining Canada. These included the 18-point List of Rights, and one final demand — that the Red River settlements be admitted as a full province, not a colony.

Early in May the Parliament, amid much furious debate, got to work on what was now known as the Manitoba Act: the new province was to be named after the Assiniboine word for "Lake of the Prairies." When the act finally passed on July 15, it incorporated nearly all the items on Riel's list. The one notable exception was amnesty for any and all actions taken during the insurrection. Macdonald lacked the political nerve for that in the face of Ontario's still raging thirst for vengeance on the "murderers" of Thomas Scott.

When news of the Manitoba Act reached Fort Garry, Riel made a speech. "I congratulate the people of the North West on the happy issue of their undertakings," he said. "I congratulate them on having trust enough in the Crown of England to believe that ultimately they would obtain their rights. For myself, it will be my duty and pleasure to bid the new governor welcome on his arrival." Riel then went on to

add: "I only wish to retain power until I can resign it to a proper government."

At that moment Riel might also have been excused for congratulating himself. He had led an almost bloodless rebellion, and seemed to have won a glorious victory. But, as he was soon to discover, he had not.

The Manitoba Act carried a codicil, adopted mainly to appease the Riel-hating Ontarians. It provided for sending into the area not only a governor but a military force of about 1,200 troops. Ostensibly the force was a constabulary, dispatched only to keep the peace and protect the colony from Indians. But its roster included a good many men to whom the very name of Louis Riel was anathema, and private thoughts of exacting satisfaction for Thomas Scott seared many a mind.

The expedition had hard going. Because the United States refused passage to an armed force through its territory, the troops had to fight their way through the roadless muskeg wilderness northwest of Lake Superior. The trip was mostly by boat and canoe, and 47 punishing portages had to be negotiated. The force was 96 days en route, sending ahead reassuring messages that they came in peace. Riel sent four boatloads of experienced Métis *voyageurs* to guide the soldiers through the forests.

The first troops appeared at Fort Garry on August 24, slogging through the gumbo on the banks of the Red River. Until that morning, Riel had planned to welcome the men personally. But at the last moment a friendly white Canadian managed to convince him that despite all protestations of peace, he would be in mortal danger if he remained. He left through the fort's front gate just as the soldiers approached the other side of the building.

It was the end of Louis Riel's first rebellion. A few days later he was a fugitive. When he received a packet of food from a man who addressed him as "M'sieu le President," Riel replied, "Tell the people that he who ruled in Fort Garry only yesterday is now a homeless wanderer with nothing to eat but two dried fish."

He fled south into the United States and exile. Not until 1875 was he granted a pardon for his insurrection, and then only on condition that he remain in exile for another five years. Three times his old followers elected him in absentia to Parliament, and he once sneaked into Ottawa to sign the register of the

House. From afar, he watched helplessly as all the fine promises went down the drain. Few of the promises of the Manitoba Act were kept. Four members of the Thomas Scott jury were murdered and another was beaten and left for dead on the American side of the border. Métis lands were stolen and Métis were harassed and bedeviled by the increasing numbers of unforgiving Ontarians. A decade later Louis Riel would arise again — and die for it.

While Louis Riel and his Métis had contrived to maintain at least a semblance of order in the Red River settlements throughout the rebellion, the rest of Rupert's Land was left in vacuum, with the Hudson's Bay Company in virtual abdication and Canada unable to assert authority. Into this vast emptiness other scourges had come to plague the infant province of Manitoba.

These pestilences — and they were truly that — were evil legacies bestowed upon the native Indian population by white men. In the autumn of 1869, an epidemic of smallpox crossed the border to visit its horrors upon the lodges of Canadian Indians. Among the afflicted a tale spread that the disease had been foisted upon them deliberately by a white trader who, having lost some horses to Indian raiders, vengefully baited the riverbank with bales of infected blankets. Possibly truer was the account of a Montana paper that a Piegan brave had unknowingly stolen an infected blanket from a Missouri riverboat.

Through that long winter, lodge after lodge was abandoned as bands of Piegans, Sarcees, Bloods and Blackfeet tried to flee. Whole families died in blizzards, leaving their bodies to their starving dogs. To an Indian, even more than to a white, the pox was unadulterated horror. The swelling, the foul odor, the delirium and disfigurement were more than an Indian's pride could endure. Young braves killed themselves to escape the ugliness, and fathers killed their wives, their children and then themselves rather than go through the degrading agony.

Sometimes the delirium stage seized whole encampments at a time and the warriors would run screaming into icy rivers, make suicidal attacks on enemy tribes or hurl themselves at the locked gates of traders' forts. Barricaded inside, the traders watched as the berserk victims tried to give the plague back to its source by rubbing their sores on gates, door handles and window frames. Others stacked their dead to windward of the white men's posts in the hope of poisoning the air. By the spring of 1870, when the epidemic subsided, the Piegans alone counted more than 1,000 dead; the Bloods and Blackfeet had lost more than 600 each. Many of the leading chiefs and warriors were gone; shorn of power and the wisdom of their elders, the tribes were in no shape to resist the further offerings of civilization that awaited the survivors.

Another pestilence, in the long run far more devastating than even the smallpox, was arriving from below the border. The fur traders of the Hudson's Bay Company had learned long since that liquor sold to an Indian could be as dangerous to the seller as to the buyer, and had eventually banned it entirely from the fur trade. In its own territory the United States was making some effort to enforce its long-standing laws against trading whiskey to Indians.

But after the Civil War, Montana was rapidly filling up with war-toughened veterans, many of them hard cases anxious to make a dollar the quickest way they could. They were well aware that most Indians would trade anything they owned for two commodities: repeating rifles and whiskey. American law rendered the trade chancy below the 49th parallel, but Rupert's Land was wide open.

The whiskey traders, as they came to be called, loaded their wagons at Fort Benton, a booming shantytown at the head of navigation on the Missouri — a "Sagebrush Sodom," as a later historian described it. Their stock in trade was the cheapest, most powerful rotgut whiskey that could be obtained from the distilleries of St. Louis. But it was seldom sold unadulterated, for the whiskey traders soon learned that the stuff would go farther and get more positive results if ingeniously doctored with various ingredients. They competed with one another in devising formulae to put more fire in the firewater. One of their more popular concoctions called for one part raw, high-proof alcohol, three parts water, a generous dose of chewing tobacco, tea leaves for color and a dash of Jamaica ginger. The concoction was heated to bring out its full bouquet. Some favored flavoring the mixture with blackstrap molasses, with the idea of making it resemble rum. Other mixtures called for additions of Hostetter's Bitters,

Perry's Famous Painkiller and, for color, red ink.

Whatever the mixture, the stuff was volcanic. Some customers died outright from poisoning or shock, but the more common result was a mass orgy, which continued until it terminated in mass unconsciousness, or until the liquor ran out. The traders, who at first did business direct from the wagon, shortly realized that a drunken Indian who was refused more liquor or who ran out of things to trade could be deadly dangerous. To establish some security, they began to build trading posts — which, by a process of evolution as the trade increased, became fortresses.

The first and most notorious of these places was the aptly named Fort Whoop-Up, built at the forks of the St. Mary and Oldman rivers, near present-day Lethbridge, Alberta. Two Montana entrepreneurs, John Healy and Al Hamilton, first erected a cluster of log cabins in 1869, and in six months made $50,000 before the place was accidentally burned down. Their new fort was squat and heavily built of squared timbers laid up horizontally. Square bastions at opposite corners mounted cannon, and firing slits for rifles were cut in the walls. Above the fort — and over Canadian soil — flew Healy's personal flag, which somewhat resembled the U.S. emblem, with stripes and Healy's monogram where the stars would ordinarily be.

Indians were seldom allowed inside the walls. Instead they traded through barred wickets beside the

A U.S. whiskey trader's flag flies over Fort Whoop-Up in Canada. Indians, seldom allowed inside, traded through barred wickets.

The Reverend George McDougall, a Methodist missionary, fought American whiskey traders by organizing a temperance society among the Indians. But the evil was so pervasive that his efforts had little effect.

heavy oaken gates — pushing in skins and taking out guns and firewater. There were even iron bars set in the chimneys to discourage unorthodox visitors.

Trading at the wickets was never orderly once the booze began to flow. Warriors fought for places in line, pushing buffalo robes, furs and bags of pemmican forward in exchange for more drink. When their trade goods were gone, and if they were still conscious, they offered their horses, their food, their wives and their daughters. Shouting, staggering braves often attempted to scale the walls and were dislodged by long pole pikes, which were kept handy by the traders. If the situation turned really ugly, the traders used their rifles or even touched off a cannon. Frequently the drunken customers turned on one another.

In the winter of 1873, a horrified missionary among the Stoney Indians reported, "In this traffic very many Indians were killed, and also quite a number of white men. Within a few miles of us, forty-two able bodied men were victims among themselves, all slain in drunk-

en rows. Some terrible scenes occurred when whole camps went on the spree, as was frequently the case, shooting, stabbing, killing, freezing, dying. Mothers lost their children. These were either frozen to death or devoured by the myriad dogs of the camp. The birth rate decreased and the poor red man was in a fair way toward extinction, just because some white men, coming out of Christian countries, and themselves the evolution of Christian civilization, were now ruled by lust and greed."

Although Whoop-Up was first in notoriety and probably in business, it was not the only trader's fortification above the border. Nor was it the only one with a descriptive name. Robber's Roost was a frank acknowledgment of what went on there. Fort Slideout memorialized an occasion when the personnel, warned that a Blood war party was headed their way, decided to slip away while the slipping was good. Fort Standoff, located inside the U.S. border, was named for the day its owner, Joseph Kipp, bluffed a United States marshal out of taking him into custody.

Another fort, raised in Rupert's Land by interlopers from Montana, served as the headquarters of a different kind of commercial enterprise. Fort Spitzee, located on the river of the same name, was a rendezvous point for men who were mortally antagonistic to the whiskey traders' traffic in firearms. It was not that these men objected to mixing Indians and whiskey, but that they had sound business reasons for objecting to the sale of guns to the Indians.

The Spitzee gang, led by two men named John "Chief" Evans and Harry "Kamoose" Taylor, were not traders, but they too were engaged in the fur business, trappers in a way. They made their living by baiting the prairie with the carcasses of buffalo seeded with strychnine. Their harvest was the pelts of wolves that came to feed on the poisoned flesh. Prime wolfskins were then selling for $2.50 to $3.00 to the traders of Fort Benton.

These men were known as wolfers, and their occupation entailed certain hazards. Because canines as a family were both ravenous and undiscriminating, the bait of the wolfers killed as many Indians' dogs as it killed wolves. While dogskins were of no value to the wolfer, the living creature that was inside one was important to its owner. Indian dogs were pack animals

that could carry up to 50 pounds in small saddlebags.

Consequently, every now and again a wolfer would fall dead to an Indian bullet fired from ambush. And, since both the bullet and the gun from which it was fired came from Whoop-Up or someplace like it, the wolfers bitterly resented the arms trade. At one point this commercial dispute came to a showdown: the wolfers under Evans and Taylor organized a party they called the Spitzee Cavalry and marched on Fort Whoop-Up to deliver an ultimatum against selling rifles to Indians. Exactly what transpired has been lost to history, but two versions of the confrontation have survived and each entails a monumental bluff by Whoop-Up's John Healy. One holds that Healy had a cannon trained on his meeting with the wolfers with orders to an assistant to touch it off if and when he gave the signal. The other is that he held a lighted cigar over an open keg of gunpowder and offered to blow up everybody, including himself, unless the wolfers cleared out. Perhaps neither is true, but the wolfers did leave.

While the Montana whiskey traders and wolfers had matters pretty thoroughly their own way through the first quarter of the 1870s, their business practices did not go unnoticed. Hudson's Bay Company protested to the provincial government that 500 American desperadoes were abroad in the land, plundering, poisoning, murdering. From Winnipeg, as Fort Garry was now called, the governor dispatched Captain W. F. Butler to bring back a first-hand account of how things stood in the Great Lone Land. Butler's report was succinct. "The region is without law, order or security for life or property; robbery and murder for years have gone unpunished; Indian massacres are unchecked; and all civil and legal institutions are entirely unknown." It would not be too much, he said, to expect the Indians to rise in one last convulsive effort to purge the land of the white man and all his works.

What the region needed desperately, concluded Butler, was an official armed force of 100 to 150 men, one third mounted, stationed at strategic posts in the region. The urgency of his report moved the militia's adjutant general, Colonel Patrick Robertson-Ross, to raise the ante. The situation, he told the government, called for a full regiment, 550 mounted men.

At last, despite his habitual reluctance to move, Prime Minister Macdonald introduced an enabling act

to the House of Commons. While drafting this legislation, he excised "Mounted Rifles" and substituted the wording "Mounted Police"; Old Tomorrow in no way wanted to affront neighborly opinion below the border with anything that could be construed as Canadian militarism.

The bill passed unopposed on May 23, 1873. Still in no great hurry, Macdonald planned to begin recruiting a force in the following year. But then an occurrence that took place almost simultaneously with the signing of the bill pushed him into what was, for him, precipitate action.

In late May a band of American wolfers, encamped a few miles north of Fort Benton in Montana, awoke one morning to find their horses gone. Reoutfitting in Benton, the "Thirteen Kit Carsons," as a Montana newspaper later described them, set off northward to recover their stolen mounts.

A few days later, on a Saturday, the wolfers were encamped in a region north of the border known as the

Fort Garry, in the fading light of a prairie sunset, fills the
background of this 19th Century oil by Winnipeg artist
W. Frank Lynn. Entitled *The Dakota Boat,* the painting shows a freight carrier on the Assiniboine River,
watched by Indians standing beside their skin lodge.

Cypress Hills. They were, fortuitously, located between two small whiskey traders' posts and, having the stuff handy, were toasting one another. The drinking went on all night and into the Sabbath. In the midst of their revels, they were joined by a Canadian named George Hammond, with whom they shared a certain community of interest. He, too, had lost a horse to Indian thieves but, by a stroke of fortune, had got it back from a friendly Assiniboine.

Now, on Sunday morning, Hammond went to check on his animal — and returned in a fury, shouting that it had been stolen again. The Canadian seized his repeating rifle and started for a nearby encampment of 40 Assiniboine lodges. The rest of the party, reinforced by six other Canadians, joined him. Later accounts held that the Indians, under a leader they called Little Soldier, were also drunk that morning. In any case, both sides started shooting.

The whites took cover in a gully, and Little Soldier's braves charged at them three times. One white man, a Canadian named Ed Grace, was killed as he rode up to join his companions. He was the only white casualty. But when the Indians finally withdrew and abandoned their camp, they left behind 30 dead.

The Cypress Hills Massacre, as the event was known throughout Canada, moved Alexander Morris, lieutenant governor of Manitoba and the North West Territories, to telegraph Ottawa: "What have you done as to Police Force stop Their absence may lead to grave disaster."

The event galvanized Old Tomorrow into action. He ordered immediate enlistment and training of 300 men to be dispatched overland to Fort Garry before the freeze. And so one of the world's most respected constabularies, the North West Mounted Police, came into being.

Their scarlet tunic was an inspiration that had occurred to Adjutant General Patrick Robertson-Ross. Remembering that a green-uniformed Canadian regiment had moved Indian leaders to look dubious and say, "We know that the soldiers of our Great White Mother wear red coats and are our friends," he urged the Mounties to adopt red as their color. His reason was simple. "Animosity is rarely, if ever, felt towards disciplined soldiers wearing Her Majesty's uniform in any portion of the British Empire," he said.

In brilliant full dress, the Mounties parade at Calgary in 1901. The pageantry honored the Duke of Cornwall, later King George V.

5 | The arrival of the Mounties

"Little as Canada might like it," said Alexander Morris in 1872, "she has got to stable her elephant." Manitoba's Lieutenant Governor was discussing the problems of the central prairie, populated by American rogues, restive Indians and struggling settlers. It was to bring law to this untamed land that the Mounties came into being.

"No more wildly impossible undertaking was ever staged," moaned one politician as the first contingent of 300 men rode west in the spring of 1874. The Toronto *Mail,* sure they would lose their scalps, bade them farewell with the small solace: "Sharp be the blade and sure the blow and short the pang to undergo."

Over the next decade, the perils of police duty cost four Mounties their lives, while each year about 12 were invalided out of service (and another dozen deserted). Yet a valiant core hung on, purging the plains of renegades and administering even-handed justice to all who lived there.

Indeed, to the Indians, so wary of the blue-coated U.S. Cavalry, the Mounties' red coat symbolized compassion and trust. Said Crowfoot, the great Blackfoot chief: "The Mounted Police have protected us as the feathers of the bird protect it from the frosts of winter."

"The Mounted Police don't scare worth a cent"

When the North West Mounted Police began assembling in 1873, the force appeared ludicrously inadequate for the awesome assignment placed before it by the government in Ottawa. Its authorized strength was scarcely 300 troopers, and except for a few commissioned and noncommissioned officers, hardly a man among them had any knowledge of police or military affairs — or of the West itself for that matter. Yet this meager handful of greenhorns was charged with imposing law and order on 300,000 square miles of untamed Canadian wilderness debauched by whiskey-trading American desperadoes and seething with discontented Indians. Indeed, if the experience of the neighboring American West was any augury, the Mounties would not only fail — they would soon be swimming in their own blood.

For decades, a steady drum roll of lurid reports from across the United States border had told of gory Indian warfare and running gun battles with outlaw bands, and it was reasonable to assume at the outset that the Mounties would find more of the same in the Northwest Territory. Surely the whiskey traders, those renegade Americans who had slain scores of Indians and ruined thousands more with smuggled alcohol, would put up a furious battle to keep their lucrative trade. Surely the Mounties would be set upon by the fierce Canadian tribes, which included several bands related or allied to the terrible Sioux who had ravaged the American West and bedeviled the U.S. Army.

To everyone's astonishment, that was not at all the way things worked out. In fact, few events in the Northwest Territory followed the pattern established below the border. The whiskey traders proved to be more slippery than fearsome, and though they caused the Mounties trouble for years, they were reduced to a relatively minor police nuisance without a fight. Even more surprising, the Mounties managed to gain dominance over the tens of thousands of restless Indian warriors without the firing of a single shot on either side.

When the Mounties did have to fight, as they did in Canada's brief but bitter civil war, they did it their own way. In the field the Mounties proved to be totally unlike either the gunfighting United States marshals or the saber-wielding blue coats of the United States cavalry. The scarlet-coated troopers were British to the core, and they won their triumphs more by their presence and persuasion than by force.

Their victories were nonetheless sensational for the lack of violence or bloodshed. Because they accomplished all they set out to do — and a great deal more — the legend that grew up painted the Mounties as supermen. But they were entirely human, "and oftentimes worse," as one veteran wryly put it. The real Mountie story had its share of life's surprises, pratfalls, loose ends, anticlimaxes and unremarkable toil. But by 1885 the troopers had delivered to Canada an enormous domain that was stable, reasonably law-abiding and ready for the onslaught of civilization.

The story had its beginning in September 1873, when recruiting notices were posted in the Eastern provinces calling for volunteers "of sound constitution, able to ride, active and able-bodied, of good character and between the ages of 18 and 40 years."

The inducements to enlist were meager at best. A subconstable — the rank of most recruits — was to be paid 75 cents a day; full constables would get one dollar. The six inspectors, each to command a division of 50 men, would earn $1,400 a year. In addition, every man who satisfactorily served out a three-year

---

The majestic head of a buffalo dominates the Mounties' first official crest. The proud motto, *Maintien le Droit* (Maintain the Right), appears in a maple leaf setting.

hitch could claim a land grant of 160 acres in the Northwest Territory.

In spite of the low pay, the appeal of high adventure brought a torrent of volunteers. The commissioner of the force, George Arthur French, set about the task of selecting the 300 most likely prospects from among no fewer than 1,500 applicants. French was a tough 32-year-old British soldier who had risen to the rank of lieutenant colonel in the Royal Artillery. He quickly noted the inexperience of the volunteers, but believed himself just the man to whip them into shape.

For his first batch of 150 recruits, French selected 46 clerks and 39 tradesmen. The rest were farmers, sailors, lumberjacks, bartenders and even a few gentlemen. One thrill-seeker, James Fullerton by name, explained that "my friends who wanted me in the cricket club tried to dissuade me from joining, but the great adventure was too big an attraction to miss."

Among French's top officers were a number of military men with international experience. Inspector William Drummer Jarvis, in command of A Division, had been with the British Army in South Africa. Ephrem Brisebois, a French-Canadian subinspector, had fought as a mercenary in Italy's peninsular wars. Inspector Jacob Carvell of E Division was a veteran of the Confederate Army in the American Civil War.

A few noncommissioned officers were also proven soldiers. One of the most promising was Sergeant Major Samuel Benfield Steele, who was destined for a long and distinguished Mountie career. Sam Steele came from a family whose menfolk had fought at Waterloo, Trafalgar and in the decisive battle at the Plains of Abraham that resulted in the fall of New France. He himself had served as a Canadian militiaman since the age of 15. Now 22, Steele was tall, fair-haired and wiry — so slender that he wore a sash under his jacket to add manly bulk to his appearance.

Steele's A Division, along with B and C, was rushed off by steamer from Toronto through the Great Lakes and then marched 450 miles farther west to

Lower Fort Garry, where they were sworn in on November 3, 1873. There Commissioner French learned to his dismay that most of his recruits had only claimed to be good riders. He assigned Steele to teach them horsemanship.

All that winter Sam Steele drove his rookies hard and picked them up often, bruised and bloody from terrible falls on the hard frozen ground. When a man complained of saddlesores, he was issued salt to rub into his wounds; the salt would form calluses. In time, one tenderfoot wrote, "We became so tough I could sit on a prickly pear."

Meanwhile, the second batch of volunteers had filled out the ranks of D, E and F divisions, and were taking their crash course in riding and marksmanship at New Fort, a Canadian army barracks in Toronto. In spite of their rigorous training, these recruits remained enthusiastic. William Parker, who had come from England and was working on an Ontario farm when he succumbed to the enlistment drive, wrote an ingenuous letter home to his parents: "I still like the life very much. I rather expect we shall have pretty good times. We shall camp out in the prairies all summer. There is most splendid shooting up there and from what I hear there is magnificent fishing, so we ought to live well."

In late spring of 1874, the commissioner issued orders to bring the two segments of his force together at Fort Dufferin, a rude little settlement 65 miles south of Winnipeg and just above the United States border. From there they would march West and establish garrisons in widely scattered points, imposing law and order on the whole ungoverned region. For Divisions A, B and C, the journey to Dufferin meant an easy march of 85 miles south along the Red River. But D, E and F had to board two special trains in Toronto for a circuitous journey West by way of Chicago, St. Paul, and Fargo, North Dakota; they had received permission to travel through United States territory provided they wore civilian clothing and kept their weapons out of sight.

The troopers left their trains at Fargo, where the rails terminated, and took to their horses for the last 160 miles to Dufferin. They completed the journey in a forced march of five days, arriving on June 19, shortly after A, B and C divisions. The troopers complained about the blistering pace, which seemed to

them pointless; their hard-driven horses bucked off riders, overturned wagons and, in two cases, simply laid down and died. But the forced march had a purpose; it was French's way of preparing the men for the hard life that lay ahead.

At Dufferin, the combined force met with more of French's toughening tactics. The commissioner tightened his discipline another notch, giving 31 faint-hearted grumblers a final excuse for deserting. To the commissioner, the loss of the malcontents was good riddance, and it afforded 20 eager reserves a chance to be full-fledged policemen. As the young troopers made last-minute preparations to depart, their excitement blotted out their many uncertainties about the mission. "I doubt," F Division Subinspector Cecil Denny later declared, "if any expedition ever undertook a journey with such complete faith and such utter ignorance." In fact, the new Mounties were about to embark on one of the longest and most grueling marches ever made across the North American wilderness.

The Great March West began with a full-dress ceremony, the last time for nearly a year that the policemen looked like proper Mounties. Late in the afternoon of July 8, 1874, Commissioner French rode out to face his force on the dusty parade ground of Fort Dufferin. Ramrod-straight and stony-faced, he watched intently as his horsemen formed ranks, snapped to attention and waited for the command that would start them on their way across 840 miles of prairie to the Rockies.

The men were impressively uniformed in scarlet Norfolk jackets, steel-gray riding breeches and gleaming black boots, white buckskin gauntlets and white cork helmets with brass-link chin straps. Their weapons — long-barreled Deane-and-Adams revolvers and Snider-Enfield carbines — were well-oiled and amply supplied with ammunition. Their horses were handsome animals, purchased for their fine appearance and distributed according to color among the six divisions.

At 5 o'clock French gave the signal. To a chorus of bellowed orders, the long line of troopers moved slowly out into the plains. "The column of route presented a very fine appearance," French later reported to his superiors in Ottawa. "First came A Division with their splendid dark bays, then B with their dark browns. Next C, with bright chestnuts, drawing the guns and ammunition. Next D with their grays, then E with their black horses, the rear being brought up by F with their light bays." Behind the troopers, strung out for a mile and a half, lumbered their support: 73 big four-wheeled wagons and 114 Red River carts; 93 head of cattle to be slaughtered for meat; and a train of field kitchens, portable forges and mowing machines for cutting fodder en route. It was, French summed up, "an astonishing cavalcade."

But the commissioner had grave private reservations. French knew all too well that his men were untested, that their field guns (two muzzle-loading nine-pounders and two brass mortars) were outmoded, and that their carbines could not match the whiskey traders' new repeating rifles.

The fact is that the regiment was even more poorly prepared and equipped than French realized. His showy horses lacked the stamina for the grueling trek; homely mules and tough Indian ponies would have been a better choice. As for the men, their physical and military training had been eminently sound as far as it went, but it had taught them precious little about the techniques of survival in the wilderness. If that was not bad enough, the Mounties' scouting reports and their half-breed guides were unreliable.

According to plan, French followed the Canada-United States border, which the Joint Canadian-American Boundary Survey Commission had been charting along the 49th parallel from Lake of the Woods to the Pacific coast. This route offered the advantages of the commission's bridges, supply depots and rough-graded road. On reaching the interior, the troopers would rout the whiskey traders around Fort Whoop-Up, then split up into small groups and fan out through the Great Lone Land to six scattered stations.

The improved route along the border did the Mounties less good than French had hoped. Day after day, the summer sun beat down, the wind burned, the dust choked and the bites of flies and mosquitoes streaked men and horses with blood. The prairie, blackened by recent fires, yielded little forage for the livestock. Water holes were few and far between, and in some of them the water was bad. Men came down with dysentery; animals sickened and died, lending credence to a boundary official's warning that the regiment would be lucky to get through with only a 40 per cent loss of its horses. To make the early days of the march thoroughly miserable, the Mounties were pelted by hailstones and attacked by a plague of locusts, which devoured even the paint off the wagons.

On July 24, just 16 days and 270 miles out of Dufferin, French mercifully called his suffering regiment to a halt at La Roche Percée, an outcropping of rocks on the bank of the Souris River. After four days of rest, the commissioner sent A Division, along with the weakest men and animals, directly to Fort Edmonton, 900 miles to the northwest; he knew it would be a desperate march, but at least it followed a well-marked traders' trail to a known destination.

But for the remaining men another ordeal lay ahead. Ottawa had warned French to turn away from the Boundary Commission trail; the United States cavalry was chasing Sioux in the border area, and the Canadian government was anxious to avoid any confrontation with either the Indians or their pursuers. So the commissioner headed northwest for the Dirt Hills, where cursing troopers had to dismount and push their field guns up slopes 1,000 feet high.

The Mounties struggled on until August 12, when a Sioux Indian came into camp and was told that the "White Chief" would gladly meet his group on the morrow. The romantic young troopers excitedly prepared for their first encounter with the fearsome savages of the plains. But they found no painted warriors, only a grubby band of about 30 wandering Indians, mostly women and children, all badly in need of a bath and a meal. Henri Julien, a correspondent accompanying the Mounties, reported to his Toronto newspaper: "They came marching in line, their wives behind, chanting something in a dirge-like monotonous tone, almost drowned in the clarion tones of our trumpets belching forth glad sounds of welcome. They were conducted to a kind of pavilion made by putting two large square tents into one. We at first met them with closed lips as we did not know what to say. The usual 'How do-you-do' would have sounded ridiculous and the 'happy-to-see-you' would have been a lie, as they were a most wretched lot. However, we soon got into the 'How' of our red brothers."

During the powwow, the Mounties set the style that would mark their relations with all Indians, whether a ragged few or a regal gathering of chiefs and

warriors. Without exhibiting the least arrogance, the Mounties smoked a peace pipe, plied their guests with gifts and made conversation through their Indian and Métis scouts. Commissioner French informed the Sioux that the Queen Mother's children came in all colors, red, black and white — a comment that the Indians seemed to consider extremely funny.

When the Mounties moved on, they discovered that the Queen's red children had left them an unwelcome gift: a generous supply of fleas and lice, which soon infested the whole regiment from the commissioner on down. To combat the pests, all ranks were ordered to strip and to rub down with oil of juniper from the surgeon's supplies. Many men deloused their clothing by consigning it to the services of predatory

local ants, a bizarre but effective technique that the policemen learned from their Métis drivers. "It was amusing," one constable wrote, "to see the men running naked over the prairie seeking anthills."

By early September, the once-crisp cavalcade was in shambles. The men were hungry, filthy, saddlesore and suffering from the first freezes of the early northern winter. Boots were worn out and sentries patrolled their posts with gunny sacking wrapped around their bare feet. The horses were in even worse shape. To protect the starving beasts from the cold, French took a blanket from every trooper, but the horses died at the rate of eight or nine a night.

Still worse lay ahead, and French realized it when an advance party reached the forks of the Bow and

Belly rivers, 780 miles out of Dufferin. This spot was reportedly the site of the nefarious Fort Whoop-Up, yet the Mounties saw nothing but three roofless shacks. Scouts searched in vain for miles around. There were only two possible explanations, both of them dismaying: either the Mounties were lost or their intelligence was faulty in the extreme. In either case, the badly needed provisions they had expected to find were nowhere to be seen.

French's first problem was to find an alternate source of sustenance for men and animals. He swung the regiment on an emergency detour about 80 miles south to the Sweet Grass Hills, where reports—accurate this time—told of good water, ample forage and plentiful game to bolster their diet. From there, the commissioner led a small detachment 80 miles farther south, across the border to Fort Benton, Montana.

With French went Assistant Commissioner James Macleod, a tall, full-bearded man of 37. Macleod had been a soldier since he had joined the first Red River expedition into Métis country as a militiaman in 1870. He was one of those rare officers who was both

Fort Walsh, an early Mountie outpost, stands in Saskatchewan's Cypress Hills. The stockade, built in 1875, was named for its commander,

tough and popular; his men admired his ability, his sense of fair play, his genial manner and the stories of his two-fisted drinking during off-duty hours. He had been a bulwark of the force since its formation, and would become even more important to it in the future.

At Fort Benton, French bought supplies and fresh horses, and finally discovered where the elusive Fort Whoop-Up really was located: 75 miles west of where he had expected to find it.

At the very end of September, the Mounties were ready to move out. They now had a new set of orders from Ottawa. Assistant Commissioner Macleod was directed to take command of the bulk of the force and resume the march west toward Whoop-Up. In the meantime Commissioner French turned back northeast with 98 men and headed for the territorial headquarters that Ottawa had chosen for him. French's destination was a site on the Swan River, 315 miles northwest of Fort Dufferin, where the march had originated back in July.

The westbound column under Macleod was now being guided by an experienced scout named Jerry

James M. Walsh, who was charged with policing Sitting Bull and 5,600 Sioux who fled the U.S. after the Little Big Horn massacre.

Potts, whom the assistant commissioner had found at Fort Benton and hired for $90 a month. Potts, who would prove an indispensable resource to the Mounties for 20 years, was a short, muscular, bowlegged half-breed, the 34-year-old son of a Scottish clerk and a woman of the Blood tribe. He had earned a reputation as an all-round plainsman, a dead shot and a ferocious defender of the Bloods and their Blackfoot allies. In one skirmish, against the Assiniboines and Crees, Jerry had taken 16 scalps. While working as a hunter and guide at various Canadian whiskey forts, Potts had learned, at great personal cost, the lawlessness and bloodshed that liquor caused among the tribes: a drunken Indian had killed his mother and half brother during a pointless melee. Potts tracked down the killer and shot him dead. He was just the man to help the Mounties root out the whiskey traders.

On the trail, Potts was nothing short of uncanny. He seemed to know every wrinkle of the terrain. But his ability to communicate was somewhat circumscribed. Though he spoke several Indian dialects perfectly and knew French well enough, he had serious trouble with English and not much use for words in any case. One day a Mountie officer, tired of the endlessly rolling prairie, rode up and impatiently asked Potts, "What do you think we'll find on the other side of this hill?" Jerry's reply: " 'Nudder hill." Even Potts's monosyllables could be eloquent. When the Mounties found a bullet-riddled Indian corpse on the trail, Jerry glanced at the body and said it all for victim and assailant in a single bitter word: "Drunk."

Later, while serving as interpreter during the Mounties' dealings with Indians, Potts irritated the chiefs by reducing their longest orations to a single phrase. On one occasion, when a band of hungry Indians approached the police, Jerry listened to the chief's lengthy speech and made no effort to translate. At last, Macleod tapped him on the shoulder and asked, "What's he saying, Potts?" Grunted Jerry, "He wants grub."

When Potts finally got the Mounties to Fort Whoop-Up on October 9, the place was strangely silent, as if the desperadoes were holding their fire until the redcoats came within easy rifle range. The Mounties wheeled their field guns into position above the fort, on the crest of a long rise. Still there was no sound or movement. With Potts at his side, Macleod trotted warily up to the fort and pounded on the stockade gate.

The log door creaked open, revealing the fort's entire garrison: Dave Akers, a goateed American in the employ of the whiskey traders. Akers politely asked Macleod in for lunch — tasty buffalo steaks served up with fresh vegetables from the fort's garden. Smoothly, Akers apologized for the fact that D. W. Davis, in charge of the post for its Fort Benton owners, was away on business. In fact, as a thorough search soon proved, the American smugglers had been forewarned of the Mounties' approach in ample time to make good their escape, taking all their whiskey with them.

For the Mounties, it was a grinding frustration after their long, harrowing march — even more anticlimactic than their first encounter with the Indians. In fact, both encounters were significant portents. The Indians could be — and would be — dealt with peaceably. In the case of the whiskey traders, Macleod and his men had already settled the basic issue by their appearance on the scene — though they could not know it immediately. These American renegades were businessmen first and fighters second. They were far too shrewd to stand and shoot it out with the law. Most of the traders, it turned out, would retire to legitimate businesses; the rest would simply go to ground until they found a chance to reappear at a later date.

The Mounties would discover all this in due time. But now they swallowed their chagrin and plodded on in search of a home. The site Potts picked for the Mounties' fort was some 30 miles north and west, on an island of 600 acres in a broad loop of the Oldman's River, where he found good pasture for the horses, groves of tall cottonwoods for timber and plenty of wild game for food. Amid plummeting temperatures and frequent snowstorms the men turned briskly to work on a stockade 200 feet square. Macleod, worried about his sick, shivering horses, ordered the stables built first, along with shelter for a few ailing men; next came the troopers' barracks. The officers' quarters went up last. By mid-December everyone was out of tents and under a roof. The place was named Fort Macleod in honor of its chief, and the proud assistant commissioner could write to French that "All ranks are as comfortable as could be wished." Soon, enterprising mechants set up general stores outside the fort. The Mounties had to buy on credit, for they had yet to receive their first pay from Ottawa; but they bought everything in sight — especially canned fruit, even priced at a dollar a can.

And it was here at last that the Mounties could point to a measure of tangible law enforcement — and erase the embarrassing memory of Fort Whoop-Up. The great Blackfoot Chief Crowfoot sent his foster brother, Three Bulls, to test the Mounties' promises of protection. He reported that some traders at Pine Coulee, about 50 miles to the north, had illegally sold him two gallons of whiskey — and bad whiskey at that — taking two of his good horses in exchange.

Ten Mounties, led by Inspector Leif Crozier and guided by Three Bulls and Jerry Potts, hurried to Pine Coulee, where they captured five surprised traders without a struggle. It was the Mounties' first arrest, and they brought back plenty of evidence to make it stick: two wagonloads of whiskey, which Macleod ordered poured out onto the ground; 10 smuggled weapons, including five repeating rifles; and, among the traders' ill-gotten gains, 116 buffalo robes, which made warm overcoats for the threadbare Mounties.

Macleod had everything he needed to convict the traders — including the right to judge them, since he foresightedly had had himself sworn in as a justice of the peace before leaving the East.

The malefactors were speedily found guilty and sentenced to fines of $200 each for the three leaders and $50 apiece for the lesser rascals.

After several more arrests, the whiskey traffic appeared to have all but disappeared. On December 1, 1874, Macleod wrote Commissioner French: "I am happy to report *the complete stoppage of the whiskey trade throughout the whole of this section of the country,* and that the drunken riots, which in former years were almost of a daily occurrence, are now entirely at an end; in fact, a more peaceable community than this, with a very large number of Indians camped along the river, could not be found anywhere."

Macleod's sanguine report (which later proved somewhat exaggerated) reached French at a time when he needed all the good news he could get. He had just learned that Inspector Jarvis' A Division, which the commissioner had sent on to Fort Edmonton, had barely managed to complete its 88-day, 900-mile trek; the troopers had finally staggered in looking like the North

West *Dis*mounted Police — propping up or even carrying, on slings between poles, the few pathetic horses that had managed to survive.

French's own men, who had traveled nearly 1,700 circuitous miles in less than four months, were not much better off at the Swan River headquarters. The place was only half-finished when French arrived on October 21, and the flimsy, windowless buildings gave the garrison scant protection from the fierce cold.

French bombarded Ottawa with angry complaints about Swan River and, to make his point unmistakably clear, he refused to use the post as his headquarters, working instead out of Winnipeg and Dufferin. His defiance, coming on top of his persistent demands for more supplies, equipment and more men, made him exceedingly unpopular with the politicians in Ottawa.

By the end of 1874, the North West Mounted Police had been deployed, as planned, in six widely scattered posts. Sixty policemen were at Dufferin, 15 at Winnipeg, 38 at Swan River, 22 at Edmonton and six at little Fort Ellice on the Assiniboine River. The key post was Fort Macleod, with 140 men and 10 officers. This post was located in the midst of the powerful, often warring, Plains tribes. If the immense interior was to be settled, and if overland travelers bound for British Columbia were to reach there directly and safely, Assistant Commissioner Macleod would have to pave the way by winning the Indians' good will and signing the rival tribes to treaties that they would keep.

Immediately on arrival, Macleod's men had given the Indians concrete evidence of their sincerity by launching their campaign against the whiskey traders. Next, the assistant commissioner sent Jerry Potts north to invite Blackfoot tribes to parley at Fort Macleod. Crowfoot, a leading chief of the great Blackfoot confederation, arrived in December. The exchange of orations, translated by Potts with uncommon loquacity, established a feeling of mutual trust between the white and red chieftains. Macleod pronounced Crowfoot a "very fine old Indian" and wrote that his chiefs were "a very intelligent lot of men." In turn, Crowfoot referred to Macleod as "Stamix-otakan," or Bull's Head, a name that had been given to him by a local Piegan chief, whose name was also Bull's Head. The chief's willingness to share his name was clearly a gesture of friendship, and one in which Crowfoot concurred.

With their Indian relations off to a promising start, the Mounties spent the early months of 1875 settling into a routine of work. On regular schedules, small groups of troopers set out on extended patrols, intercepting and searching traders for contraband liquor and repeating rifles. Their patrol duties led inevitably to new and unexpected chores. To return stolen or lost livestock to the rightful owners, the policemen became impromptu wranglers. They delivered letters sent to the few remote early settlers in care of the fort. When a prairie fire threatened a settler's cabin, they raced out to fight the flames. They did what they could, in their own interests as well as the Indians', to improve sanitation and prevent epidemics among the tribes. They worked hard as justices of the peace to make fair decisions for both Indians and whites; and when a Mountie's knowledge of the law failed him, he improvised. "We make up the law as we go along," one inspector calmly informed an irate whiskey trader whom he had arrested.

In every isolated wilderness post, the Mounties found that time weighed heavily on their hands. With nowhere to go in their off-duty hours, they washed and mended their clothes, patched leaks in the roof, wrote letters home, read dog-eared novels and out-of-date newspapers, and griped about unnecessary drills, the pay, the weather and above all the food — which for the garrison at Macleod consisted of an unending round of buffalo patties, pork and beans, flapjacks and tea. One bright spot on the calendar came on Christmas, when the men sat down to turkey and plum pudding, shipped up from Fort Benton. In the mess hall that first Christmas, Macleod tacked up a sign that paid his men a well-deserved compliment: "Pioneers of a Glorious Future." But the Mounties would have welcomed a less arduous present.

To relieve the tedium, policemen gamely played at sports in frigid weather. Cricket was popular, though gopher holes and sagebrush made it hard to lay out a proper pitch. At some posts the men favored rugby football and tug-of-war. Troopers at the Swan River barracks, where temperatures for January 1875 averaged 21° below zero, did gymnastics indoors on crude horizontal bars. But their exercises hardly qualified as recreation; the men were simply trying to get warm. ◉

Four years after the signing of Treaty No. 7 in 1877 at Blackfoot Crossing, the Blackfoot confederacy gathers for a second great council at the same site. The occasion is a viceregal visit by Governor-General Lord Lorne, who brings greetings from his mother-in-law, Queen Victoria.

170

The relationship between Superintendent James M. Walsh *(left)* and Sitting Bull *(above)* went well beyond the cool exchanges of official business. The Mountie, who preferred a frontier outfit to formal uniform — although he did cherish his sword — became the Sioux chief's trusted adviser and admirer. "He is the shrewdest and most intelligent living Indian, has the ambition of Napoleon and is brave to a fault," Walsh wrote. "In war he has no equal, in council he is superior to all,"

Lacking any real social life, the Mounties spared no effort to arrange periodic celebrations. The little detachment at Fort Edmonton prepared for Christmas Eve by collecting a month's pay from each man and inviting every settler and trader for a hundred miles around to a gala supper and ball.

Of course the Mounties could not let Queen Victoria's birthday, May 24, pass without some sort of patriotic festivities. In 1875, the troopers at Swan River paid their respects to Her Majesty by staging a snake-killing competition, which cleared the post of 1,110 reptiles. Then the men turned out in their best tattered uniforms for an inspection by Commissioner French, whom Ottawa had flatly ordered to operate out of Swan River, and not Forts Dufferin or Winnipeg. It was reported that French took one look at the ragtag ranks, exclaimed "Good God," and returned to his quarters. The commissioner then pestered Ottawa until he got the men new uniforms and, for good measure, a piano and small library. Ottawa later authorized the Swan River men to form a band "to provide entertainments during the long winter." Though the musicians were obliged to buy their own instruments and pay the freight by dog sled from Winnipeg, they held their first concert the next spring, again on Victoria's birthday. The red-coated musicians thrilled their guests with a recognizable rendition of "God Save the Queen."

But between the two springs, the Mounties' morale occasionally hit bottom, and with distressing results. Though the policemen were duty bound to protect the Indians from the ravages of alcohol, they themselves often drank enough to gladden any whiskey trader's heart. Booze of any sort would do for men tormented by boredom. When smuggled — or confiscated — whiskey could not be had, incorrigible drinkers made do with bay rum, liniment and alcohol purloined from the surgeon's supply. At Battleford in the winter of 1882, several noncommissioned officers were so desperate they drank ether. "The effect was most disastrous," reported the commander. "Sergeant Waltham for the time being was a regular lunatic."

The troopers who drank were an insoluble problem for their superiors, many of whom were known to take a dram or two themselves. Responsible officers insisted on public abstinence, and even at the mess hall with no guests present, they would drink toasts of cold water or hot tea. But, realizing that no man could make a teetotaler out of another, most officers would look away if their troopers drank quietly in the privacy of their barracks, where bootleg liquor usually could be had at five dollars a bottle.

Predictably, private imbibing sometimes led to a public outrage. After one clandestine drinking bout in his barracks, Bugler W. Martin staggered out to the parade grounds, blew a few squawking notes of "Last Post" and then passed out cold — a flagrant performance that earned him three months' hard labor and a $10 fine. During the 1880s, when several forts had acquired satellite settlements for the Mounties to visit, drunken troopers became a hazard in town. In the village outside Fort Macleod, two inebriated policemen held up a traveler at gunpoint to get money to buy more booze. And one night in 1886, a whole troop of drunken redcoats terrorized the citizens of Lethbridge.

Another concern for the force was a high desertion rate, which spared no post commander, not even the much-admired James Macleod. More than 10 per cent of the assistant commissioner's Fort Macleod garrison — 18 men — went AWOL in the winter of 1874-1875, slipping over the border to work in the Montana gold mines. But Macleod conceded that the men had a legitimate complaint: they had not been paid, in spite of his efforts, since they had left Dufferin more than six months before.

Finally in March of 1875, Macleod got the bureaucrats to arrange for a payroll of $30,000; all he had to do was ride 300 miles south to pick up the money at a bank in Helena, Montana. The trusty Jerry Potts led him and three troopers through a howling blizzard, a huge herd of buffalo and a border patrol of American soldiers who mistook them for whiskey smugglers. At Helena, Macleod collected a bag full of dollars and also seven of his runaways, who had had their fill of the miner's life. Because of the mitigating circumstances, Macleod restored the deserters to duty with no penalty, except the loss of pay for their time away.

On another occasion, Macleod was also involved in one of the nasty little mutinies that briefly crippled operations at various Mountie posts during the pioneer period. In the early days at Fort Macleod, when everyone was overworked, many of the men refused to fall out for extra security duty after one whiskey trader had escaped from the fort lockup. The assistant commissioner showed the iron fist, reducing the ringleader in rank, but it was again his forbearance that won the day. He went through the barracks discussing grievances with the mutineers, and, he reported with obvious relief, "They all cheered me most heartily as I left each room." Macleod's star was definitely on the rise.

The fall of another officer brought the Mounties' shakedown period to a close. Commissioner French, having rubbed too many Ottawa politicians the wrong way, was summarily dismissed on July 22, 1876. His departure caused regret among his troopers: although they regarded him as something of a martinet, they recognized his effectiveness as an officer. He was, said Constable E. H. Maunsell, "a man who would never inspire those serving under him with love, but who gained increasing respect the longer we knew him." French's Swan River headquarters' garrison, particularly indebted for their improved living conditions, chipped in to give him a gold watch and a banquet. Then French moved on — to distinguished service and the rank of major general in the British Army.

Whatever French's merits or shortcomings, the time had come for a different sort of top policeman. With the Mounties now solidly established in more than a dozen posts in the Northwest Territory, Canada needed a tactful, imaginative administrator who would cooperate with civil authorities in signing the Western Indians to a fair and permanent peace. Since Assistant Commissioner James Macleod had demonstrated those qualities, and had earned the Indian chiefs' respect to boot, he was appointed to the post.

Just after Macleod took over as commissioner, the Canadian government signed the Cree tribes to the sixth treaty it had concluded with various Indian groups since 1871. In return for annual payments and supplies, the Crees ceded 120,000 square miles of terrain around both branches of the Saskatchewan River. This accord focused the government's attention on the last great Indian confederation to retain its ancestral land rights in the Northwest Territory: the Blackfoot tribes and their allies, the Bloods, North Piegans and Sarcees, as well as their enemies the Stonies, or Northern Assiniboines. These tribes inhabited an area of some 50,000 square miles that hugged the

Rockies and extended along the international boundary. Macleod, therefore, moved Mountie headquarters from remote Swan River to Fort Macleod where he could keep a closer eye on the Indians and police the delicate situation along the border. The commissioner trusted that the friendly patriarch Crowfoot would bring about Indian acceptance of a final treaty, known as Treaty No. 7 (and designed to give the government control over the territory and the tribes).

However, Macleod had made the common mistake of overestimating the importance of a single chief. Far from being able to dictate policy to his confederation, Crowfoot was merely the leading chief of one of several autonomous tribes of the Blackfoot Nation. His brother-in-law Red Crow of the Bloods was actually more powerful than Crowfoot, and Red Crow resented being treated as Crowfoot's inferior.

To complicate matters further, Crowfoot insisted that the treaty conference be held in his home territory, at Blackfoot Crossing, some 80 miles north of Fort Macleod. This site would mean a considerable journey for the Bloods and Piegans, who lived south of the fort, and when Macleod agreed to Crowfoot's demand, Red Crow refused to make the trip. The commissioner had no assurance that several other dissident chiefs would attend the talks, and without the approval of all the important Indian leaders the treaty would be invalid.

During the first three weeks of September 1877, the Canadians and most of the Indians assembled in a broad, beautiful meadow beside Blackfoot Crossing. On one side of the Bow River stood the tents of the treaty team: Territorial Governor David Laird, Commissioner Macleod and two magistrates. Camped nearby was their Mountie escort of 108 men and officers, including the military band from Swan River and a small artillery unit.

On both sides of the river the Indian encampment grew steadily as some 4,000 warriors, women and children trailed in from all directions. Inspector Cecil Denny wrote, "There must have been a thousand lodges. Their horses covered uplands to the north and south of the camp in thousands. It was a stirring and picturesque scene; great bands of grazing horses, the mounted warriors threading their way among them and as far as the eye could reach the white Indian lodges glimmering among the trees along the river bottom.

To amuse the folks back home, a pair of
Mounties perform a quick-change act in
1879, having their photograph taken first
in uniform and then, with an Indian to
provide added color, in fancy buckskins.

Never before had such a concourse of Indians assembled on Canada's western plains."

On September 17, with many of the tribesmen still absent, the treaty negotiators asked the chiefs for a postponement of two days to wait for Red Crow. But by September 19, Red Crow still had not made an appearance. Nevertheless, a loud boom from one of the Mounties' nine-pounders announced that the time had come for talk. From their lodges, the tribes filed slowly on foot up the meadow, led by chiefs in ceremonial dress: Old Sun and Heavy Shield of the Blackfoot, Bull Head of the Sarcees, Bear's Paw and Big Stony of the Mountain Assiniboines, Sitting-on-an-Eagle-Tail of the North Piegans. As the chiefs approached the big treaty tent, the band welcomed them with rousing performances of "Hold the Fort" and "The Maple Leaf Forever."

Suddenly, more than a thousand Blackfoot warriors rode their ponies over the skyline of a nearby hill,

whooping and firing their rifles as they charged. David Laird later described it as a sight that would make any man's throat go dry. But the Mounties' honor guard—50 troopers in spotless scarlet jackets and white helmets—stood their ground behind the treaty table with scarcely the twitch of a waxed mustache as the warriors swooped downhill and reared thunderously to a halt before the big tent.

At this point Crowfoot strode forward grandly, holding up his hand. Then with the other chiefs nearby, he sat cross-legged on a buffalo robe, lighted a peace pipe and passed it ceremoniously to the governor. After taking a puff, Laird started a business-like speech of the sort that won him the Indian name The Man Who Talks Straight.

"In a few years," Laird said, "the buffalo will probably all be destroyed, and for this reason the Queen wishes to help you live in the future in some other way. She wishes you to allow her white children to come and live on your land, and should you agree to this she will assist you to raise cattle and grain, and thus give you the means of living when the buffalo are no more. The Queen will also pay you and your children money every year, which you can spend as you please."

Laird went on to spell out the details. They more or less followed the pattern of the six previous treaties. In return for relinquishing territory, the Indians would receive their own land reserves, based on a formula of one square mile for each five persons in a tribe. Every Indian would also receive $12 in the first year of the treaty and five dollars every year thereafter. In addition, the Indians would be allowed to hunt on government land, and would be given a supply of ammunition. To prepare the tribes for the time when the buffalo disappeared, the Queen's men would give them cattle, seed potatoes and plows, and teach them farming, reading and writing.

The chiefs asked some questions, then returned to their lodges to hold their own councils. A few chiefs were in favor of the terms. Eagle Calf, leader of the Many Children band of the Blackfoot tribe, said that since the whites were coming anyway, the Indians might as well get something for their land. But a number of chiefs demurred. Eagle Ribs, leader of the Blackfoot Skunk band, threatened to withdraw from the talks unless the whites offered better terms. Facing a deadlock, the chiefs looked to wise old Crowfoot, but he refused to express his opinion until his brother-in-law Red Crow arrived.

At last, on the fourth day of the conference, Red Crow and the Bloods made their appearance at Blackfoot Crossing; the importance of the talks had overcome his annoyance. After an all-night council, Red Crow made his decision. Little as he might like it, the treaty was preferable to a long, bloody and futile war. With a consensus arrived at, Crowfoot would speak for all the tribes.

That morning, September 21, the chiefs silently filed into the treaty tent, and all save Crowfoot took seats on the buffalo robes. The old chief stood before them and spoke: "We are the children of the plains, it is our home, and the buffalo has been our food always. I hope you look upon the Blackfeet, Bloods and Sarcees as your children now, and that you will be indul-

gent and charitable to them. If the Police had not come to the country, where would we all be now? Bad men and whiskey were killing us so fast that very few, indeed, of us would have been left today. I wish them all good and trust that all our hearts will increase in goodness from this time forward. I am satisfied. I will sign the treaty."

Now the other chiefs stepped forward. "Three years ago," said Red Crow, "when the Mounted Police came to my country, I met and shook hands with Stamix-otokan at the Belly River. Since that time he has made me many promises and has kept them all — not one of them has been broken. Everything that the Mounted Police have done has been for our good. I trust Stamix-otokan and will leave everything to him. I will sign with Crowfoot."

One by one, the chiefs filed to the table. All touched or pointed to a pen, and the recorder made a mark for them. Though the terms of the treaty were fraught with unknowns, the chiefs had trusted the word and the honor of the white man Macleod. What they signed was a pact of faith.

The Canadian delegation then added their signatures. To conclude Treaty No. 7, the police band played "God Save the Queen," and the chiefs were presented red coats, flags and medals commemorating the occasion. The Canadians had won their treaty without shedding a drop of blood.

The signing of Treaty No. 7 came in the nick of time for both the Canadians and the Indians. American Sioux, whose great leader Sitting Bull had annihilated General Custer's Seventh Cavalry at Little Big Horn back in June, were fleeing north to escape the vengeful wrath of the U.S. Army. Small parties of Sioux, whose 30 bands totaled about 50,000 people, began crossing the Canadian border in November; the tribes had always done so freely during buffalo hunts, but now they were using the border as a "medicine line" that pursuing American soldiers dared not cross. More and more Sioux approached the border in the Cypress Hills region, not far from the site of the 1873 massacre and just across from the Mounties' recently built post, Fort Walsh.

Any large-scale border crossing by the Sioux would pose two dire threats. The lesser of these was a crisis

The Mounties' Sherlock Holmes

In 1877, after a series of successful Mountie forays against American desperadoes operating across the border, the Fort Benton, Montana, *Record* wrote admiringly that the Mounted Police had "fetched their man every time." Like most legends, the always-get-their-man stories grew in the telling; in truth, the Mounties were often as flummoxed as lawmen anywhere. But one redcoat whose exploits burnished the image of the Mountie as the implacable nemesis of miscreants was a constable with the splendid name of Alick Pennycuick, who patrolled the Yukon at the turn of the century.

A onetime British Army officer, the 30-year-old Pennycuick had seven years of Mountie experience when he was assigned in 1900 to investigate the 11-day-old disappearance of three wealthy travelers making their way down the Yukon Trail. The natural suspect was one George O'Brien, a bad-acting ex-convict in the area. But there was little to link him to the missing men.

In the depths of winter, Pennycuick and an assistant undertook a systematic search of 40 square miles along the river trail. One day while combing likely ambush spots, they were alerted by a sled dog pawing at the snow. Digging down, Pennycuick came on a patch of frozen blood.

Now he did something surprising: he sent for O'Brien's dog. Showing the animal the blood, he turned him loose — and followed him straight to an abandoned riverside campsite.

There, after six weeks of sifting through the snow, Pennycuick began to turn up the evidence he needed. First he found some charred clothing, bits of moccasin and cartridge cases. Nearby, out on the river, he found a disturbed spot in the ice where bodies might have been stuffed through. Fur-

GEORGE O'BRIEN

ERNEST CASHEL

ther searching uncovered a piece of human skull and a broken tooth embedded in a bullet.

That spring when the river ice melted, the bodies of the three men washed up. In one of their jawbones was a tooth stump that fitted the fragment discovered at the campsite.

O'Brien was tried and swiftly convicted; never, said the judge, had he seen more conclusive evidence. The killer died unrepentant, railing from the gallows against the Mounties and cursing Constable Pennycuick.

Two years later, the redoubtable Pennycuick did it again. A Calgary rancher named J. R. Belt had vanished, and the only hint of suspicion involved one Ernest Cashel, a shady

American to whom Belt had recently given shelter. Tracing Cashel's movements, Pennycuick found that he had spent some time in a settlement of half-breeds near Calgary. There Pennycuick discovered a coat that belonged to Belt — and, lo, it matched the trousers Cashel was wearing. The policeman also learned that Cashel had been flashing a gold certificate identical to one missing from Belt's house. Final proof came when the rancher's body was found in a nearby river: the cause of death was a bullet from Cashel's pistol.

For these and other exploits, Pennycuick won promotion to sergeant — and the accolade "The Sherlock Holmes of the Mounted Police."

in Canadian-American relations. Far more serious was the possibility of a West-wide war between the Sioux refugees and their ancient enemies of the Blackfoot confederation. Though the 102 Mounties at Fort Walsh could hardly have prevented the mightiest of all Indian nations from crossing the border in full force, they patrolled vigorously nonetheless, keeping a close watch on the Sioux's movements. The Fort Benton *Record* was impressed: "The Mounted Police don't scare worth a cent. Parties of two and three men are scouting along the line looking for Sitting Bull!"

Early in December 1876, word reached Fort Walsh that some 3,000 Sioux had crossed the border and were setting up camp near the trading post at Wood Mountain, 150 miles east of Cypress Hills. At that, Inspector James M. Walsh, the tough former cavalryman for whom the post had been named, rode out with a dozen men to see if the report was true. Reaching Wood Mountain, the little band of redcoats rode straight into a great Indian encampment.

Walsh sat down in solemn council with a group of Sioux leaders. The Mountie officer went straight to the point: the Sioux were now in the country of the Great White Mother, and while they remained they must obey her laws. There would be no fighting, no horse-stealing — and no raids back across the border.

The chiefs assured Walsh that they were tired, starving, sick of war; they wanted only peace. They remembered their grandfathers saying that the British would protect them, that once, long ago, they had been "British Indians," children of the Crown. Walsh chose to believe them sincere. He allowed them to stay and to barter with the local traders for supplies and enough ammunition for hunting.

But more Sioux came. Early in 1877, bands of Teton Sioux and their allies the Yanktons were intercepted along the Frenchman Creek. Walsh went out to put them on warning. "The warriors were silent and solemn," he noted, then added sadly, "War had made the children forget how to play." At last, late in May, news reached Fort Walsh that a large band of Sioux had entered Canada at Pinto Horse Buttes. The leader was Sitting Bull himself.

Walsh immediately made his usual visit and dictated the same terms he had given the other chiefs. Sitting Bull denounced the American cavalry in soar-ing, bitter rhetoric. But he told Walsh he would do no wrong in the land of the Great White Mother. He had "buried his weapons on the American side."

Though the Sioux refugees remained quiescent through the summer of 1877, the added pressure they put on the dwindling herds of buffalo raised the specter of famine and increased the chances of a fateful clash between competitive hunting parties of Canadian and American Indians.

Commissioner Macleod, who was fully aware that his handful of Mounties was powerless to prevent an explosion of violence, warned Ottawa that the situation was "very grave." But the Canadian government, strapped for funds and manpower, could only urge Macleod to send Sitting Bull's people back to the United States. Ottawa suggested to Macleod — as if there were a choice in the matter — that "Our action should be persuasive, not compulsory."

The state of emergency — with frantic messages speeding constantly between the Mountie forts, Ottawa, Washington and London — was to persist for four jittery years. Sitting Bull's followers, peaking at well over 5,000, showed no inclination to leave their new haven. The United States government, vastly relieved to be rid of the Sioux, was in no rush to get them back. The Canadians, trying to be humane to their unwelcome guests, only managed to prolong their stay by failing to act decisively.

It took Ottawa until late August of 1877, to persuade the United States government to start negotiating with the Sioux for their return, and it took Walsh still longer to talk Sitting Bull into meeting with the Americans. At once the conference was imperiled by two American blunders. First, in a stroke of bureaucratic stupidity, Washington appointed as its top negotiator Brigadier General Alfred H. Terry, the very man who had led the reprisals against the Sioux after the Custer massacre. And second, little groups of Nez Percé Indians, who had refused to accept a drastically reduced reservation in Idaho, staggered half-dead across the border after a 1,700-mile flight from American cavalry units. The pathetic condition of the Nez Percé struck Sitting Bull as an example of what his people would suffer if they returned to the United States. Nevertheless, both parties showed up at the appointed time and place, October 17, at Fort Walsh.

General Terry, whose party had been escorted from the border by Commissioner Macleod himself, was already in the conference room—the officers' mess hall—when the Sioux arrived. Newspapermen from New York and Chicago giddily described the garb of the numerous chiefs, especially Sitting Bull, who wore a wolfskin cap and a black shirt with large white polka dots, and Spotted Eagle, who was stripped to the waist and wore white war paint and an eagle feather in his hair. The negotiating teams never quite met; when Sitting Bull entered he glanced contemptuously at the Americans, and brushed by to shake hands warmly with Macleod and Walsh. With the chiefs came an Indian woman—a calculated insult, since females were not permitted to attend serious warriors' councils.

To start the conference, General Terry explained to the chiefs that the President in Washington wanted a "lasting peace," and promised full pardons to all Sioux who surrendered their arms and horses and reported to their assigned Indian agencies. Spotted Eagle's reaction was set down by one reporter: "The chief turned to the Mounties and *winked* several times."

After Terry had said his brief piece, Sitting Bull delivered a scathing reply: "For 64 years you have persecuted my people. You come here to tell us lies. We do not want to hear them. You can go back. Take your lies with you. I will stay with these people. The country we came from belonged to us. You took it from us. We will live here."

One after another, the other chiefs ridiculed Terry's proposals, and then, as a supreme affront, they let the woman speak. "I wanted to raise my children over there," she said disdainfully, "but you did not give me time to breed." Finally the meeting broke up and Terry headed south the next day. The chiefs stayed on at the fort for a few days. They were treated as honored guests, enjoyed a band concert and consumed, among other things, a vast amount of tasty plum pudding at the officers' mess.

The conference had changed nothing, and now conditions worsened steadily. The buffalo herds continued to dwindle. The Blackfoot tribes and other Canadian Indians, who had not yet learned to support themselves as farmers and cattle raisers, blamed their plight on the Sioux. Following a winter of light snowfall in 1877-

1878, the plains were so parched that most of the remaining buffalo grazed their way south into the United States. American hide-hunters set grass fires behind the herds to prevent them from drifting back into Canada. Indian hunters had stripped the Canadian plains of the remaining game by the summer of 1879, and their families were eating grass, mice, carrion, and their bony dogs and horses.

When Ottawa realized that Indians were actually starving to death, it sent the Mountie posts emergency shipments of provisions, and troopers in oxcarts trundled about distributing tons of beef, bacon and flour. But the relief shipments made barely a dent in the epic hunger of thousands of Indians; at Fort Walsh alone, 5,000 Sioux, Crees, Blackfeet and Bloods were begging for food. The post commanders gave out the Mounties' emergency provisions, and the policemen went so far as to share food from their own meals. Table scraps from the mess halls were a prize Indians would fight for.

Desperation drove many Indians to break the law. At Fort Qu'Appelle, 220 miles west of Winnipeg, a group of emaciated Cree Indians broke into the police storehouses and helped themselves to the provisions. Around Fort Macleod, lone Indians regularly raided the settlers' cattle, which they impudently referred to as "pinto buffalo." And, most conspicuously, the Sioux broke their pledge not to use Canada as a base for sorties to the south. Their border crossings, which started out as innocent hunting expeditions, sometimes ended up as impromptu raids.

Superintendent Walsh, whom the American press had dubbed "Sitting Bull's Boss," did the best he could to keep his eminent charge in check and also to persuade him to surrender. But his efforts, as Canadian officials came to realize, had quite the opposite effect; the admiration that Walsh and Sitting Bull had for each other made them friends and encouraged the chief to resist to the bitter end. To break the strange symbiotic alliance, Ottawa in July 1880 transferred Walsh from his namesake post to Fort Qu'Appelle, 160 miles away. The government also announced that it was halting all food handouts to the Sioux.

Disconsolate at the loss of his friend, Sitting Bull drifted from place to place, seeking a home, voicing his despair to whomever would listen. He stopped in peri-

Inspector Samuel B. Steele, every inch the indomitable
officer, sits with his detachment at Beavermouth, where
in 1885 they kept peace among 1,000 railroaders. Wrote
Steele: "We were rarely to bed before two or three a.m.,
and were up in the morning between six and seven."

odically at Fort Walsh, but the new commander, Inspector Leif Crozier, was completely unsympathetic; he solemnly repeated Ottawa's new get-tough order, telling the chief that the Sioux would get no more food. Still Sitting Bull held grimly on. Now his people were abandoning him, drifting sick and starving across the border to surrender to United States troops. He railed at them to stay, but his personal following shrank to 100 family lodges by the summer of 1880.

In the spring of 1881, Sitting Bull made a trip to Fort Qu'Appelle to see Walsh, who happened to be away in Eastern Canada. The chief then went to nearby Wood Mountain Fort, where the Mountie in charge told him that he would receive nothing more than a ration of bullets. "I am cast away!" the old warrior cried out.

At last, with all hope gone, Sitting Bull steeled himself, led his wretched little band of 187 across the border, and on July 21, 1881, surrendered to the hated Americans at Fort Buford, Montana.

With the Sioux's tragic sojourn at an end, the North West Mounted Police were free to attend to pressing chores that had been neglected during the famine. One task was to conclude arrangements for the tribes that had signed Treaty No. 7. During the recent confusion, several tribes had failed to report to, or to stay in, their allotted reserves in the fertile riverlands near the Battle River where they could more easily learn to become self-sufficient farmers. A few bands balked at making the final move. When persuasion failed, the Mounties used a weapon that always succeeded: food. They would refuse to give the hungry recalcitrants their allotment of government provisions until the whole band was en route to its appointed reservation.

For some Indians, hunger alone was not enough to force submission. A proud band of Crees offered a curious sort of symbolic resistance; they fought the transcontinental railroad, whose track-laying crews were making rapid progress across the plains in the early 1880s. The intelligent Cree chief, Piapot, knew that the railroad would bring more and more white settlers, and he may well have sensed that nothing could stop the trains or the remorseless westward progress of civilization. All the same, in 1882 he sent his warriors to uproot 40 miles of railroad survey stakes west of Moose Jaw. Some months later, he ordered his followers to pitch their lodges directly in the path of construction crews at Maple Creek.

On learning of this human roadblock, the police sent in two Mounties including a daring young corporal named William Brock Wilde, to break it up.

Exuding self-confidence, Wilde and his companion trotted to Piapot's lodge in the Cree camp and told the chief that he must move his camp away from the railroad's right-of-way. Piapot called the Mounties' attention to his armed warriors, clustered all around.

Wilde took out his pocket watch, studied it intently and then informed the chief that he had exactly 15 minutes to move. Angry warriors began jostling the Mounties provocatively, but the two young men sat unperturbed on their black horses.

At length, Wilde glanced at his watch for the last time and called out cheerfully, "Time's up!" Then, leaping from his steed, he strode up to Piapot's lodge and yanked it apart, bringing the painted buffalo skins down on the startled women inside. As the Crees looked on dumbfounded, Wilde marched about the camp, collapsing lodges as he went. Prizing courage above all things, the Crees were so impressed by the troopers' appearance of utter fearlessness and invincibility that they yielded. Piapot ordered his people to break camp and clear out, making way for the rails.

Not just for the Indians, but for every Canadian on the Western plains, the coming of the Canadian Pacific Railway was the dominant fact of life as the 1880s wore on. It brought civilization (as Piapot had feared) and also (as the Mounties had feared) the endless complications of organizing many newcomers into law-abiding communities. Besides hordes of construction workers, the Canadian Pacific Railway brought self-willed farmers from the East, polyglot immigrants from Europe, rambunctious cowboys from the United States with cattle to start Canadian herds—and, from almost everywhere, resurgent whiskey traders, ambitious harlots, imaginative confidence men and unscrupulous merchants, who gave Indians the labels from canned goods as change for their annuity dollars.

The Mounted Police, outnumbered more than ever before, had to cope with many new and complex problems—such as putting down strikes by underpaid rail-

hands, suppressing gambling and enforcing prohibition in a 10-mile-wide strip along the tracks. Among other things, that last requirement involved the arrest of a certain Mrs. Hobourg, who smuggled booze under her clothing in a rubber bag that made her appear to be perpetually pregnant.

The Mountie in charge of law enforcement all along the line was none other than Sam Steele, who had first come west as an up-and-coming young sergeant with the newly recruited force in 1874. Since then, Steele had served with zeal and distinction in several posts, rising to the rank of inspector. The special detachment he now commanded kept one jump ahead of the rails, leaving behind a trooper or two to keep order at intervals along the route. As the tracks neared the Rockies and a linkup with crews building from west to east, Sam meted out Mountie justice wherever he could find a place. At Regina, he held his hearings in a tent, and at Swift Current his court jounced along on top of a squealing Red River cart.

As winter took hold in 1884, the Canadian Pacific Railway was piercing the Rockies. Steele had set up his advance headquarters at a rugged site called Beavermouth, west of Kicking Horse Pass. The approach of the construction gangs created a boom town of crude frame saloons and brothels just outside the 10-mile limit, and the Mounties worked themselves to a frazzle just to maintain a semblance of Canadian law.

The rail crews did work just as taxing and even more dangerous, and a stern Mountie might sympathize with them in spite of the problems they caused. In many places, the workers had to blast the roadbed out of solid rock and later enclose it in miles of wooden sheds to guard against thunderous avalanches, which could carry a quarter of a million cubic yards of snow down a mountainside and bring along great cedars, huge boulders and cyclonic winds, crushing men, equipment and livestock. To handle engineering operations such as the construction of these shed-sheltered roadbeds, the Canadian Pacific Railway strained the technology of the day, to say nothing of the financial resources of private bankers and, indeed, of the Canadian government itself. But Canada's future depended heavily on the rail line, and the Mounties were duty bound to see that the tracks went through, even if they had to clash with work crews who were driven to disorderly conduct by their many legitimate grievances.

A strike that threatened to stop the Canadian Pacific on the last leg of its journey confronted Sam Steele on April 1, 1885. Angry workers left the job and came to Sam's headquarters to put him on warning: they had received no pay for many months. Sam pleaded with them to be patient a little longer, but he knew they would not take his advice. In a wire to Ottawa he said that a strike might turn into a riot.

At this critical juncture, Sam was laid low by a virulent fever; he could barely lift his head from his pillow to question his men as they reported in. Their news was grim. Almost 1,200 workers had joined the strike, and some 300 of them, many armed with revolvers and rifles, were marching toward the railhead to stop the work of nonstriking teamsters, bridge-builders and track-laying crews. The strikers managed to halt a trainload of workers. But James Ross, in charge of mountain construction, mounted the engine himself, ordered full steam and drove through the mob while bullets ricocheted off the cab.

To protect the tracklayers at their work, Steele sent in four or five Mounties, all he could spare. They were led by his second-in-command, a little bulldog of a sergeant named Billy Fury. Fury chose to make his stand in a gorge not much wider than the tracks, on the theory that it could be defended by only a few men. As the Mounties blocked the tracks, the strikers advanced, shouting and firing their pistols in the air. Fury roared that he would shoot anyone who tried to pass. The strikers continued their noisy demonstration, but when they failed to intimidate the Mounties they retired to Beavermouth, allowing the trackmen to complete their day's work.

By the time Sergeant Fury had reported to Steele at his bedside, however, a new uproar had begun. A constable, attempting to arrest a troublemaker in the workers' shantytown, had been roughed up by the hostile crowd. Steele sent Fury with a couple of troopers to take the culprit prisoner, but the sergeant came back empty-handed, with his uniform and dignity in tatters. No sooner had Fury reported than Steele sent him back again, this time with three constables and orders to shoot anyone who interfered with the arrest.

To keep Steele in his sickbed, the local magistrate, George Johnston, stood at the window and delivered a running account of the showdown. Now the four Mounties were crossing the bridge between their barracks and the shantytown. But now they turned a corner and disappeared behind a cabin. Moments later, Sam heard a shot. Johnston cried, "There is one gone to hell, Steele!"

Sam crawled from his bed to the window, just in time to see two of his men hauling their prisoner across the bridge, with Fury and the fourth Mountie at their heels, trying to hold back the surging mob at gunpoint.

It was one of those moments when a small thing could decide the course of events for years to come. Steele, weak as he was, took command. Grabbing his boots and his Winchester, he staggered to the bridge, arriving just as the mob began to rush up the other side. Sam leveled his rifle and ordered the strikers to halt. "They answered with curses and cries," he later recounted, "but they halted."

At this point Johnston arrived with a copy of the Riot Act, and Steele yelled out above the hooting of strikers. "Listen to this," he cried, "and keep your hands off your guns!" The magistrate read the cautionary act, which authorized the use of practically any means to suppress a disturbance that threatened the public welfare. To underscore the warning, eight Mounties slammed home cartridges in their rifles. Sam finished with a promise: "If I find more than 12 of you standing together or any large crowd assembled I will open fire upon you and mow you down! Now disperse at once and behave yourselves!"

In the face of the determined Steele the strikers backed down. Next day, he could report: "All along the line was as quiet as a country village on Sunday."

The episode ended with a fair amount of justice dispensed. The company paid the strikers their overdue wages, and the ringleaders, pursued and brought in by the redcoats, were given a choice of a $100 fine or six months' hard labor.

Once again the Mounties had won the day. The railroad went through, bringing Canada's two coasts ever closer. The nation would still have to experience a period of violent convulsion—mercifully brief—before the Great Lone Land of the prairies could finally be declared tamed. But thanks largely to the redcoats' efforts, a rock-solid foundation had at last been laid for a dominion that stretched unbroken from sea to sea.

6 | "All aboard for the Pacific"

The many opponents of a transcontinental railroad decried the idea as "an act of insane recklessness," while its champions, notably Prime Minister John Macdonald, insisted that it would "give us a great and united Canada." The debate went on for years, but at last, in February 1881, the young dominion committed itself to 2,900 miles of railroad building across the vast land from Montreal to Vancouver.

With a $25-million government subsidy, the Canadian Pacific began work that spring. In the terrible geography of British Columbia, 22,000 men slaved to build 600 bridges and trestles, as well as to blast 27 tunnels through the Coast Mountains. At times the awesome task claimed a life a day — for an advance of barely six feet. Yet in the East, the connecting line from Lake Superior came west at astonishing speed. Sweating, cursing and singing "Drill, Ye Tarriers, Drill!" 7,600 men had, by the end of 1882, laid 417 miles of track to Colley, Saskatchewan. By 1884, the road was virtually complete across the prairies to the Rockies.

It took another two years to drive the rails through that colossal range. In the meantime, the Canadian Pacific carried a fighting army west: the original claimants of the Great Lone Land, the Indians and Métis, resisted the coming of Eastern civilization. Sadly, a bitter uprising and a tragic civil war preceded the triumphant Canadian cry, "All aboard for the Pacific!"

The Selkirk Mountains fill the sky at Rogers Pass, a Canadian Pacific construction town that was almost abandoned by 1887.

A work gang takes a break from roadbed construction along the Kicking Horse River in British Columbia. To prevent floods from eroding the track, this heavy timber cribwork was ballasted with stones.

Buffalo bones, vestiges of a dying era, are stacked beside the CPR track. The railroad paid Métis and Indians $4.50 to $5.00 a ton to gather the bones, then sold them at $7.00 in Minneapolis for fertilizer.

Graders prepare to move out on the road's 675-mile scrape across the prairies in 1882. To cope with winter snowdrifts, engineers laid the tracks atop a four-foot-high embankment flanked by wide ditches.

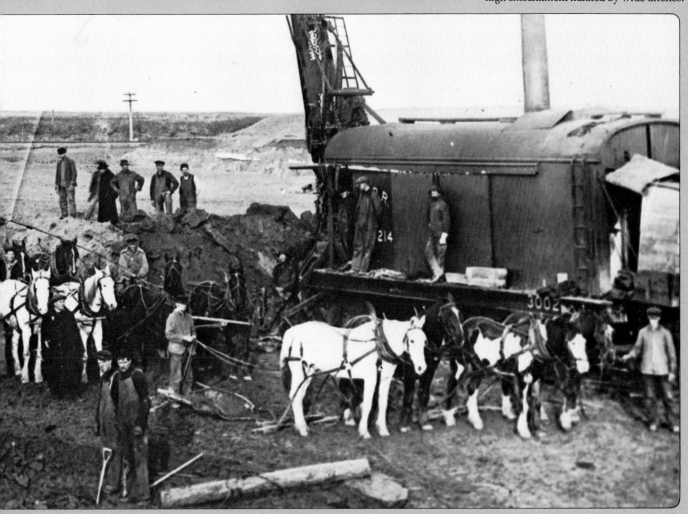

The Canadian Pacific trunk line sags just a bit as it passes Calgary in 1884. One of more than 800 prairie towns fostered by the railroad, Calgary began life as a cluster of tents, its entrepreneurs living under canvas while waiting to see where the track would come through. When the depot *(far left)* went up, permanent construction commenced.

An excursion train out of Fort Yale, British Columbia, in June 1884, bears celebrants across a trestle on their way to mark completion

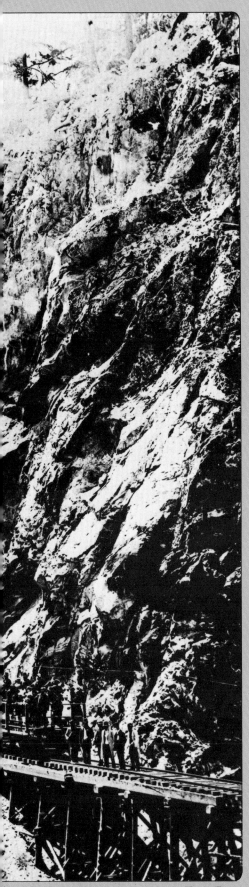

of a steel cantilever bridge over the Fraser River.

Surveyors perch atop one of 54 snowsheds built in the Selkirks in 1887. Two winters before, snowslides had buried some sections 39 feet deep, forcing construction of five miles of shelters at $43 a foot.

Timber towers set in concrete support the Stoney Creek Bridge, at 292 feet the highest structure of its kind in North America. The truss was built over a gorge cut by the melting glaciers of the Selkirks.

A Canadian Pacific train clears an engineering

marvel, the 1,086-foot-long Mountain Creek Bridge across a Selkirk canyon. The bridge contained two million board feet of lumber.

The Loop, three miles of track laid in a giant inverted S to avoid snowslide areas, winds through the spectacular Illecillewaet Valley. With completion of the railroad in 1885, tourists had access to this area, which became the 521-square-mile Glacier National Park the following year.

The brave last stand of Louis Riel

The year 1885 was one that Canadians will never forget. In nine short months, between the snows of March and the snows of November, a series of climactic events brought together all the actors in the drama of Canada's West—Indians and whites, French Catholics and English Protestants, builders and bureaucrats, Mounties and militiamen and, in a central, tragic role, the Métis, mixed-blood sons of the fur traders and the *voyageurs*. Before it was over Canada had seen a half-breed rebellion, an Indian uprising, a victorious army of suppression and a rebel martyr swinging from a gallows rope. In 1885 as well, Canada emerged from the era of the birchbark canoe and Red River cart, and entered the age of the iron horse as the last spike of a transcontinental railroad was driven in a spur of the Rockies.

The final confrontation was inevitable. As civilization rolled westward, many Indians at first believed they could share the land with white men like brothers. But the treaties they signed became articles of betrayal. "The Indian was blind in regard to making the treaty," cried a speaker at an 1884 tribal council. "Governor Morris comes and tells the Indian we are not coming to buy your land. We come here to borrow the country, to keep it for you. The Indians therefore understand that the country is only borrowed, not bought."

By this time, Indian ownership of the traditional hunting grounds was becoming academic in any event. After years of unremitting slaughter by whites, the buffalo, on which the Indian had always depended for food, clothing, shelter and fuel, was nearly extinct. "What shall we do?" a young Dakota Sioux cried despairingly. "What shall we do? The buffalo is our only friend. When he goes, all is over with the Dakotas."

The Indians had been told that the government would feed them. But in 1883, when the exchequer was low, one of the first things cut back was Indian rations. Later that year, an Indian agent called his charges "mere skeletons." Wrote an interpreter in the winter of 1884: "The Indians are starving very badly. I fear that many of these people will not see spring."

Most whites shrugged off the Indians' predicament. A few understood that it was a prelude to chaos. "It is poor, yes, false economy to cut down the expenditure so closely in connection with the feeding of the Indians," warned Superintendent Leif Crozier of the Mounted Police in 1884. "It would seem as if there was a wish to see upon how little a man can exist. They should be humored a little. My firm conviction is, if some such policy as I have outlined is not carried out, there is only one other, and that is to fight them."

The condition of the mixed-blood Métis was even more troubled — and dangerous — than that of the pureblood Indians. Those who had remained in Manitoba after the first Riel resistance found themselves overwhelmed by the flood of immigration from the East. Those who had fled west seeking sanctuary and a resumption of their old ways on the Saskatchewan River were now feeling pressure from the land speculators and homesteaders who followed hard on their heels.

The main cause of the rising Métis anger was the half-breeds' fear of losing lands they regarded as their patrimony, their natural inheritance from Indian ancestors. When the Canadian government bought the Western wilderness from the Hudson's Bay Company, it took the position that all lands not specifically granted to individuals belonged to the Crown. By this rea-

Louis Riel came out of exile to lead a second Métis revolt in 1885. Convinced by visions that the half-breeds would triumph over the government with divine assistance, Riel told his followers, "The Holy Ghost is with you in my person."

soning, the Métis were squatters on land they had farmed and improved for generations. Under the new homestead law, they had to register their holdings as if they were brand-new settlers and then wait three years before being granted "patents," or deeds.

Eventually, Ottawa acknowledged that the Métis had a natural title to the land they worked. But the government was slow to survey their holdings, and slower still to issue official patents. Worse yet, government surveyors insisted on charting square lots instead of the long, narrow ones the Métis had laid out to intersect rivers and streams. And access to water was only one of the survey problems. In 1884 a priest named Father Végreville complained to Ottawa that "these inflexible limits, right-lines and parallels will traverse fields, pass through houses, cut off farm houses from the fields connected with them. What serious hardships, what deplorable results must flow from all this."

In petition after petition the Métis pleaded with Ottawa for sensible surveys, prompt ownership patents and, above all, a voice in their own affairs. But the appeals were denied or simply ignored. In desperation the Métis turned to the one man who had been able to stand up for their rights. They sent for Louis Riel, the miller's son who had led the Red River rebellion 15 years before, and had won concessions from the government — only to see himself forced into exile.

Since his banishment from Canada, Riel had wandered through the United States, living largely on the charity of French-Canadian sympathizers and increasingly subject to mystical visions and irrational outbursts. In 1884, he was in Judith Basin, Montana. He had become an American citizen, had married a half-breed girl named Marguerite Monet and was passing his days teaching Indian children in a mission school.

He turned 40 that year. Not surprisingly, since he was only one-eighth Indian, he looked distinctly French, with pale skin and a thin, straight nose. Slender, almost frail of build, he could not ride, shoot or hunt as skillfully as most half-breeds. His great gift as their leader was that he could articulate their deepest fears, resentments and longings. To his compatriots, as Father Vital Fourmond of Batoche observed, Riel was "a Joshua, a prophet, even a saint."

Louis Riel himself was obsessed with the idea that he was God's chosen instrument for accomplishing the deliverance of the Métis. He recounted a vision that had come to him some years before: "The same spirit who showed himself to Moses in the midst of fire and cloud appeared to me in the same manner. I was stupefied; I was confused. He said to me, 'Rise up, Louis David Riel. You have a mission to fulfill.' Stretching out my arms and bending my head, I received this heavenly messenger."

And so it was hardly a surprise to Riel when, on Sunday morning, June 4, 1884, the call came to his divine mission. Riel was in church at St. Peter's Mission when he was told that four horsemen attended him outside. The leader was Gabriel Dumont, renowned along the Saskatchewan as a horseman, sharpshooter and longtime chief of the buffalo hunt.

At 47, Dumont was a swarthy, handsome figure of a man, whom his admirers called "the prince of the prairies." According to Sam Steele of the Mounties, "One might travel the plains from one end to the other and never hear an unkind word said of Dumont. He would kill bison by the score and give them to those who were either unable to kill or had no buffalo. Not until every poor member of the hunting-parties had his cart filled with meat would he begin to fill his own. When in trouble the cry of all was for Gabriel."

Dumont spoke no English, and in any case he had no gift for oratory. No one, Dumont least of all, believed that he alone could unite the Métis against the Canadian government. That was why he and his companions had ridden nearly 700 miles from the Saskatchewan valley to plead with Louis Riel to take up the old cause, and to assure him that French, English and Indians alike would rally to his side.

After a few days, Riel packed his wife, two young children and their few possessions on a Red River cart, and with his escort commenced the long trek north. At Fort Benton the little party stopped to ask the blessing of Father Frederick Eberschweiler, a Jesuit who had befriended Riel. When he heard the purpose of the journey, the good father pleaded with Riel not to precipitate a conflict the Métis could not possibly win. Louis assured the priest that he went in peace. But Eberschweiler later recalled that he had last seen Riel staring at the crest of a nearby hill. "Father," Louis had called to him, "I see a gallows on top of that hill, and I am swinging from it." It was one vision that

With rifle and pony, famed buffalo hunter Gabriel Dumont typifies the self-sufficient Métis plainsman. A shrewd tactician and a crack shot, Dumont was Louis Riel's chief lieutenant during the Métis rebellion.

the troubled messiah of the Métis saw all too well.

In early July, Riel and his friends approached Batoche, the major Métis settlement on the South Saskatchewan River. A crowd of horsemen galloped out to meet them, cheering wildly and firing their buffalo guns into the air. Louis and his family were escorted to the home of a cousin, Charles Nolin. And with that as a headquarters, Riel spent the next few months addressing meetings of half-breed and white settlers in nearby communities, calling on them to defend their interests by firm but peaceful means.

A fresh bill of rights was drafted and sent to Ottawa in December. It demanded deeds to existing riverfront farms, scrip entitling original settlers to additional land, local government with representation in the Dominion Parliament, reduction of tariffs, more liberal settlement of Indian claims, and a new railroad to link the Saskatchewan region to ports in Hudson Bay.

Ottawa acknowledged receipt of the petition but Prime Minister Macdonald took no official action. He did, however, send a secret message to Donald Smith of the Hudson's Bay Company, asking for the loan of the company's buildings at Fort Carlton, 20 miles west

of Batoche, as emergency quarters for additional Mounted Police.

All through the winter, Riel's agitation gathered momentum. In early February, Father Alexis André, a Batoche priest who disliked Riel and was spying on him for the government, sent an urgent message to Ottawa that the Métis' "great indignation might easily lead them to extreme acts." Indeed, Riel was by now convinced that constitutional appeals were useless. On March 5, he and Gabriel Dumont announced: "We are going to take up arms for the glory of God, the honour of religion and for the salvation of our souls."

To strengthen the resolve of his unsophisticated followers Riel employed a bit of sorcery. On March 15, he assured a gathering that he had heaven's highest blessing. As a sign of divine approval, he predicted that "God will draw His hand over the face of the sun." Shortly after he spoke, the sky darkened. Riel had consulted an almanac and knew he could count on a partial eclipse. To his followers it seemed like a powerful omen.

A few days later, Riel gambled on repeating the bold moves that had worked at Red River to bring

Big Bear (*center*), a Cree chieftain, attends a deceptively peaceful trading session at Fort Pitt just before joining the Métis rebellion.

Ottawa to terms. He formed the "Provisional Government of the Saskatchewan," with Dumont as commander of the army, in charge of organizing 400 tough Métis into squadrons of cavalry. The guerrillas went into action at once. They cut the telegraph line at Batoche, ransacked government stores and seized several hostages, including an Indian agent. Then, seeking to take over a fortified headquarters as he had done at Red River, Riel issued an ultimatum to Major Leif Crozier and the 50 Mounties who had been sent to Fort Carlton.

Riel offered safe conduct if the Mounties surrendered. If they refused, he swore to "commence without delay a war of extermination upon all those who have shown themselves hostile to our rights."

But Riel, in hoping to duplicate his earlier success, had ignored a number of changed circumstances. In 1869, there had been no North West Mounted Police, and no railroad to bring regular Canadian army troops into the Great Lone Land. Now, the Mounties were in Saskatchewan in force. And the transcontinental railroad begun in 1881 had pushed its steel rails as far as the Rockies. Moreover, in 1869, Can-

ada's grip on the vast plains of the Northwest had been tenuous in the extreme. Riel and his followers had had an inherent right to form their own government to protect their lives and property. In 1885, by contrast, the Canadian government was very much in evidence in the Northwest, and Riel's actions could only be regarded as rebellion.

At Fort Carlton, Crozier decided to move swiftly against Riel. The site he chose for the confrontation was the trading post at Duck Lake, 13 miles to the east, which had been occupied by Métis and Indians under Gabriel Dumont. On March 26, Crozier led 55 Mounted Policemen out of Fort Carlton to uphold the authority of the dominion and the queen. With them went 43 hastily assembled volunteers, one seven-pounder cannon and 20 horse-drawn sleighs.

Because of the deep, sticky spring snow, Crozier's task force had to march in file along the hard-packed trail. As the column approached Duck Lake, the troopers noticed with alarm that they were slowly being encircled by Métis slipping wraithlike through the woods on snow shoes. The Mounties, as Corporal John Donkin later recalled, were in "a wretched position, lying

Inspector Francis Dickens, son of the novelist, musters his garrison at Fort Pitt. But Dickens was not a fighter and fled the Crees.

in an exposed hollow and surrounded on three sides by scrubby bush."

Crozier quickly drew his sleds across the path as a barricade, then advanced with John McKay, his Scottish half-breed interpreter, to parley under a white flag borne by an Indian and Dumont's brother Isidore. It soon became apparent to the major, however, that the Métis were merely playing for time so that more of their men could creep up on his flanks and rear. Crozier abruptly turned to break off the talk. At that, the Indian made a grab for McKay's rifle. "Fire away, boys!" Crozier yelled. In a storm of bullets, Isidore Dumont toppled from his horse, mortally wounded.

As Mounties and volunteers scrambled for cover behind their sleighs, Crozier realized that he had fallen into a clever trap. One of the volunteers later remembered blazing away at caps and Indian headdresses barely visible over the top of the snow—only to discover that his targets were decoys propped up on sticks while their owners were somewhere else, firing at *him*. An apparently deserted cabin on the right turned out to be a nest of snipers, who poured a murderous fire at the exposed troopers. Crozier ordered his cannon unlimbered, but after the artillerymen had gotten off three misaimed shots, an excited gunner rammed home a shell ahead of its powder charge and put the piece out of action.

By now 150 or more Métis fighters had swarmed in over the hill. Suddenly, Louis Riel himself appeared on horseback, brandishing a large crucifix he had taken from the little church at Duck Lake. When the troopers fired at him and missed, he gestured with the cross, and roared, "In the name of God the Father who created us, reply to that!" His inspired followers sent fresh volleys into the demoralized enemy below.

After half an hour of unequal struggle, Crozier desperately called the retreat. Five rebels had been killed and three wounded. But 10 volunteers and Mounties lay dead, with another 14 wounded—almost a quarter of the entire contingent. As the troopers frantically clambered aboard the sleighs, Gabriel Dumont, blood streaming down his face from a scalp wound, shouted to his men to destroy the fleeing force once and for all. Riel countermanded the order. "For the love of God, kill no more of them," he cried.

That afternoon the Métis walked slowly among the dead collecting guns and cartridge belts. Then they car-

ried the bodies into the little cabin and sent word to Crozier that anyone coming to recover them would not be harmed. In fact, when a group of Mounties arrived, the rebels helped them load their dead into a wagon.

Scarcely more than an hour after Crozier's beaten detachment had staggered back through the gates of Fort Carlton, a fresh force of Mounties arrived from the territorial capital of Regina—108 men under the command of Commissioner A. G. Irvine. Prudently, Irvine decided not to mount another foray against the deadly Métis, or even to try to defend Fort Carlton. The fort was built for trading, not military action; the stockade was flimsy, and the interior was exposed to fire from a hillside to the rear. Irvine decided to concentrate his forces at nearby Prince Albert, which was a major settlement and thus a greater potential prize for Riel. On March 27, he ordered the evacuation of 350 Mounties, volunteers and residents; as a final indignity to hurry them on their way, the fort caught fire from a hay mattress set too close to a stove.

Of course, the Métis scouts reported everything, and Dumont immediately planned an ambush where the trail passed through a dense grove of trees. But once more an opportunity was lost. "We could have killed a lot of them," Dumont later reported regretfully, "but Riel, who was always restraining us, formally opposed the idea."

In a period of a few days a wooden stockade was thrown up around Prince Albert's Presbyterian church and manse. Into this small defense perimeter poured the townsmen and terrified refugees from the surrounding countryside. Soon there were 1,800 people jammed into the area. "Every open window of the large brick manse was filled with anxious women's faces, the eyes of many being dim with tears," Corporal Donkin wrote. "The enclosure was filled with sleighs and a restless, surging throng. The interior of the ecclesiastical edifice was simply a vast nursery of noisy children and screaming females. Some were ministering to the young fellow of ours whose feet were frozen, and who was laid on a sort of dais near the pulpit. Two long tables stretched the entire length of the kirk, with benches on each side. Here the hungry ones were demolishing a varied assortment of viands. It was a strange sight. One strong man was weeping piteous-

ly for the loss of his brother in the recent fight."

To defend the Prince Albert stockade, Irvine could count on 200 policemen and 300 home guardsmen. The garrison was evidently formidable enough to deter the Métis, for they never attacked the settlement. Though there is no record, Riel may have had second thoughts about his rebellion. Thus far, the revolt had produced a tactical victory but a strategic defeat. The Métis had the blood of a dozen white men on their hands and a shock wave of raging public opinion in Eastern Canada to cope with as citizens read lurid tales of a savage rebellion spreading through the Northwest.

To many Canadians, the greatest threat was that the half-breed uprising might spread to Indian reserves all over Western Canada and even the United States, bringing on the catastrophe of an Indian war. Riel had already exhorted his followers to "stir up the Indians," and after the Duck Lake battle he sent notes to several chiefs, addressing them as "dear relatives" and urging them to "capture all the police you possibly can."

The major tribes were deeply disturbed by news of the half-breed revolt. Most of them, including the

203

An 1885 lithograph shows the "battle" at Fort Pitt, which actually fell without a shot. Among the loot for the Crees was a glass eye; when it did not restore the full sight of a one-eyed warrior, a captured settler coolly said the blue eye was "the wrong color for an Indian."

Blackfoot tribe under Crowfoot, saw no profit in war against the Queen and her sturdy redcoats. Two bands of Cree Indians were notable exceptions. One was led by Poundmaker, Crowfoot's adopted son, who had grown to detest life on the reserve. The other was headed by Big Bear, a small, wizened chieftain around whom had gathered many disgruntled braves skilled at extracting government rations while ignoring the farmwork they were supposed to undertake.

Barely two days after the Duck Lake debacle, white settlers at Battleford, a hundred miles to the west, learned that 200 warriors led by Poundmaker were heading for the town. More than 500 men, women and children took refuge in the Mounties' fortress-like barracks just outside Battleford, crowding in with its garrison of 43 men. The Indians arrived, fearsomely decked out in war paint, and loudly demanded food, clothing and ammunition.

Battleford's Indian agent hastily telegraphed his superiors for authority to issue the rations. But the impatient warriors refused to wait; they began looting the Hudson's Bay store and other buildings in the abandoned town. Because Battleford lay beyond the range of the fort's cannon, the police could only stand helplessly by while the rampaging braves tore the place apart, smashing furniture, killing livestock and capering in the streets in silk shirts, ladies' bonnets and top hats. Outlying farmhouses were sacked and burned, and a white settler who had tarried too long was murdered.

For three weeks, Poundmaker and his Crees laid siege to the Mountie fort, which was jam-packed with townspeople. Providentially, the refugees had brought with them plenty of food, and the Indians, wearying of the game, eventually departed.

An even more terrifying episode was brewing another 150 miles up the North Saskatchewan, 30 miles back in the hills behind Fort Pitt. At the tiny hamlet of Frog Lake, near a reserve where Big Bear and his followers had spent a wretched winter, a party of warpainted Crees burst in during mass at the Catholic mission. They ransacked the Hudson's Bay Company store and ordered all 13 white settlers to go as prisoners to their camp. The Frog Lake Indian agent, a lanky Minnesotan named Thomas Trueman Quinn, refused to lead the way. Big Bear's war chief, Wandering Spirit, stepped up to Quinn. A fierce warrior known for his open hatred of whites, Wandering Spirit was in full war regalia; his eyelids, lips and chin were painted a hideous yellow, and on his head he wore a lynx-skin bonnet decorated with eagle plumes, one for each of the five enemies he had killed. "If you love your life, you will do as I tell you," he hissed. "My place is here. I will not go," said Quinn. Wandering Spirit raised his rifle, screamed, "I tell you — go!" and fired point-blank. Big Bear rushed up crying, "Tesqua! Tesqua!" ("Stop! Stop!")

He was too late. Wandering Spirit had taken command. Dancing and waving his rifle in triumphant frenzy, he shouted, "Nipuhao! Nipuhao!" ("Kill! Kill!") The other Crees took up the chant: "Nipuhao! Nipuhao!" The whites were herded out of the church into the road. The Crees opened fire. The first to fall were a half-breed carpenter named Charles Gouin and a mechanic, John Williscroft. John Gowanlock, a miller, was next. Then, as farm instructor John Delaney went down, his wife flung herself over his body and screamed for help. Father François Fafard knelt beside the dying man. As the priest was making the sign of the cross, Wandering Spirit shot him in the back of the neck. Father Felix Marchand ran to Fafard, and was himself slain. Just four of the 13 whites in the church survived. Taken away as captives were the widows of Delaney and Gowanlock, along with William Cameron, a young Hudson's Bay clerk. One other man, the Indian agent's nephew, Henry Quinn, escaped to carry the news of the massacre to Fort Pitt.

Prodded by a nationwide wave of patriotic fervor and fear, the government in Ottawa reacted to all this with rare determination and speed. Indeed, in the weeks before Duck Lake, when it was apparent that matters were coming to a head, Ottawa had already thought to mobilize a militia battalion in the Winnipeg area. Immediately after the March 26 debacle, orders went out to muster units throughout Canada. Quebec mobilized 1,000 men, including the Montreal Garrison Artillery and the French-speaking 65th Rifles and 9th Voltigeurs. Ontario furnished 2,000 troops, among them the 7th Fusiliers, the Queen's Own Rifles and the Royal Grenadiers. From Nova Scotia came the Halifax Battalion, 400 men strong. Manitoba, which had already turned out its 90th Infantry Battalion, now added the 91st and Light Infantry Regiments — more than 1,000 men all told. Farther west impromptu units were formed and given rousing names like the Rocky Mountain Rangers and the Moose Mountain Scouts.

Counting staff and supply detachments, a North West Field Force of close to 8,000 men was rapidly assembled to reinforce the beleaguered Western settlements. The army's heavy artillery consisted of nine cannon, some so old their wooden carriages had rotted under several coats of paint. But there were also two brand-new Gatling machine guns brought in on trial from the United States; they were formidable-looking weapons with revolving barrels that could fire an astounding 1,200 rounds per minute.

Against this force of citizens and professionals, the Saskatchewan rebels could count on 1,000 men at most, French and English half-breeds armed mainly with old shotguns and smoothbore hunting pieces, short on supplies and ammunition and often wondering whether they should be fighting Canada at all. A larger question mark on the plains was the Indian population, which numbered 20,000 or more. Only a tiny fraction — Big Bear's and Poundmaker's Crees, perhaps 400 warriors in all — had thus far risen in arms. To keep the vast tribes of Blackfeet, Stoneys and Saulteaux loyal — or at least quiescent — the Canadian government hastily dispatched fresh provisions of flour, beef, tea and tobacco to them.

To move its soldiers and supplies into the field, the government turned to the new Canadian Pacific Railway. By now, at least theoretically, the line reached all the way to the Rockies, but a 250-mile section along the north shore of Lake Superior was riddled with gaps where its builders still struggled with the rock ledges and quaking muskeg of the Canadian Shield. The railroad was on the verge of bankruptcy, unable to meet payrolls and begging Ottawa for a government-backed loan. So far both Macdonald and the Montreal bankers had turned deaf ears to these appeals.

Now, the Canadian Pacific's general manager, William Van Horne, saw his chance to prove the railroad's value to Canada and thus win financial support from Parliament. He told the government he would transport its troops over the 86 miles of gaps in the line and out onto the prairies in 11 days flat if Ottawa would give him two days' notice of each troop shipment. The units from the East started entraining near Ottawa on March 30.

The first gap in the line was a 45-mile segment at Dog Lake, about 750 miles west of Toronto, and there the ordeal began. Van Horne had provided a shuttle of horse-drawn sleighs, which lurched down rough construction roads, bouncing off boulders and into deep holes, frequently pitching their occupants into puddles of icy water or six feet of deep snow. One sleigh overturned 13 times before reaching the next stretch of track.

In temperatures that dropped to ⁻35° F., many ill-clad troopers suffered frostbite. Of the eight-hour trek across the glare ice of Lake Superior, a member of the Queen's Own Rifles wrote to his family: "We dared not stop an instant as we were in great danger of being frozen, although the sun was taking the skin off our faces. One man of our company went mad and one of the regulars went blind from snow glare."

Troops who slogged over the same ground at night endured hardships of another sort. "You have heard of soldiers in the Sudan wandering away from the column while in a somnambulistic condition," wrote one artilleryman. "Well that is just how our men were. The night was dark, the temperature freezing and a heavy snow storm with a wild, piercing wind made the march a fearful undertaking." Though Van Horne had provided tons of food and gallons of hot coffee at the transfer points, many of the men were too exhausted to eat. They fell sprawling in the snow until their comrades picked them up and threw them into open flatcars for the next leg ahead.

Nevertheless, by mid-April, all units of the North West Field Force had reached their staging points along the railway beyond Winnipeg. The plan called for a three-pronged offensive into the heart of the Saskatchewan River — Métis country. The main force, led by the expedition's commander, Major General Frederick Dobson Middleton, had already started marching north on April 6 from Qu'Appelle against the rebel headquarters at Batoche. A second force under Colonel William Otter was gathered farther west at Swift Current with orders to proceed directly to the relief of Battleford. The third battalion, under Major General Thomas Bland Strange, was to move north from Calgary in the Far Western prairies to pacify the area around Edmonton, then veer east in a pincer movement with Middleton to subdue the Crees led by Big Bear and Poundmaker near Fort Pitt.

Though Middleton's strategy appeared to be sound enough on paper, its execution depended on swift maneuver and decisive attack, which were not the general's forte. The portly, white-whiskered commandant of Canadian militia was a Sandhurst graduate who had helped put down the Maoris in New Zealand and the sepoys in India. In Canada, a country where horsemen and sharpshooters had the obvious advantage of mobility and concealment, he retained an unshakable faith in ponderous infantry advances for attack and the massed British square for defense. Moreover, he obviously had little confidence in his largely citizen army, which did nothing to improve its fighting spirit.

With time out for drill, it took Middleton three weeks to march his force 150 miles north to within 20 miles of Batoche. He had 800 men in two columns of infantry, but he had left most of his cavalry behind to guard supply depots and protect the railway. Thus, he had lost his ability to maneuver — and against the Métis it would cost him dearly.

On the morning of April 24, Gabriel Dumont concealed a force of 130 half-breeds and Indians in the small ravine of Fish Creek, a few miles from Middleton's camp. He ordered his men to dig rifle pits, facing uphill, among the trees and brush. Gabriel, the wily hunter, planned to catch Middleton's troopers on the brow of the hill, where they would be silhouetted against the sky, and turn it into a bloody killing ground.

Some undisciplined young Métis horsemen gave away their presence by chasing stray cattle, leaving tracks for Middleton's scouts to pick up. Nevertheless, Middleton pressed blindly on, and as the orderly ranks of soldiers rolled over the crest of the hill, they were greeted by sheets of fire from the rebels hidden below. The Canadians wheeled up two artillery pieces but the muzzles could not be depressed far enough, and their shrapnel shells exploded harmlessly in the treetops beyond the Métis rifle pits.

Twice the Canadians attempted a bayonet charge, and each time reeled back under the weight of Métis fire. Dumont walked among his men. "Don't be afraid of bullets; they won't hurt you," he told them. One Métis began to sing "The Falcon's Song," an old half-

Canadian soldiers, among them factory workers and clerks who had volunteered to fight the rebels, sprawl in a day coach taking them across

the plains. This was the easy part of the trip. Over some incomplete stretches, the troops suffered the bitter cold in sleighs or on foot.

breed fighting song. Another took up the melody on the flute he had carried with him into battle. When nightfall finally ended the engagement, the Canadians withdrew and the Métis claimed the battlefield. Someone brought Dumont a medical kit dropped by a Canadian field doctor. It included two bottles of medicinal brandy. "To the good doctor's health," toasted a grinning Dumont, as he and his Métis drank them down.

Although outnumbered by 5 to 1, Dumont had lost only four dead and two wounded. Canadian casualties were almost 10 times as great: 50 men dead or wounded. Middleton was so shaken that he stopped for two weeks to regroup and think things over.

The same day that Dumont savaged Middleton at Fish Creek, the second prong of 543 men under Colonel Otter marched into Battleford to the lusty cheers of its inhabitants. The colonel rested his troops for a few days, and then set out to teach the town's erstwhile besiegers a lesson, taking with him a force of 325 men, including 75 Mounties, two seven-pounder cannon and one Gatling gun. Otter hoped to surprise Poundmaker's Cree warriors at daybreak in their camp on Cut Knife Creek, 38 miles away. However, the Indians were far too alert, and while the cannon and Gatling futilely pounded the tipis, most of the Indians faded away into the brush. Within 20 minutes the Canadians found themselves on the defensive, almost surrounded by warriors. Poundmaker's 300 braves were armed only with old rifles and bows and arrows. Yet for seven hours they kept Otter's wildly firing troops pinned down. At length, the Canadians managed to fight their way back to Battleford. This new disaster had cost the North West Field Force another eight dead and 15 wounded.

By the end of the first week of May, General Middleton was at last ready to make his push on the rebels' main stronghold at Batoche. To the astonishment of nearly everyone, the Britisher had dreamed up a navy to accompany his land forces the last few miles down the South Saskatchewan. It consisted of the flat-bottomed sternwheeler *Northcote,* which had been puffing up and down inland waterways delivering supplies to Hudson's Bay Company posts. For heavy weapons, Middleton mounted a seven-pound cannon and a Gatling gun on *Northcote;* 35 troopers with ri-

fles would supply the light armament. The plan was for *Northcote* to sail downriver and bombard Batoche, while Middleton's main force launched a frontal attack.

Naturally, Métis scouts had observed every detail of *Northcote*'s transformation, and by the time the gunboat approached Batoche early on May 9, Dumont had prepared a warm welcome. As the pilot nursed the balky steamer through a narrow channel at the edge of town, a barrage of gunfire exploded from both banks of the river. With bullets splintering the superstructure, *Northcote*'s crew frantically poured on steam.

But Dumont was just beginning. As the steamer chugged through the settlement, belching sparks from her stacks, the captain saw too late that the Métis had rigged a trap with two ferry cables that spanned the river several hundred feet apart. As *Northcote* passed under the first cable, soldiers and crew watched in helpless fascination while the thick strand of wire dropped into the water astern, sealing off retreat. Now the other cable began to fall ahead, closing the trap. But the Métis' timing was slightly off. Instead of hitting the water, the heavy steel rope scraped across the top of the pilot house, yanking off the smokestacks, whistle, mast and loading spars, and flinging them in a tangle to the wooden deck, which began to burn. Desperately ducking Métis bullets, *Northcote*'s crew manned a bucket brigade to put out the fire. At last, the steamer slipped around a bend and out of sight of the Métis. The comic-opera engagement was over. If Middleton was to take Batoche, he would have to do it without naval support.

Later that morning, Middleton's advance guard marched into the outskirts of the village. Artillery was moved into position and began shelling the town, which stretched away down a sloping hillside into a ravine below. It was as if the place had been abandoned. Not a single Métis could be seen anywhere.

Middleton ordered his infantry forward. Suddenly, 30 yards in front of the advancing troops, the ground erupted in puffs of smoke. It was Fish Creek all over again, with the soldiers silhouetted on the skyline and the Métis dug in below—this time virtually invisible in an elaborate network of camouflaged pits and trenches. As the troopers tried flanking movements, dry brush and grass on both sides crackled into flames, causing the men to choke and cough, and forcing them to stumble around blindly. The Gatling gunner could only crank away grimly into the haze, hoping the spray of bullets would discourage a Métis charge.

At dusk, Middleton ordered his men back to the safety of a zareba, or stockade improvised from transport wagons. No fires were permitted, so the exhausted troopers dined on hardtack and cold water. All night long the Métis sent sporadic fire into the compound, compelling the men to duck under the wagons and threatening to stampede the animals. To top off the evening's entertainment, Dumont sent a large rocket arching up over the zareba at midnight. It exploded with a colossal bang and an eye-searing flare, further unnerving Middleton's troops.

The next day, a Sunday, the militiamen warily threw out early morning skirmish lines. But no one ventured within 200 yards of the hooting, cheering Métis in their trenches. As the two sides settled down to a waiting game, Dumont exhorted his men to conserve ammunition, which was running dangerously low. Louis Riel appeared in the trenches, and crept back and forth among his followers, praying with them and telling them to keep up their courage for the glory of God.

For two more days the stalemate continued. Middleton's officers pleaded with their general to order a bayonet attack and overwhelm the Métis. He had, after all, 900 men under his command by now, which was more than four times the number of Métis. Even Gabriel Dumont said afterward that he could not understand why the English general had not quickly overwhelmed the 200-odd buffalo hunters by sheer numbers in one all-out charge.

But Middleton, twice burned by Métis tactics, was thrice careful. At last, on the fourth day, an exasperated Ontario colonel named A. T. H. Williams took matters into his own hands. While Middleton was in the zareba eating lunch, Williams led his Midland Battalion forward en masse. The cheering, running men were joined by the 90th Winnipeg Rifles and Toronto's Royal Grenadiers. Sputtering with rage, Middleton roared to his bugler to sound the recall. But the troops ignored the signal, and Middleton was forced to

Following the path of the telegraph line, Major-General Frederick Middleton leads his troops to the Métis stronghold at Batoche.

Middleton's men *(numbered on the picture 16-28)*, who were kept off balance for three days at Batoche by Métis sharpshooters *(8-15)*, crush the rebels with an all-out charge. While the Métis were forced to retrieve spent bullets from the battlefield at night, the militia drew from supplies of 1.5 million rifle bullets and 70,000 Gatling rounds.

Big Bear *(standing)* and Poundmaker, another Cree chief who joined the rebellion, pause with priests and a warden at the door of Stoney Mountain prison after their surrender, conviction and sentencing to jail.

bring up the rest of his units to support the charge.

The Métis, now so short of bullets they were firing nails, pebbles, even metal buttons, could not reload fast enough to keep the soldiers from the first line of trenches. Most of the rebels held until the last second, then raced back to the next trench down the hill. Many ran barefoot, having taken off boots and moccasins during the long, cramped hours in the pits. Leaping into a trench, one young volunteer stared at the body of a defender who had fought to the end. He was a wrinkled, white-haired Métis of 93 named Joseph Ouellette. Dumont later recounted that he had pleaded with the old man to fall back. "Several times I said to him, 'Father, we have to retreat.' And this simple man replied, 'Wait, I want to kill another Englishman.'"

When the Métis were dislodged from the last trenches, they crouched and fired from the ruins of the shelled town and then from trees along the river. But by 7 o'clock that evening it was over. Métis women and children emerged from cellars and riverbank caves, followed by the men, who had finally gone to ground. The victorious troopers milled around, some boasting, but many silent and shaken. Poking around for a souvenir, one man came across a shrine in a grove of poplars where the villagers had met daily to hear Riel's prayers and exhortations. The shrine was merely a cheap lithograph of the Sacred Heart of Jesus, mounted on cardboard and draped in a scrap of white muslin. The man thought of taking it home, then stopped. He left the sad little symbol where he had found it, nailed to a tree in the shattered village of Batoche.

Casualties at Batoche, though slight compared to the slaughter at Gettysburg or Shiloh in the United States Civil War, were nevertheless severe for Canada's civil war: eight dead and 46 wounded among Middleton's soldiers, 16 dead and 30 wounded among Dumont's Métis, fully 10 per cent of all those engaged. Dumont himself was unhurt, and refused to surrender. Skilled in the hunt and the ways of the plains, he evaded the patrols sent out to capture him and eventually reached safety in Montana. He later became a star attraction in Buffalo Bill Cody's Wild West Show.

Louis Riel pondered his fate while hiding in the nearby woods. Then, three days after the battle, he gave himself up to a party of mounted scouts, who es-

corted him to Middleton. "I found him a mild-spoken and mild-looking man with a short brown beard," the general recounted. "He had no coat on and looked cold and forlorn and as it was still chilly out of the sun, I commenced proceedings by giving him a military greatcoat of my own." Middleton asked how Riel could ever have dreamed of waging war against the mighty British Crown? Riel replied wearily that there had been no hope of defeating Canada or the Queen; he had tried only to make one last stand, to take hostages and convince the government that it must deal fairly with people of the territories and their long-neglected rights. After a week in camp, awaiting word of what Ottawa had decided to do with him, Riel was taken by steamer to Saskatoon, and then in a heavily guarded wagon caravan and a special train to the territorial capital of Regina, where he was placed in the Mounted Police guardhouse to await trial.

His affairs at Batoche concluded, Frederick Dobson Middleton led a triumphal march to relieve the stockaded inhabitants of Prince Albert. Then, dressed in his best white helmet and tweed shooting clothes, he went on *Northcote* to Battleford, where he received the unconditional surrender of Poundmaker and his Crees.

There was but one more episode to be played out in Canada's civil war. While Middleton was capturing Batoche and Otter was relieving Battleford, the third column of the North West Field Force set out to avenge the massacre at Frog Lake and the capture of Fort Pitt by Big Bear's rampaging Crees. On May 25, some 500 men under General Thomas Strange arrived in the vicinity of Fort Pitt after a 250-mile march from Edmonton. In addition to 375 infantry troops, the force included three Stoney Indian scouts, 100 ranch hands and settlers who could handle a horse and gun, and 25 Mounties wearing cowboy outfits because, Strange complained, the policemen's red coats were too conspicuous and made his eyes ache. Called down from his railway duties in the Rockies to lead the Mounties was that legendary figure Samuel Benfield Steele, dressed, unlike his men, in full regalia. Strange reported that Steele, "a splendid-looking fellow, could not give up the swagger of his scarlet tunic, and I did not ask him to make the sacrifice."

On May 26 the scouts picked up the trail of Big Bear's 200 warriors, and two days later Strange brought them under fire at Frenchmen's Butte. After an initial frontal attack, he ordered his cavalry to commence a flanking maneuver — to which a number of Cree horsemen responded with an encirclement of their own. At this point Strange decided to break off the battle. He had already suffered a number of casualties, and his respect for Indian tactics and fighting prowess made him wary of "committing Custer," as he put it.

Strange's concern was for his untried troops, not his personal safety, for he was courageous to a fault. At one point during the skirmishing, he reproved an officer for abandoning a dying militiaman near the Indian lines. "General, I have been shot at quite enough today," the officer replied, "and I am damned if I go down there again." Strange went himself, taking two stretcher-bearers and a priest to administer the last rites. Afterward the general recalled, "I must admit some impatience, which the good priest did not seem to share, during the confession of sin, and suggested to the brave padre the desirability of lumping the lot, which he did; putting the dying man into the stretcher, the party moved up the hill, and I brought up the rear with the man's rifle. The fire grew hotter as we ascended the hill; the rear man dropped his end of the stretcher and I took his place."

On June 3, Middleton joined Strange with 200 troops, and assumed overall command. But by now Big Bear had prudently decided to retreat into the swampy, virtually impenetrable northern wilderness. Steele's Mounties and scouts caught up with the Crees once more at Loon Lake. In a fierce little fight, Sergeant Billy Fury was wounded in the chest and several Indians were killed before the rest slipped away.

That was the last spasm of resistance. On June 18 Big Bear's band, now starving, released a number of white prisoners with a little food, some moccasins and a message pleading for "our Great Mother, the Queen, to stop the Government soldiers and Red Coats from shooting us."

Gradually the Indians straggled in to Fort Pitt to give themselves up. Big Bear also surrendered, but not without a final gesture. Accompanied only by his 12-year-old son and a councillor, he made his way on foot 100 miles eastward, right under the noses of police and militia, and on July 2 turned himself in at Fort Carlton to an astonished police sergeant, who was one of the few men in the Canadian Northwest not out searching for him.

Looking smaller and more wizened than ever, the famed chieftain was taken to the police barracks at Prince Albert "in a pitiable condition of filth and hunger," according to one of his escorts, Corporal John Donkin. There he got his first decent meal in nearly two weeks. In addition, Donkin said, "He was given a good scrubbing in a tub. Big Bear's horror of the cleansing process was comic. His breech-clout had done duty for a decade and was as black as the ace of spades which, by the way, it rather resembled."

All told, about 80 whites and perhaps an equal number of Métis and Indians had lost their lives in battle. Putting down the uprising, trying its leaders and paying various claims cost the young confederation five million dollars, a sum it could ill afford. Among the items were $14,500 for rental of *Northcote* for 58 days, as well as $15 for five gallons of good rye whiskey consumed at a victory reception honoring General Middleton. Hardtack, of which the soldiers had seen enough to last a lifetime, had been paid for at the bargain price of five cents a pound, and came to $3,400.

The cost to the losers was far harder to bear. In Regina, 18 Métis were convicted of treason and given prison terms of up to seven years. Eleven Indians were tried for murder at Battleford and sentenced to death. Three were reprieved, but the remaining eight, including Wandering Spirit, were hanged from a common scaffold. As a gesture of magnanimity, Big Bear and Poundmaker were spared the gallows. Instead they were each sentenced to three years' imprisonment. "I would rather prefer to be hung at once than to be in that place," cried Poundmaker despairingly. He and Big Bear were freed after two years. Physically ill and crushed in spirit, they both died within six months of their release.

And what of the man who had started it all, who had galvanized the Crees and Métis and led them in rebellion? What of Louis Riel? On July 28, 1885, the messiah of the Métis sat in the prisoner's dock in a makeshift courtroom in Regina. As the trial began, the prosecutor commented that it was probably "the most serious that has ever taken place in Canada." Louis

Riel's counsel thought the case was important enough to deserve trial in the East before at least a provincial court. Instead, Riel faced a part-time territorial magistrate and a jury of six white settlers.

The room was hot and crowded. A special table had been provided for a dozen newspaper reporters and a section set aside for the ladies, all of them, including General Middleton's wife, dressed in their Sunday finery. Riel, flanked by four red-coated Mounties, wore a black frock coat, black tie, and a fresh white shirt. The magistrate, the prosecutor and Riel's four-man defense team, paid for by the donations of sympathizers in Quebec, were robed and bewigged.

The proceedings opened with the reading of the solemnly worded indictment: ". . . not regarding the duty of his allegiance, nor having the fear of God in his heart, but being moved and seduced by the instigation of the devil as a false traitor against our said Lady the Queen. . . ." To this accusation of high treason, the ultimate crime against the state, Louis Riel responded in a firm voice: "I have the honor to answer the court I am not guilty."

While the spectators listened intently, a procession of witnesses marched to the stand. It was not difficult to show that Riel had indeed stirred up and led an armed rebellion. The prosecution read to the jury the letter in Riel's own handwriting in which he had threatened a war of extermination against the whites. From the witness stand, the Scottish half-breed Thomas McKay quoted Riel as saying, "You don't know what we are after — it is blood, blood. Everybody that is against us is to be driven out of the country."

Under the circumstances Riel's lawyers despaired of proving that he had not incited a revolt. To save their client's life, they hoped to prove instead that he was not guilty by virtue of insanity. Two doctors testified that he was a victim of "megalomania, the mania of ambition." But they could not agree as to the precise degree of his mania, or whether he could distinguish right from wrong. As for Riel himself, he preferred the scaffold to what he described as "the stain of insanity." Several times he disrupted the trial to protest the effort to brand him insane. "I cannot abandon my dignity!" he once cried out. "Here I have to defend myself against the accusation of high treason, or I have to consent to the animal life of an asylum."

The most dramatic moment of the trial came when Riel rose to defend himself in a long and sometimes dis-

Members of Riel's council stand handcuffed in Regina. For pleading guilty to treason, they were all imprisoned rather than hanged.

connected address to the jury. A newspaper account gave the incident full justice: "At the outset, Riel spoke in a quiet and low tone, many of his statements carrying home conviction to his hearers. Gradually as he proceeded, his eyes sparkled, his body swayed to and fro as if strongly agitated, and his hands accomplished a series of wonderful gestures as he spoke with impassioned eloquence. His hearers were spellbound, and well they might be, as each concluding assertion with terrible earnestness was uttered with the effect and force of a trumpet blast. That every soul in Court was impressed is not untrue, and many ladies were moved to tears."

According to the observers' accounts, Riel began by saying, in his stilted English, "It would be an easy matter for me today to play the role of a lunatic. The excitement which my trial causes me is enough to justify me in acting in the manner of a demented man. Although a man, I am as helpless today as I was a babe on my mother's breast. But the Northwest is also my mother and I am sure that my mother will not kill me. . . . She will be indulgent and will forget. . . .

"When I came here from Montana, I found the Indians starving. The half-breeds were subsisting on the rotten pork of the Hudson's Bay Company. This was the condition, this was the pride, of responsible Government! What did Louis Riel do? I did not equally forget the whites. I directed my attention to assist all classes, irrespective of creed, colour or nationality. We have made petitions to the Canadian Government, asking them to relieve the state of affairs. We took time with the object of uniting all classes. . . .

"Even if I am to die I will have the satisfaction of knowing that I will not be regarded by all men as an insane person. . . . A monster of irresponsible, insane government had made up their minds to answer my petitions by surrounding me, and by suddenly attempting to jump at me and my people in the fertile valley of the Saskatchewan. I acted reasonably and in self-defense, while the Government, my aggressor, cannot but have acted madly and wrong; and if high treason there is, it must be on its side, not on my part. I say humbly through the grace of God, I believe I am the prophet of the new world."

On the fifth day of the trial, the jurors retired to deliberate. Riel dropped to his knees, praying in French

218

Riel, whose indictment charged that he did not have "the fear of God in his heart," speaks at his trial. "Though it might take 200 years," said the Roman Catholic half-breed, "my children's children will shake hands with the Protestants of the new world in a friendly manner."

One of Riel's last messages appears on Mountie memo paper, handed to him by a reporter just before his execution. The newsman is said to have posed as a prison worker to foil death-row security.

I have devoted my life to my country. If it is necessary for the happiness of my country that I should now soon cease to live, I leave it to the Providence of my God.

Louis Riel.

and Latin in a soft monotone until the jury returned to the courtroom one hour and 20 minutes later. "We find the defendant guilty," foreman Francis Cosgrave pronounced solemnly. He then asked the court for clemency for Riel: "Your Honor, I have been asked by my brother jurors to recommend the prisoner to the mercy of the Crown."

When the magistrate answered it was to address Riel. "I cannot hold out any hope to you that Her Majesty will open her hand of clemency to you. All I can advise you is to prepare to meet your end. It is now my painful duty to pass the sentence. On the 18th of September next you will be taken to the place appointed for your execution, and there be hanged by the neck till you are dead."

The news of Riel's conviction ignited a controversy that very nearly tore the new, fragile Canadian confederation apart. French Catholics defended the half-breed leader as a patriot; English Protestants damned him as a traitor. Quebec City's *L'Electeur* eulogized Riel: "History will reserve a glorious page for you. . . . Joan of Arc! Napoléon! Chénier! Riel!" *The Selkirk Herald* thought otherwise: "We consider that such lives as that of Riel are blots and stains on our humanity which ought to be summarily removed by the hand of justice in like manner as the dangerous cancer is re-

moved from the human body by the hand of the surgeon." In that Prime Minister Macdonald heartily concurred: "He shall hang though every dog in Quebec bark in his favor."

Riel's lawyers appealed to higher courts in Ottawa and London. The hearings dragged on until November, through one stay of execution after another. But the verdict and sentence were always upheld. A three-man medical commission was appointed to examine Riel once again. A doctor reported, "He suffers under hallucinations on political and religious subjects, but on other points I believe him to be quite sensible and can distinguish right from wrong."

Gabriel Dumont hoped to the last to free his beloved leader by staging a bold jailbreak and escaping to the United States. With the help of other Métis, Gabriel set up an underground network of relay stations, one every 10 or 20 miles on the 450-mile route from Regina to Lewistown, Montana. Each station was stocked with a supply of food and fresh horses and was manned by armed escorts. They were never used. Perhaps because officials got wind of the escape plan, the guard around Riel was strengthened and the break was never attempted.

During his last days, Riel did not even have the comfort of a visit from his wife, Marguerite. The trauma of the trial and the death of a third child after its premature birth in October had been too much for her; she had refused to eat and was slowly dying. Riel did receive occasional visits from his mother and from his brother Alexandre. Most of his time was spent praying and writing. His letters were often incoherent. But he wrote a lucid *Last Memoir,* in which he extolled the Métis way of life, especially the hunt, with "the coursers rearing, neighing, dancing, digging at the ground with eager hooves."

The day of execution on November 16 dawned cold and brilliantly clear in Regina. Carrying a small crucifix, Riel walked slowly with a deputy sheriff and two priests out onto the prison gallows platform. His face was pale and beaded with perspiration but he walked with dignity, and when one of the overwrought priests stumbled he murmured softly, "Courage, mon père." With the priests he repeated the Lord's Prayer, in English, as the hangman dropped a white hood over his head and adjusted the noose. At the words "lead us not into temptation, but deliver us . . ." the trap opened abruptly and Louis Riel plunged nine feet to his death. The body was placed in a rough pine box and taken east on a Canadian Pacific train to Winnipeg, where it was buried in the quiet, tree-shaded cathedral yard of St. Boniface. Above the grave was erected a simple granite shaft, provided by sorrowers in Quebec and inscribed with the simple legend: RIEL, 16 NOVEMBRE, 1885.

Although Riel's conviction and execution scarred relations between French- and English-speaking Canadians — and between plainsmen and Easterners — for generations, another event of 1885, that watershed year, symbolized Canada's growing strength and sense of nationhood. On November 7, just nine days before the Métis leader met his doom, the Canadian Pacific Railway was at last completed, connecting the Atlantic and Pacific coasts of Canada across 2,900 miles of difficult terrain.

Ironically, the Métis, who stood to suffer most from the encroachment of railroad-borne settlers, had been instrumental in the completion of the last links. Canadian Pacific General Manager William Cornelius Van Horne had sought to prove his railroad's worth by transporting troops to put down the Riel rebellion.

And he had succeeded handsomely. On July 20, a grateful Parliament in Ottawa had approved a multimillion-dollar package of aid in the form of direct loans, guarantees and permission to substitute a bond issue for unsold shares. The assistance enabled the Canadian Pacific to finish work on the eastern section and to lay the last 175 miles of track westward from the summit of the Selkirks and eastward from Kamloops. The railroad also used the funds to complete track ballasting, build stations and provide locomotives and rolling stock.

Now General Manager Van Horne stood with a group of workers and notables at a place called Craigellachie, ready to join the final section of track over which would pass the inhabitants and commerce of a new Canadian West. Some of the witnesses to the symbolic ritual of driving the last spike insisted afterward that it had been made of gold. It had not. "The last spike," Van Horne had announced, "will be just as good an iron one as there is between Montreal and Vancouver, and anyone who wants to see it driven will have to pay full fare."

Sandford Fleming, engineer-in-chief of the Canadian Pacific Railway, recalled the scene as Donald Smith, the eldest of the line's directors, drove the iron spike home. A crowd of workmen, many of whom had seen the line cross the continent, watched as the official put the culminating touch to their long ordeal. At first, apart from the clang of the spike hammer and the rippling of a mountain stream, stillness reigned. "It seemed as if the act now performed had worked a spell on all present. Each one appeared absorbed in his own reflections," recalled Fleming. Then a cheer broke out. "It was no ordinary cheer. The subdued enthusiasm, the pentup feelings of men familiar with hard work, now found vent."

All at once the crowd demanded of Van Horne, "Speech! Speech!" Again Van Horne's response was characteristically simple: "All I can say is that the work has been done well in every way."

It had indeed. For centuries, men had vainly sought after a Northwest Passage across the rim of the immense continent. Now there was one, not via water and bark canoe, but overland and built of steel. Canada was no longer an impenetrable wilderness dotted with a few isolated settlements. It had become a nation.

English immigrants, mostly cityfolk totally unprepared for life on the plains, shelter in government tents at Saskatoon in 1903.

Populating the prairies with a mosaic of people

When Canada's government pondered the sort of settler to seek for the prairies, one official knew just the type. Clifford Sifton, Minister of the Interior in 1896 said: "I think a stalwart peasant in a sheep-skin coat, born on the soil, whose forefathers have been farmers for ten generations, with a stout wife and a half-dozen children, is good quality."

In the decades after Canada's unification, many thousands of prairie pioneers who fitted this description came from the Ukraine, Scandinavia, Germany and Holland. But the offer of 160 acres of virgin farmland virtually for the asking touched a broad chord in all sorts of people. Hundreds of Londoners, city-dwellers to the core, crossed the Atlantic to try life on the plains; they were joined by Polish miners, Swedish loggers and Norwegian fishermen. Eastern Canadians left shops and factories, and Americans poured across the border to take advantage of Canadian generosity.

Western Canada became a promised land as well for religious dissidents of every sort: Hutterites and Mormons from the United States, Mennonites from Russia, Jewish survivors of the Czarist pogroms.

The result was a wave of newcomers who did not consider themselves constituents of a "melting pot," as in the United States, but part of what was called a new "mosaic of people." By 1911, the population of Canada's West had soared from a few thousand to more than a million. The pioneer era was over. It was time for these individualistic people to turn the prairie's oceans of grass into fields of grain and make Canada a breadbasket for the world.

With mattresses piled high, a rocking chair on top, and the next generation clustered in the stern, English colonists begin the 250-mile float down the North Saskatchewan River from Edmonton to Lloydminster. Upon arrival, the scow was dismantled to provide building material.

225

A settler from Eastern Canada comes to collect his family and their belongings from a Canadian Pacific train at a prairie whistle stop. Male immigrants usually went out alone to select a homestead and build a log cabin or sod hut before sending for their kin the following year.

227

Working like draft horses, Doukhobor women pull a plow across their acreage in Saskatchewan. When 7,000 members of this Russian sect immigrated in 1898, most of the men took railroad jobs, or used their horses to haul logs for cabin construction. Therefore the tilling fell to the ladies.

A Galician settlement in Manitoba around 1900 is a cluster of poplar pole huts thatched with hay. These Austro-Hungarian peasants, skilled at growing wheat, were so highly regarded that Canada paid brokers a bonus of $2 per person and $5 for each family head.

Itinerant harvesters take a break from threshing grain on a British Columbia farm around 1900. Their steam-powered, belt-driven machine was said to be under repair two days for every one it worked—during which time the crew often ate the farmer out of house and home.

ACKNOWLEDGMENTS

The index for this book was prepared by Gale Partoyan. The editors give special thanks to the following persons: Keith Wheeler, who edited portions of the book and Hugh A. Dempsey, Director of History, Glenbow-Alberta Institute, Calgary, Alberta, who read portions of the text. The editors also thank Georgeen Barrass, Assistant Chief Archivist, Linda Bartz, Curatorial Assistant, Rona Fleising, Education Assistant, Sheilagh Jameson, Archivist, and Andrew Oko, Assistant Curator, Glenbow-Alberta Institute, Calgary, Alberta; Jim Burant, National Photography Collection, Yvan Goudreau, Dominion Lands Specialist, Public Records Division, Monica McNeil, Lise Gobeil and Natalie Clerk, Picture Division, Gary Maunder, Archivist, Manuscript Division, Public Archives of Canada, Ottawa, Ontario; Ed Clark, Liaison Branch, Stan Horrall, Historian, Royal Canadian Mounted Police, Ottawa, Ontario; Ann Davis, Curator of Canadian Arts, Nancy Mato, Registrar, David Wagar, Curatorial Assistant, The Winnipeg Art Gallery, Winnipeg, Manitoba; J. Robert Davison, Jerry Mossop and Alan R. Turner, Archivists, The Provincial Archives, Victoria, British Columbia; Lynn Freeman, Photo Editor, Royal Ontario Museum, Toronto, Ontario; John Gilpin, Photo Collection, Provincial Museum of Alberta, Edmonton, Alberta; Jean Goldie, Photography Collection, Saskatchewan Archives, University of Regina, Regina, Saskatchewan; Barry Hyman, Assistant Archivist, Provincial Archives of Manitoba, Winnipeg, Manitoba; Henri Letourneau, Curator, St. Boniface Museum, St. Boniface, Manitoba; Michael E. Moss, Curator of Art, West Point Museum, United States Military Academy, West Point, New York; Ed Ogle, Vancouver, British Columbia; Robert Oleson, Public Relations Officer, and Shirlee Smith, Hudson's Bay Company, Winnipeg, Manitoba; James A. Shields and Omer Lavallée, Canadian Pacific Limited, Pointe Claire, Quebec; Stanley G. Triggs, Curator of Phototography, Notman Photographic Archives, Montreal, Quebec; Elizabeth Virolainen, Museum Technician, British Columbia Provincial Museum, Victoria, British Columbia; Garron Wells, Assistant Archivist, Hudson's Bay Company Archives, Winnipeg, Manitoba. Quotations from *Strange Empire, A Narrative of the Northwest*, by Joseph Kinsey Howard, 1952, reprinted with permission from James Lorimer and Company, Toronto, Canada.

PICTURE CREDITS

The sources for the illustrations in this book are shown below. Credits from left to right are separated by semicolons, from top to bottom by dashes.

Cover: Paulus Leeser from *Shooting the Rapids* by Frances Ann Hopkins, courtesy the Public Archives of Canada. 2—Benjamin Baltzly, courtesy Notman Photographic Archives, McCord Museum. 6,7—Courtesy the Public Archives of Canada (PA-9170). 8,9—Frederick Dally, courtesy Provincial Archives of British Columbia. 10,11—Courtesy the Public Archives of Canada (PA-9240). 12,13—E. Brown Collection, courtesy Provincial Archives of Alberta. 14 through 17—The Stoess Collection owned by Taylor Stoess, West Vancouver, Canada. 18—Courtesy Notman Photographic Archives, McCord Museum. 20—Courtesy Rare Book Division, The New York Public Library, Astor, Lenox and Tilden Foundations. 22,23—Courtesy Science and Technology Research Center, The New York Public Library, Astor, Lenox and Tilden Foundations. 24,25—George Porter from the National Audubon Society Collection/Photo Researchers, Inc. (2)—Courtesy Science and Technology Research Center, The New York Public Library, Astor, Lenox and Tilden Foundations (2); George Porter from the National Audubon Society Collection/Photo Researchers, Inc.—Courtesy Science and Technology Research Center, The New York Public Library, Astor, Lenox and Tilden Foundations; the National Audubon Society Collection/ Photo Researchers, Inc. 26,27—Map by Robert Ritter. 28—Maurice Hodge, courtesy Oregon Historical Society (2). 30,31—Courtesy Royal Ontario Museum, Toronto, Canada. 34,35—Courtesy of The National Map Collection, the Public Archives of Canada (C-16082). 37—H. A. Ogden, "At the Portage," in *Picturesque Canada*, Vol. I, p. 308, courtesy the Public Archives of Canada (C-82974). 39—Courtesy Rare Book Division, The New York Public Library, Astor, Lenox and Tilden Foundations. 40,41—Courtesy the Public Archives of Canada (C-1229). 43—Courtesy West Point Museum Collections, United States Military Academy. 44,45—Ron Marsh, courtesy Glenbow-Alberta Institute. 46,47—*Canoe Manned by Voyageurs* by Frances Ann Hopkins, I-21, courtesy the Public Archives of Canada. 48,49—Courtesy Royal Ontario Museum, To-

ronto, Canada. 50,51—Paulus Leeser from *Canoe Party Around Camp Fire* by Frances Ann Hopkins, courtesy the Public Archives of Canada. 52,53—Crown Copyright, reproduced by permission of the Controller, Her Majesty's Stationery Office, London. 54—Courtesy the National Gallery of Canada, Ottawa. 57—Courtesy National Maritime Museum, Greenwich Hospital Collection, London. 60—Map by Robert Ritter. 62,63—Courtesy Picture Collection, the Branch Libraries, The New York Public Library; courtesy the National Portrait Gallery, London; courtesy Picture Collection, the Branch Libraries, The New York Public Library—Courtesy General Research and Humanities Division, The New York Public Library, Astor, Lenox and Tilden Foundations. 64,65—Courtesy General Research and Humanities Division, The New York Public Library, Astor, Lenox and Tilden Foundations except bottom right, courtesy Royal Ontario Museum, Toronto, Canada. 66,67—Derek Bayes, courtesy National Maritime Museum, Greenwich, London. 70,71—Courtesy the National Portrait Gallery, London; courtesy Rare Book Division, The New York Public Library, Astor, Lenox and Tilden Foundations. 74,75—Courtesy British Columbia Provincial Museum. 76,77—Courtesy The American Museum of Natural History. 78,79—Courtesy British Columbia Provincial Museum. 80,81—Courtesy Library of Congress. 82,83—Courtesy The American Museum of Natural History. 84,85—Courtesy British Columbia Provincial Museum. 86,87—Courtesy Library of Congress. 88,89—Courtesy Provincial Archives of British Columbia. 90—Courtesy the Public Archives of Canada (PA-61930). 93,94—Courtesy Provincial Archives of British Columbia. 96,97—Courtesy the Public Archives of Canada (C-4964). 99 through 103—Courtesy Provincial Archives of British Columbia. 104,105—Courtesy Provincial Archives of British Columbia except top left, Council Annette Islands Reserve, Metlakatla Indian Community. 108,109—Courtesy Provincial Archives of British Columbia. 111—Courtesy the Public Archives of Canada (C-19423). 112 through 129—Courtesy Provincial Archives of British

Columbia. 130,131—Courtesy Royal Ontario Museum, Toronto, Canada. 132—Courtesy Provincial Archives of Manitoba. 134, 135—Ron Marsh, courtesy Glenbow-Alberta Institute. 138 through 141—Courtesy Royal Ontario Museum, Toronto, Canada. 143—Courtesy Provincial Archives of Manitoba (2). 144—Jerry Pace, courtesy Ottawa Public Library from *Canadian Illustrated News,* Saturday, April 23, 1870. 146,147—*Expedition to the Red River in 1870 Under Sir Garnet Wolseley, Advanced Guard Crossing a Portage* by Frances Ann Hopkins, courtesy the Public Archives of Canada. 148—Jerry Pace, courtesy the Public Archives of Canada, Records of the Department of the Interior, RG 15, Volume 1618. 151—Courtesy Royal Canadian Mounted Police. 152,153—Courtesy United Church Archives, Victoria University; courtesy the Public Archives of Canada (C-22762). 154,155—Collection of the Winnipeg Art Gallery, donated by Mr. and Mrs. Sam Cohen. 156,157—Courtesy Glenbow-Alberta Institute. 158—Courtesy Royal Canadian Mounted Police. 160—Courtesy the Public Archives of Canada. 163—Courtesy Glenbow-Alberta Institute. 164,165—Courtesy the Public Archives of Canada (C-6547). 166—Courtesy Glenbow-Alberta Institute. 169—Courtesy the Public Archives of Canada (C-1871). 170,171—Courtesy Glenbow-Alberta Institute. 172—Courtesy Royal Canadian Mounted Police (2). 175—Courtesy Glenbow-Alberta Institute (2). 177—Courtesy Royal Canadian Mounted Police except lower right, courtesy Glenbow-Alberta Institute. 180,181—Ross, Best & Co., Winnipeg, courtesy Glenbow-Alberta Institute. 184,185—William McF. Notman, courtesy Notman Photographic Archives, McCord Museum. 186,187—Courtesy Glenbow-Alberta Institute; courtesy Canadian Pacific Railroad—courtesy the Public Archives of Canada (PA-38679). 188,189—William McF. Notman, courtesy Notman Photographic Archives, McCord Museum. 190,191—Courtesy Provincial Archives of British Columbia; William McF. Notman, courtesy Notman Photographic Archives, McCord Museum. 192,193—Courtesy Notman Photographic Archives, McCord Museum; courtesy the Public Archives of Canada (PA-66576). 194,195—William McF. Notman, courtesy Notman Photographic Archives, McCord Museum. 196—Courtesy Saskatchewan Archives. 199—Courtesy Glenbow-Alberta Institute. 200, 201—Courtesy the Public Archives of Canada (C-6692); courtesy Saskatchewan Archives. 203—Courtesy Royal Ontario Museum, Toronto, Canada. 204,205—Courtesy Glenbow-Alberta Institute. 208,209—Courtesy Canadian Pacific Railroad. 211—Courtesy the Public Archives of Canada (C-1876). 212,213—Courtesy the Public Archives of Canada. 214—Courtesy Glenbow-Alberta Institute. 217—Courtesy Provincial Archives of Manitoba. 218,219—Courtesy the Public Archives of Canada (C-1879). 220—Courtesy Glenbow-Alberta Institute. 222,223—Courtesy the Public Archives of Canada (PA-38667). 224,225—Ernest Brown, courtesy Provincial Archives of Alberta. 226,227—Courtesy Provincial Archives of Manitoba. 228,229—Courtesy Saskatchewan Archives. 230,231—Courtesy the Public Archives of Canada (C-6605). 232,233—Courtesy Notman Photographic Archives, McCord Museum.

TEXT CREDITS

For full reference on specific page credits see bibliography.

Chapter 1: Particularly useful sources for information and quotes in this chapter were: Marjorie Wilkins Campbell, *The Nor'Westers,* Macmillan, 1971; Harold A. Innis, *Peter Pond: Fur Trader and Adventurer,* The Ryerson Press, 1930; Douglas MacKay, *The Honourable Company,* McClelland and Stewart Limited, 1966; Eric W. Morse, "Canoe Routes of the Voyageurs," Quetico Foundation of Ontario and Minnesota Historical Society pamphlet, 1962; Eric W. Morse, *Fur Trade Routes of Canada/Then and Now,* National and Historic Parks Branch of the Department of Indian Affairs and Northern Development, 1971; Arthur S. Morton, *A History of the Canadian West to 1870-71,* University of Toronto Press, 1973; Grace Lee Nute, *The Voyageur,* Minnesota Historical Society, 1972; Walter O'Meara, *The Savage Country,* Houghton Mifflin Company, 1960; Gordon Speck, *Northwest Explorations,* Binfords and Mort, 1970; Norah Story, *The Oxford Companion to Canadian History and Literature,* Oxford University Press, 1968; and Washington Irving, *Astoria,* Author's Revised Edition, George P. Putnam, 1849; 19—*voyageurs* as Sinbads, *Astoria,* 1964 edition, p. xlv; 23—Pond's manner, Mead, p. 51; 28—innocence of Pond and clerk; 29—McTavish nickname, Rich, p. 154; 36—canoe race, Morton, *The Journal of Duncan M'Gillivray,* p. 11; 36, 38—trading formalities, Morton, *The Journal of Duncan M'Gillivray,* p. 30; 38—fictitious requirements to endure cold, Rasky, p. 137; 42—Harmon accepts a wife, Harmon, p. 98, Harmon's thoughts on family, Harmon, pp. 194-195; 45—*voyageur* hardships, Howard, p. 201, happiness of *voyageurs,* Howard, p. 40.

Chapter 2: Particularly useful source: W. Kaye Lamb, *The Journals and Letters of Sir Alexander Mackenzie,* Macmillan of Canada, 1970; 39—Tanner on effects of liquor, James, pp. 70-71; 57—Cook on trading wares, Russian chart, Barrow, pp. 343, 373; 62—Hearne on fasting, Hearne, p. 16; 65—discovery of skeletons, Mowat, p. 314; Franklin on ice conditions, Franklin, pp. 169-170; 78—Meares on Indian lodge, Hays, p. 19. Chapter 3: Particularly useful sources: Art Downs, *Wagon Road North,* Foremost Publishing Company Ltd., 1973; Bruce Hutchison, *The Fraser,* Clarke, Irwin and Company Limited, 1950; Margaret A. Ormsby, *British Columbia: A History,* Macmillan of Canada, 1958; Dorothy Blakey Smith, *James Douglas,* Oxford University Press, 1971; James K. Smith, *David Thompson,* Oxford University Press, 1971; 102-103—Indian quote, Begg, p. 22; Duncan on condition of natives, Usher, p. 43; Duncan on cannibal scene, Begg, p. 7; 107—Begbie letter to Douglas, Pettit, p. 5. Chapter 4: Particularly useful sources: Joseph Kinsey Howard, *Strange Empire,* William Morrow and Company, 1952; Douglas Hill, *The Opening of the Canadian West,* Longman Canada Limited, 1967; Alexander Ross, *The Red River Settlement,* Smith, Elder and Company, 1856; Paul F. Sharp, *Whoop-Up Country,* University of Oklahoma Press, 1973; George F. G. Stanley, *The Birth of Western Canada,* University of Toronto Press, 1961; 140—Mactavish on local rule, Salagnac, p. 43; 152—missionary on whiskey trade, Horrall, p. 18; 153—Kit Carsons, Sharp, p. 57; 155—Morris on need for police, Horrall, p. 21. Chapter 5: Particularly useful sources: Ronald Atkin, *Maintain The*

Right, Macmillan, 1973; Pierre Berton, *The National Dream* and *The Last Spike,* McClelland and Stewart Limited, 1974; Hugh A. Dempsey, *Crowfoot: Chief of the Blackfeet,* University of Oklahoma Press, 1972; Commissioners of the RNWMP, *Opening Up the West,* Coles Publishing Company, Coles Canadiana Collection, 1973; Samuel B. Steele, *Forty Years in Canada,* Herbert Jenkins Limited, 1914; John Peter Turner, *The North West Mounted Police, 1873-1893,* two volumes, King's Printer, 1950; 166—dialogue between officer and Potts, Dempsey, *Jerry Potts, Plainsman,* p. 14; Mcleod to Potts, Dempsey, *Jerry Potts, Plainsman,* p. 16; 176—Sioux evaluation of boundary, Dempsey, *Men in Scarlet,* p. 69; 178—Sioux seeing themselves as British, Dempsey, *Men in Scarlet,* p. 69; Sitting Bull's pledge to Walsh, Horrall, p. 71; 179—Indian woman's words at conference, Sharp, p. 276; pinto buffalo, Sharp, p. 155. Chapter 6:

Particularly useful sources: Ronald Atkin, *Maintain The Right,* Macmillan, 1973; Pierre Berton, *The Impossible Railway: The Building of the Canadian Pacific,* Alfred A. Knopf, Inc., 1972; Peter Charlebois, *The Life of Louis Riel,* NC Press Limited, 1975; John G. Donkin, *Trooper and Redskin in the Far North-West,* Coles Publishing Company, Coles Canadiana Collection, 1973; Joseph Kinsey Howard, *Strange Empire,* William Morrow and Company, 1952; Omer Lavallée, *Van Horne's Road,* Railfare, 1974; George F. G. Stanley, *The Birth of Western Canada,* University of Toronto Press, 1960; *The Story of Louis Riel: The Rebel Chief,* Coles Publishing Company, Coles Canadiana Collection, 1970; 198—Steele describes Dumont, Steele, p. 93; 200—Riel eclipse quote, Campbell, p. 222; 222—Sifton quote, Cook, Ricker and Saywell, p. 144.

BIBLIOGRAPHY

Anderson, Bern, *Surveyor of the Sea: The Life and Voyages of Captain George Vancouver.* University of Washington Press, 1960.

Atkin, Ronald, *Maintain the Right.* Macmillan, 1973.

Barrow, John, *Captain Cook's Voyages of Discovery.* E. P. Dutton and Co. Inc., 1944.

Begg, Alexander, *A Sketch of the Successful Missionary Work of William Duncan, 1858-1901.* Victoria, 1901.

Berton, Pierre: *The Impossible Railway.* Alfred A. Knopf, Inc., 1972.

The National Dream and *The Last Spike.* McClelland and Stewart Ltd., 1974.

Birrell, A. J., *Into the Silent Land.* Information Canada, Ottawa, 1975.

Brown, George W., ed., *Canada.* University of California Press, 1950.

Cameron, William Bleasdell, *Blood Red the Sun.* Kenways Ltd., 1950.

Campbell, Marjorie Wilkins: *The North West Company.* St. Martin's Press, 1957.

The Nor'Westers, The Fight for the Fur Trade. Macmillan, 1954.

The Saskatchewan. Rinehart and Co., Inc., 1950.

Cashman, Tony, *An Illustrated History of Western Canada.* Hurtig Publishers, 1971.

Charlebois, Dr. Peter, *The Life of Louis Riel.* NC Press Ltd., 1975.

Commissioners of the RNWMP, *Opening Up the West.* Coles Publishing Co., 1973.

Cook, Ramsay, with John C. Ricker and John T. Saywell, *Canada: A Modern Study.* Clarke, Irwin and Co., Toronto, 1963.

Davidson, Gordon Charles, *The North West Company.* University of California Press, 1918.

Davidson, William McCartney, *Louis Riel, 1844-1885.* The Albertan Publishing Company Ltd., 1955.

David Thompson's Narrative 1784-1812. Edited with an introduction and notes by Richard Glover. The Champlain Society, 1962.

Dempsey, Hugh A.: *Crowfoot.* Hurtig Publishers, 1972.

Jerry Potts, Plainsman. Glenbow-Alberta Institute, 1966.

Men in Scarlet. Historical Society of Alberta, McClelland and Stewart Ltd., 1974.

Dodge, Ernest S., *Northwest by Sea.* Oxford University Press, 1961.

Donkin, John G., *Trooper and Redskin in the Far North-West.* Coles Publishing Company, 1973.

Downs, Art: *Paddlewheels on the Frontier,* Vol. I. Foremost Publishing Co. Ltd., 1967-1971.

Wagon Road North. Foremost Publishing Co. Ltd., 1973.

Driver, Harold E., *Indians of North America.* The University of Chicago Press, 1969.

Drucker, Philip, *Indians of the Northwest Coast.* The Natural History Press, 1963.

Fetherstonhaugh, R. C., *The Royal Canadian Mounted Police.* Carrick and Evans, Inc., 1938.

Fleming, Freeda, "Rocky Mountain House," *The Beaver.* December 1949.

Ford, Alice, compiler and ed., *Audubon's Animals: The Quadrupeds of North America.* The Studio Publications with Thomas Y. Crowell Co., 1951.

Franklin, John, *Narrative of a Journey to the Shores of the Polar Sea in the Years 1819, 20, 21, and 22.* Charles E. Tuttle Co., 1970.

Goodchild, Fred H., *British Columbia.* George Allen and Unwin Ltd., 1951.

Harmon, Daniel Williams, *Sixteen Years in the Indian Country.* W. Kaye Lamb, ed., Macmillan, 1957.

Harper, J. Russell, ed., *Paul Kane's Frontier.* University of Texas Press, 1971.

Hays, H. R., *Children of the Raven: The Seven Indian Nations of the Northwest Coast.* McGraw-Hill Book Co., 1975.

Hearne, Samuel, *Coppermine Journey.* Farley Mowat, ed., McClelland and Stewart Ltd., 1958.

Hill, Douglas, *The Opening of the Canadian West.* Longman Canada Ltd., 1967.

Horrall, S. W., *The Pictorial History of the Royal Canadian Mounted Police.* McGraw-Hill Ryerson Ltd., 1973.

Howard, Joseph Kinsey, *Strange Empire.* William Morrow and Co., 1952; James Lorimer and Co., 1974 (paperback).

Hutchison, Bruce, *The Fraser.* Clarke, Irwin and Co. Ltd., 1950.

Innis, Harold A.: *The Fur Trade In Canada.* University of Toronto Press, 1970.

Peter Pond: Fur Trader and Adventurer. The Ryerson Press, 1930.

Irving, Washington: *Astoria or, Anecdotes of an Enterprise beyond the Rocky Mountains.* Revised Edition, George P. Putnam, 1849.

Astoria. Edgeley W. Todd, ed., University of Oklahoma Press, 1964.

James, Edwin, ed., *A Narrative of the Captivity and Adventures of John Tanner.* Baldwin and Cradock, 1830.

Jamieson, F. C., *The Alberta Field Force of '85.* Canadian North-West Historical Society, 1931.

Johnson, Alice M., "Edward and Frances Hopkins of Montreal," *The Beaver.* Autumn 1971.

Kerr, D. G. G., and R. I. K. Davidson, *An Illustrated History of Canada.* Thomas Nelson and Sons Ltd., 1966.

Lamb, W. Kaye, *The Journal and Letters of Sir Alexander Mackenzie.* Macmillan of Canada, 1970.

Lavallée, Omer, *Van Horne's Road.* Railfare, 1974.

Leechman, Douglas, " 'Comodityes besides Furres'," *The Beaver.* Spring 1974.

MacEwan, J. W. Grant: *Between the Red and the Rockies.* University of Toronto Press, 1952.

Macfie, Matthew, *Vancouver Island and British Columbia.* Coles Publishing Co., 1972.

MacKay, Douglas, *The Honourable Company.* McClelland and Stewart Ltd., Toronto, 1966.

MacLennan, Hugh: "By Canoe to Empire," *American Heritage.* October 1961.

The Rivers of Canada. Scribners, 1962.

MacNair, Peter L., "Kwakiutl Winter Dances," *artscanada,* Vol. XXX, Nos. 5 and 6. December 1973/January 1974.

Marshall, Carrie, and James Stirrat, *Vancouver's Voyage.* Mitchell Press Ltd., 1955.

Martin, Horace T., *Castorologica.* William Drysdale and Co., 1892.

Mead, Robert Douglas, *Ultimate North.* Doubleday, 1976.

Morse, Eric W.: "Canoe Routes of the Voyageurs." Quetico Foundation of Ontario and the Minnesota Historical Society, 1962.

Fur Trade Canoe Routes of Canada/Then and Now. National and Historic Parks Branch of the Department of Indian Affairs and Northern Development, Ottawa, 1971.

Morton, Arthur S.: *A History of The Canadian West To 1870-71.* University of Toronto Press, 1973.

Ed., *The Journal of Duncan M'Gillivray.* Macmillan of Canada, 1929.

Morton, W. L., ed., *Alexander Begg's Red River Journal.* The Champlain Society, Toronto, 1956.

Mowat, Farley, ed., *Ordeal by Ice.* Little, Brown and Co., 1960.

Neatby, Leslie H., *In Quest of the Northwest Passage.* Thomas Y. Crowell Co., 1958.

Neering, Rosemary, *Gold Rush.* Fitzhenry and Whiteside Ltd., 1974.

Nevitt, R. B., *A Winter at Fort MacLeod.* Glenbow-Alberta Institute/McClelland and Stewart Ltd., 1974.

Nute, Grace Lee: *The Voyageur.* Historical Society, St. Paul, 1972.

"Voyageurs' Artist," *The Beaver.* June 1947.

O'Meara, Walter: *The Last Portage.* Houghton-Mifflin Co., 1962.

The Savage Country. Houghton-Mifflin Co., 1960.

Ormsby, Margaret A., *British Columbia: A History.* Macmillan of Canada, 1958.

Pethick, Derek, and Susan Baumgarten, *British Columbia Recalled.* Hancock House Publishers Ltd., 1974.

Pettit, Sydney G., "Frontier Judge," *The Beaver.* September, 1948.

The Pioneers: An Illustrated History of Early Settlement in Canada. McClelland and Stewart Ltd., 1974.

Reid, J. H. Stewart, *Mountains, Men and Rivers.* Bouregy and Curl, Inc., 1954.

Reid, J. H. Stewart, Kenneth McNaught and Harry S. Crowe, *A Source-Book of Canadian History.* Longmans, Green and Co., 1959.

Rich, E. E.: *The Fur Trade and the Northwest, to 1857.* McClelland and Stewart Ltd., 1967.

Hudson's Bay Company 1670-1870, Three Vols. Macmillan, 1960.

Robertson, Heather, ed., *Salt of the Earth.* James Lorimer and Co., 1974.

Ross, Alexander, *The Red River Settlement.* Smith, Elder and Co., London, 1856.

Salagnac, Georges Cerbelaud, *La Révolte des Métis: Louis Riel, héros ou rebelle?* Les Dossiers Ressuscités, Maison Mame, Tours, France, 1971.

Sharp, Paul F., *Whoop-Up Country.* University of Oklahoma Press, 1973.

Smith, James K.: *David Thompson.* Oxford University Press, 1971.

Alexander Mackenzie, Explorer: The Hero Who Failed. McGraw-Hill Ryerson Ltd., 1973.

Smith, Dorothy Blakey, *James Douglas.* Oxford University Press, 1971.

Speck, Gordon, *Northwest Explorations.* Binfords and Mort, 1970.

Stanley, George F. G.: *The Birth of Western Canada.* University of Toronto Press, 1961.

Louis Riel. Ryerson Press, 1963.

Steele, Samuel B., *Forty Years in Canada.* Herbert Jenkins Ltd., 1914.

The Story of Louis Riel the Rebel Chief. Coles Publishing Co., 1970.

Story, Norah, *The Oxford Companion to Canadian History and Literature.* Oxford University Press, 1967.

Thomas, Lewis G., general ed., *The Prairie West to 1905: A Canadian Sourcebook.* Oxford University Press, 1975.

Thomson, George Malcolm, *The Search for the North-West Passage.* Macmillan, 1975.

Turner, John Peter, *The North-West Mounted Police 1873-1893,* Two Vols. King's Printer, 1950.

Usher, Jean, *William Duncan of Metlakatla: A Victorian Missionary in British Columbia.* National Museums of Canada, 1974.

Wherry, Joseph H., *The Totem Pole Indians.* Thomas Y. Crowell Co., Inc., 1974.

Williams, Glyndwr, "Highlights of the First 200 Years of the Hudson's Bay Company," *The Beaver.* Autumn 1970.

Williams, Stanley T., *The Life of Washington Irving,* Vols. I and II. Oxford University Press, New York, 1935.

The Winnipeg Art Gallery, *150 Years of Art in Manitoba.* An exhibition for the Manitoba Centennial, 1970.

Woodcock, George: *Canada and the Canadians.* Stackpole Books, 1970.

Gabriel Dumont. Hurtig Publishers, 1975.

Woollacott, Arthur P., *MacKenzie and His Voyageurs, by Canoe to the Arctic and the Pacific, 1789-93.* J. M. Dent and Sons Ltd., 1927.

Wright, Jim F. C., *Saskatchewan, The History of a Province.* McClelland and Stewart Ltd., 1955.

Printed in U.S.A.